Language Testing in Practice:

Designing and Developing Useful Language Tests

Lyle F. Bachman and
Adrian S. Palmer

D1124750

Oxford University Press

OXFORD

UNIVERSITY PRESS

Great Clarendon Street, Oxford OX2 6DP

Oxford University Press is a department of the University of Oxford.
It furthers the University's objective of excellence in research, scholarship,
and education by publishing worldwide in

Oxford New York

Auckland Cape Town Dar es Salaam Hong Kong Karachi
Kuala Lumpur Madrid Melbourne Mexico City Nairobi
New Delhi Shanghai Taipei Toronto

With offices in

Argentina Austria Brazil Chile Czech Republic France Greece
Guatemala Hungary Italy Japan Poland Portugal Singapore
South Korea Switzerland Thailand Turkey Ukraine Vietnam

OXFORD and OXFORD ENGLISH are registered trade marks of
Oxford University Press in the UK and in certain other countries

ISBN 978 0 19 437148 3

Typeset by Wyvern Typesetting Ltd, Bristol

Printed in China

This book is printed on paper from certified and well-managed sources

Contents

Acknowledgments

This book has been in gestation for over five years, and during that time we have benefited from a great deal of support, criticism, and suggestions from our students, from friends and colleagues, and from our spouses (actual and virtual). Probably the most important feedback has been that received in the crucible of teaching courses in language testing, which has provided the acid test of our ideas and the way we have presented them. Between the two of us, we have probably used this book, in its various incarnations, as a classroom text with over ten different classes of students, in our regular testing courses at UCLA and The University of Utah, as well as in numerous summer courses, seminars, and workshops we've conducted. It has been in the classroom, in the presence of our students, that many a half-baked concept and rube-goldberg diagram bit the dust. Our students have given us many original insights and have pushed us to go further and deeper into some issues than we might originally have felt comfortable with.

We thus would first like to thank our students, who provided us both inspiration and criticism as they worked through various drafts our book. We would particularly like to thank Nancy Horvath, Gary Ockey, and Gini Smith for their detailed reviews of early versions of the entire manuscript, as well as Jim Purpura, Jungok Bae, Ruey Jiuan (Regina) Wu, and Shichi (Greg) Kamei, who provided extensive feedback and suggestions for improvements.

We would also like to thank the following colleagues who have used parts of this book with their language testing classes and who have given us invaluable feedback: Caroline Clapham, Carol Chapelle, Andrew Cohen, Fred Davidson, Antony Kunnan, and Jim Purpura.

In addition, the following colleagues have given us valuable criticism and suggestions: Barbara Hoekje, Michael Milanovic, Nick Saville, John Schumann, and John Oller. We would also like to thank George Trosper for his help in designing several of the illustrative test development projects.

Finally, we would like to thank the staff of OUP, Henry Widdowson, several anonymous reviewers, and Carol Chapelle for their very helpful comments and suggestions for improving the book as we came into the final stretch.

The publishers and authors would like to thank Mr Howard P. Sou and the Hong Kong Education Department for permission to reproduce parts of a test.

Every effort has been made to trace the owners of copyright material in this book, but we should be pleased to hear from any copyright holder whom we have been unable to contact. We apologize for any apparent negligence. If notified, the publisher will be pleased to rectify any errors or omissions at the earliest opportunity.

PART ONE

Conceptual bases of test development

1 Objectives and expectations

Introduction: Some common misconceptions about language testing and resulting problems

The primary purpose of this book is to enable the reader to become competent in the design, development, and use of language tests. Over the years we have worked with a wide range of individuals—language teachers who want to be able to use tests as part of their classroom teaching, applied linguists interested in developing tests for use as research instruments, people who are involved in large-scale language testing programs, and graduate students in fields such as applied linguistics, English as a second/ foreign language, bilingual education, and foreign language education. In virtually every group we have worked with, we have found misconceptions about the development and use of language tests, and unrealistic expectations about what language tests can do and what they should be like, that have prevented people from becoming competent in language testing. Furthermore, there is often a belief that 'language testers' have some almost magical procedures and formulae for creating the 'best' test. These misconceptions and unrealistic expectations, and the mystique associated with language testing, constitute strong affective barriers to many people who want and need to be able to use language tests in their professional work. Breaking down this affective barrier by dispelling misconceptions, helping readers develop a sense of what can reasonably be expected of language tests, and demystifying language testing is thus an important part of this book.

Perhaps the best way to illustrate this is with an example from our own experience with language testing. We first started working together in language testing about 25 years ago, when we were in similar situations in which we needed to develop language tests for a particular purpose. We were both involved in developing tests for use in placing students into an appropriate level or group in English as a foreign language (EFL) courses in tertiary-level institutions in Thailand, where, at that time, English was not the medium of instruction for education, and was not widely used in the society at large. Neither of us had had any formal training in either language testing or psychometrics, and we had come to the task with different backgrounds—one in theoretical linguistics and the other in English language and literature. On the other hand, we had both had experience in teaching English as a second/foreign language, and considerable understanding of what was then known, in terms of theory and research, of second/foreign language teaching. In addition, we shared a common concern: to develop the 'best' test for our situations. We believed that there was a model language test and a set of straightforward procedures—a recipe, if you will—that we could follow to create a test that would be the best one for our purposes and situations.

What we did, essentially, was to model our tests on the large-scale EFL tests that were widely used at that time, which included sections testing English grammar, vocabulary, reading, and listening comprehension. Following this model, we employed test development procedures that had been developed for psychological and educational tests to produce, rather mechanically, tests that both we and our colleagues believed were 'state-of-the-art' EFL tests, and hence the 'best' for our needs. We had started with the 'best' models and had used sophisticated statistical techniques in test development, so that our tests were definitely state-of-the-art at that time, but now, in retrospect, we wonder whether they were the best for those situations. Indeed, we wonder if there is a single 'best' test for any language testing situation.

In developing those tests, we believed that if we followed the model of a test that was widely recognized and used, it would automatically be useful for our particular needs. These tests had been designed and developed by the 'experts' in the field, who were assumed to know more than we did. There were, however, several questions we did not ask. Were our situations different enough from the ones for which these large-scale tests were developed to make them inappropriate? Were our test takers like the ones who took those large-scale tests, or would the results of our tests be used to make the same kinds of decisions? We did not even ask whether the abilities tested in those tests were the ones we needed to test.

Given what was known (and not known) about the nature of language use, of language learning, and of language testing at that time, these were questions that simply never occurred. Language ability was viewed as a set of finite components—grammar, vocabulary, pronunciation, spelling—that were realized as four skills—listening, speaking, reading, and writing. If we taught or tested these, we were teaching or testing everything that was needed. Language learners were viewed as organisms who all learned language by essentially the same processes—stimulus and response, as described by behaviorist psychology. Finally, it was assumed that the processes involved in language learning were more or less the same for all learners, for all situations, and for all purposes. It is not surprising, then, that we believed that a single model would provide the best test for our particular test takers, for our particular uses, and for the areas of language ability that were of interest in our particular situation.

As it turned out, the two groups of test takers for whom we developed essentially the same kind of language test were quite different. One group consisted of first-year students entering a university in which very little of their academic course work would involve the use of English. Most of them would be required to take at least one English course as part of their degree requirements. Though all of the students had had some exposure to English in their secondary school education, most had very little control of the language, and almost none of them had had any exposure to English outside of the EFL classroom. Few had ever spoken English with a native speaker or had any opportunity to use English for any non-instructional purpose.

The other group consisted of university teachers, many of whom were quite senior, from many different universities, and representing a wide range of academic disciplines, who had been selected as recipients of scholarships to continue work on advanced degrees in countries where English is the medium of instruction. They were much more highly specialized in their knowledge of their disciplines than were the first-year university students, were considerably older, on average, and were more experienced.

The programs into which these test takers would be placed by means of the tests were also quite different. The program into which the university students would be placed consisted of four levels of non-intensive (five hours per week) English instruction during their first and second years of university work. The program focused primarily on enabling the students to read academic reference works written in English. Students were placed in courses at one of the four levels by general ability level and not according to their area of academic specialization. Most of the English classes were taught by teachers who had learned English as a foreign language, and much of the classroom instruction was carried out in the students' native language.

The university teachers, on the other hand, would be placed into a ten-week intensive (40 hours per week) course at a national English language institute where they would be required to speak nothing but English between the hours of about eight until five every working day. They would take classes in all four skills, but would be divided into groups according to broad classifications of their academic disciplines, such as agriculture, engineering and sciences, medical sciences, and economics. Unlike the university English program, the teachers in this program were all native speakers of English, and all classroom instruction was carried out in English. This program was thus much more intensive than that of the university students: the curriculum was focused on English for specific purposes and involved a great deal more actual use of English.

This example illustrates the most common misconception that we find among those who ask for advice about their specific testing needs. In our experience, many people believe, as we did, that there is an ideal of what a 'good' language test is, and want to know how to create tests on this ideal model for their own testing needs. Our answer is that there is no such thing as a 'good' or 'bad' test *in the abstract*, and that there is no such thing as the one 'best' test, even for a specific situation. To understand why this is so, we must consider some of the problems that result from this misconception.

If we assume that a single 'best' test exists, and we attempt either to use this test itself, or to use it as a model for developing a test of our own, we are likely to end up with a test that will be inappropriate for at least some of our test takers. In the example above, the test developed for the university students might have been appropriate for this group, in terms of the areas of language ability measured (grammar, vocabulary, and reading comprehension), and topical content, since this was quite general and not specific to any particular discipline. The test developed for the university teachers, however, was probably not particularly appropriate for this group, since it did not include material related to the teachers' different disciplines or to the areas of ESP that were covered in the intensive course. This test was also of limited appropriateness because it did not include an assessment of students' ability to perform listening and speaking tasks, which was heavily emphasized in the intensive program.

Because of these limitations, the test for the teachers did not meet all of the needs of the test users (the director of and teachers in the intensive program). Specifically, teachers in the intensive course reported that students who were placed into levels on the basis of the test were quite homogeneous in terms of their reading, but that there were considerable differences among students within a given level in terms of their listening and speaking. These differences made it quite difficult for teachers to find and use listening and speaking activities that were appropriate for a given group. Teachers felt that the test should be able to accurately predict students' placement into the listening and speaking classes, as well as into the reading classes, and urged the test developer to remedy this situation.

In an attempt to address this problem, a dictation was added to the test as a way of assessing the students' ability to perform listening tasks. In this task the test takers listened to a passage presented with a tape recorder, and were required to write down exactly what they heard. This particular task was added largely because it had been used previously, and was considered to be a 'good' way to test listening. At the same time, the director of the intensive program agreed to group students homogeneously into listening and speaking groups on the basis of their scores on the dictation. This seemed to work well as a program modification, and teachers felt that it facilitated both their teaching and their students' learning.

It is not clear that it was the dictation test or the program change—grouping students homogeneously into listening and speaking classes—that solved the problem with the listening and speaking classes. What is clear, however, is that adding a dictation test created another problem. Most of the listening tasks in the intensive course were interactive, conversational tasks involving a give and take, in which responses were generally oral, and these tasks were quite different from the dictation test task, which involved no interaction and required only written responses. Thus, although the addition of the dictation did, perhaps, provide some general information about the students' ability to listen and understand spoken language, the test task itself was quite different from the kinds of listening tasks the students would be engaged in in the intensive course, and both the test takers and the test users frequently complained that the test was very artificial and bore no relationship to what students actually did in the intensive course. The teachers were frustrated because even though the test seemed to be providing useful information for placing students into groups, the tasks that were included in the test bore little, if any, resemblance to class work. The teachers expected the test to provide completely accurate information for placement purposes and at the same time to include test tasks that were very similar to those they incorporated into their teaching. The test developer was frustrated because he felt that he had done everything he could to make this the best test possible. He had used as models two types of tests that were widely used by language testers, and had followed standard test development procedures that were used and prescribed by measurement specialists.

To summarize, Table 1.1 shows some of the misconceptions and resulting

Misconceptions	Resulting problems
1 Believing that there is one 'best' test for any given situation.	1 Tests which are inappropriate for the test takers.
2 Misunderstanding the nature of language testing and language test development.	2 Tests which do not meet the specific needs of the test users.
3 Having unreasonable expectations about what language tests can do and what they should be.	3 Uninformed use of tests or testing methods simply because they have become popular.
4 Placing blind faith in the technology of measurement.	4 Becoming frustrated when one is unable to find or develop the perfect test.
	5 Loss of faith in one's own capacity for developing and using tests appropriately, as well as a feeling that language testing is something that only 'experts' can understand and do.
	6 Being placed in a situation of trying to defend the indefensible, since many students, as well as administrators, have unreasonable expectations.

Table 1.1:   Some misconceptions and resulting problems

problems that are illustrated by the above example, which we have found to be very common among individuals who want to be able to use language tests but feel that they do not have the knowledge or competence to do so.

Why it is important to be competent in language testing

We believe that being competent in language testing will help readers to avoid some of the misconceptions described above and to develop a set of reasonable expectations for any given language test they may need to use. In addition, this will give a sense of confidence in one's own knowledge and skills in this endeavor. Language tests can be a valuable tool for providing information that is relevant to several concerns in language teaching. They can provide evidence of the results of learning and instruction, and hence feedback on the effectiveness of the teaching program itself. They can also provide information that is relevant to making decisions about individuals, such as determining what specific kinds of learning materials and activities should be provided to students, based on a diagnosis of their strengths and weaknesses, deciding whether individual students or an entire class are ready to move on to another unit of instruction, and assigning grades on the basis of students' achievement. Finally, testing can also be used as a tool for clarifying instructional objectives and, in some cases, for evaluating the relevance of these objectives and the instructional materials and activities based on them to the language use needs of students following the program of instruction. For these reasons, virtually all language teaching programs involve some testing, and hence, language teachers need to be able either to make informed judgments in selecting appropriate language tests or to plan, construct, and develop appropriate tests of their own.

What does competence in language testing involve?

As already stated, the primary purpose of this book is to give the reader increased competence in the design, development, and use of language tests. Table 1.2 shows what we believe competence in language testing involves.

An approach to language test design and development

The approach to language testing that we present in this book is not a 'cookbook' approach, with a miscellany of templates for test tasks, along with a list of recipes and procedures for developing and using language tests. Thus, it does not include examples of all types of test items that have been used in language tests. Nor is this is a book about 'everything you always wanted to know about language testing but were afraid to ask'.

Competence in language testing involves the following:

1 An understanding of the fundamental considerations that must be addressed at the start of any language testing effort, whether this involves the development of new tests or the selection of existing language tests;

2 An understanding of the fundamental issues and concerns in the appropriate use of language tests;

3 An understanding of the fundamental issues, approaches, and methods used in measurement and evaluation;[1]

4 The ability to design, develop, evaluate and use language tests in ways that are appropriate for a given purpose, context, and group of test takers;

5 The ability to critically read published research in language testing and information about published tests in order to make informed decisions.

Table 1.2: Requirements for competence in language testing

Thus, it does not include definitions for all the technical terms in language testing and measurement.

We believe that our approach to language testing will provide two things:

1 a theoretically grounded and principled basis for developing and using language tests, and

2 an understanding that will enable readers to make their own judgments and decisions about either selecting or developing a language test that will be useful for a particular language testing situation.

To facilitate this, we provide examples that clearly illustrate specific points, principles, and concepts that are important to our approach. Furthermore, we limit our use of technical terms to those essential to our approach, and provide clear definitions and/or examples to make these terms clear to readers.

Our approach to language test development and use incorporates recent research in language testing and language teaching, and is based on two fundamental principles:

– *The need for a correspondence between language test performance and language use*:
In order for a particular language test to be useful for its intended purposes, test performance must correspond in demonstrable ways to language use in non-test situations.

– *A clear and explicit definition of the qualities of test usefulness*:
Test usefulness, consisting of several qualities (reliability, construct validity, authenticity, interactiveness, impact, and practicality), is an overriding consideration for quality control throughout the process of designing, developing, and using a particular language test.

We will discuss the first principle in this chapter, and elaborate on this in Chapters 3 and 4. We discuss the notion of test usefulness in detail in Chapter 2.

Correspondence between language test performance and language use

If we want to use the scores from a language test to make inferences about individuals' language ability, and possibly to make various types of decisions, we must be able to demonstrate how performance on that language test is related to language use in specific situations other than the language test itself. In order to be able to demonstrate this relationship, we need a conceptual framework that enables us to treat performance on a language test as a particular instance of language use. That is, we need a framework that enables us to use the same characteristics to describe what we believe are the critical features of both language test performance and non-test language use.

To illustrate the need for such a framework, let us consider a typical situation in which there is the need to develop a language test. Suppose you need to develop a test to determine if undergraduate students of Spanish as a foreign language at a North American university are ready, in terms of their language ability in Spanish, to spend a year studying entirely in Spanish at a university in Spain. You may already know that one use of Spanish will be in comprehending academic lectures, so you initially decide to include such a task in your test.

When you begin designing the actual test tasks, however, there are a lot of characteristics of the academic lecture that you will need to specify. For example, how long will the lecture be? In what discipline? At what level, introductory or advanced, in terms of its topical content? In addition to characterizing the input—the lecture—of your test task, you will need to specify what test takers will be asked to do with this input. For example, will they be asked to summarize the lecture, or to answer short questions? If the latter, how long will these questions be, and how complex, in terms of their language (e.g. syntax, vocabulary)? Will the questions be presented aurally or in writing? And what about the responses you expect from the test takers? Will they respond by selecting the best answer from among several choices that are presented, or will they construct their responses? If the responses are to be constructed, how long will you expect these responses to be? Will test takers be expected to respond in writing, or by speaking? In Spanish or in their native language? Clearly, then, in order to adequately describe a given language use task, such as listening to an academic lecture, a whole range of specific task characteristics must be considered.

How should one attempt to answer all of these questions? One way might be to identify and analyze the tasks these students will need to accomplish, using Spanish, in what you have identified as the target language use domain—in this case, an academic program at a Spanish university.[2] In analyzing specific tasks in this target language use situation, you will undoubtedly find it very useful to either begin with or to derive a set of specific characteristics, such as the length of the language samples provided in the input to test takers, the grammatical, textual, functional and sociolinguistics characteristics of the input, and so on, for identifying similarities and differences across the wide range of individual tasks you might choose to analyze.

Another set of questions that you will need to address in designing your test pertains to the characteristics of the language users, or your potential test takers. For example, how much knowledge are they likely to have about the topical content of the lecture, and at what level? Do they have positive or negative emotions and feelings about the lecture, the lecturer, the topic, or the setting? Are they overly anxious about their ability to cope with this task? You will also need to address some questions about the nature of the areas of language ability you want to measure. For example, although you may have some general notions about this, you may decide to use a current theory of language ability or of listening to help you identify specific abilities involved in listening comprehension tasks.

As this example illustrates, when we design a language test we need to consider the characteristics of the language use situation and tasks and of the language users and test takers. We need to consider task characteristics in order to insure and demonstrate the ways in which our test tasks correspond to language use tasks. We need to consider characteristics of individuals in order to be able to demonstrate the extent to which these characteristics are involved in language use tasks and test tasks. Thus, two sets of characteristics that affect both language use and language test performance are of central interest. One set, the characteristics of individuals, is relevant to the construct validity of any inferences we make about language ability. The other set, the characteristics of the tasks, is relevant to determining the domain to which these inferences generalize. The effects of these two sets of characteristics on language use and language test performance are illustrated in Figure 1.1.

As indicated above, the correspondence that is of central concern in designing, developing, and using language tests is that between language test performance and non-test language use, illustrated by the horizontal arrow labeled 'A' in Figure 1.1. In order to demonstrate this correspondence, either in tests that we design and develop ourselves, or in tests that we may want to select for possible use, we need to be able to demonstrate the correspondences between both the characteristics of the language use situation and tasks and those of the test situation and tasks, illustrated by

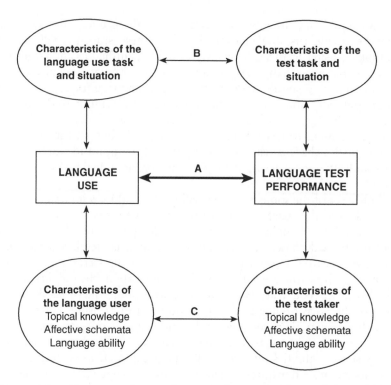

Figure 1.1:   Correspondences between language use and language test performance

the arrow labeled 'B' in Figure 1.1, and the characteristics of individuals as language users and as test takers, illustrated by the arrow labeled 'C' in Figure 1.1.

The characteristic of individuals that is of primary interest in language testing is language ability, since this is what we want to make inferences about. Other individual characteristics that we also need to consider are topical knowledge, or knowledge schemata, and affective schemata. We include these in our discussion for two reasons. First, we believe that these characteristics can have important influences on both language use and test performance. Second, we believe that it is possible to design language tests so that these characteristics facilitate, rather than impede, test takers' performance.

What does our approach have to offer?

In addition to these two principles, the approach we present in this book is based on the tenets of our philosophy of language testing as

---

Our philosophy of language testing

1 Relate language testing to language teaching and language use.

2 Design your tests so as to encourage and enable test takers to perform at their highest level of ability.

3 Build considerations of fairness into test design.

4 Humanize the testing process: seek ways in which to involve test takers more directly in the testing process; treat test takers as responsible individuals; provide them with as complete information about the entire testing procedure as possible.

5 Demand accountability for test use; hold yourself, as well as any others who use your test, accountable for the way your test is used.

6 Recognize that decisions based on test scores are fraught with dilemmas, and that there are no universal answers to these.

Photocopiable © Oxford University Press

Table 1.3: Our philosophy of language testing

shown in Table 1.3. We have attempted to incorporate these into every part of this book.

Who can benefit from this approach to language testing?

We believe that a wide range of individuals can benefit from our approach to language testing. This belief is based not only on our experience in teaching this approach to our students, but also on having used it successfully in consulting with individuals and institutions in many parts of the world in the actual design and development of language tests. We have worked with language teachers who need to select, adapt, or develop tests for classroom use, with testing specialists developing tests for wider use within particular language teaching programs, and with material developers and textbook writers who need to include appropriate tests or suggestions for test development in the materials they produce. We have also worked with professional test developers in organizations that are responsible for producing high-stakes tests. Finally, we have worked with researchers in various areas of applied linguistics who need to select or develop language tests that are appropriate to their research needs.

Overview of the book

The book is organized into three main parts. Part One presents a conceptual framework that provides the theoretical basis for designing, developing, and using language tests. This framework includes a set of principles for describing and assessing test usefulness, presented in Chapter 2, as well as models of test task characteristics and language ability, presented in Chapters 3 and 4 respectively. While this framework is grounded in theoretical research in applied linguistics, it is not simply theoretical, but is practical as well. Its primary purpose is to guide the design, development, and use of language tests.

Part Two presents a detailed discussion, with extensive examples, of the test development process, from planning to pretesting and test administration to scoring. This section begins with an overview of the test development process in Chapter 5. Chapter 6 discusses considerations and procedures for describing the specific purposes of the test, the tasks in the language use situation beyond the test itself, and the characteristics of the test takers, as well as for defining the abilities to be measured. Chapter 7 focuses on developing a plan and a set of procedures, both conceptual and empirical, for evaluating the usefulness of the tests we develop. Chapter 8 discusses practical issues in the allocation and management of resources that are needed in the development and use of language tests. Chapter 9 deals with writing test tasks and creating blueprints for tests, while Chapter 10 discusses the writing of effective instructions. Chapter 11 discusses the considerations to be made in scoring, as well as a wide range of scoring methods. Finally, Chapter 12 discusses procedures for administering tests and the process of collecting feedback for assessing the usefulness of tests.

The chapters in Parts One and Two include, in addition to the main discussion, a summary, discussion questions/exercises and suggestions for further reading. The specific types of exercises vary from chapter to chapter, and include activities such as the analysis of a particular language testing need with suggestions for how to address this, tests and test items to critique, and objectives for which the reader will write test items. These exercises and activities can be used in a variety of ways, depending upon the particular situation. For example, they can be used to stimulate discussion by an entire class, by students working in small groups, or by students working in pairs. They can also be used as the basis for self-reflective writing activities or individual homework assignments.

In the last part of the book, Part Three, we provide a number of illustrative test development projects which take the reader through the entire test development process. These projects have been taken from our own work in developing language tests over the years, as well as from projects that our students have completed in the testing courses we teach. They thus constitute genuine instances of test development which we hope will provide a rich source of activities that readers can pursue either as part of a class or on their own, so as to learn how to use and adapt our approach to their own language test development needs.

Exercises

1   Examine the list of misconceptions and unrealistic expectations about the development and use of language tests listed in this chapter. Which

of these misconceptions did you hold? How have these misconceptions affected the ways in which you have developed or used language tests? Have others with whom you have worked held any of these misconceptions? What problems have their misconceptions created for them, and for you?

2   What experience have you had with the belief that there exists such a thing as the 'best' test for a given situation? What was the situation and what did you imagine this 'best' test had to look like? What were the bases for your opinions?

3   Re-read the description of the authors' experience with the placement test they developed and the problems they encountered. Then think of a situation in which you used a language test with which you were dissatisfied, and describe it. Make a list of specific ways in which you were dissatisfied with the test. Are any of these ways related to a mismatch between the kinds of information the test provided and the kinds of information you needed—as was the case in the authors' example? Did you make any attempt to modify the test to provide more useful information? If so, what?

4   Recall an experience in which you used a test that had been developed 'locally'. Who developed the test and what were their qualifications? Then read the description of what it means to be 'competent in language testing'. In your opinion, how competent in general were the test developers? In what areas do you believe the test developers were or were not competent?

5   Think of a situation in which you both taught a second language and tested students in that language. Describe the situation. In your opinion, how well did the way the students were tested reflect the course objectives? In addition to providing you with a measure of the students' control of the language, what other kind of impact do you believe the test had on the teacher, the students, or the instruction? Were you satisfied with this impact? Why or why not?

6   Re-read the description of the authors' philosophy of language testing. To what extent does this philosophy correspond with your own? Has your philosophy of language testing already changed as a result of reading this chapter? If so, how?

7   Read the introduction to Project 1 in Part Three, and consider what specific misconceptions and unrealistic expectations might arise among teachers in the writing program, program administrators, and test developers. Why might these groups have different kinds of misconceptions and unrealistic expectations?

8   Read the Design Statement for Project 1 in Part Three. What specific areas of competence in language testing do you think this illustrates?

9   Read the blueprint and the actual test described in Project 1 in Part Three. To what extent do these incorporate the tenets of the philosophy of testing presented in this chapter?

Notes

1   Statistical techniques and procedures for measurement and evaluation are not discussed in this book. References to these are provided in Chapters 2, 5, and 11.

2   The term 'target language use domain' is defined in Chapter 3.

2 Test usefulness: Qualities of language tests

Introduction

The most important consideration in designing and developing a language test is the use for which it is intended, so that the most important quality of a test is its usefulness. This may seem so obvious that it need not be stated. But what makes a test useful? How do we know if a test will be useful before we use it? Or if it has been useful after we have used it? Stating the question of usefulness this way implies that simply using a test does not make it useful. By stating the obvious and by questioning it, we wish to point out that although usefulness is of unquestioned importance, it has not been defined precisely enough to provide a basis for either designing and developing a test or for determining its usefulness after it has been developed.

We believe that test usefulness provides a kind of metric by which we can evaluate not only the tests that we develop and use, but also all aspects of test development and use. We thus regard a model of test usefulness as the essential basis for quality control throughout the entire test development process. We would further argue that all test development and use should be informed by a model of test usefulness. In this chapter we propose a model of test usefulness that includes six test qualities—reliability, construct validity, authenticity, interactiveness, impact, and practicality. We also propose three principles that we believe are the basis for operationalizing our model of usefulness in the development and use of language tests. This model, along with the three principles, provides a basis for answering the question, 'How useful is this particular test for its intended purpose(s)?' We first describe the model and principles, and then discuss each of the six qualities of test usefulness, providing examples to illustrate each. In Chapter 7 we provide specific questions that might be asked, during the test design and development process, for evaluating these qualities for specific testing situations.

Test usefulness

The traditional approach to describing test qualities has been to discuss these as more or less independent characteristics, emphasizing the need to maximize them all. This has led some language testers to what we see as the extreme and untenable position that maximizing one quality leads to the virtual loss of others. Language testers have been told that the qualities of reliability and validity are essentially in conflict (for example, Underhill 1982; Heaton 1988), or that it is not possible to design test tasks that are authentic and at the same time reliable (for example, Morrow 1979, 1986). A much more reasonable position, expressed by Hughes (1989), is that although there is a tension among the different test qualities, this need not lead to the total abandonment of any. It is our view that rather than emphasizing the tension among the different qualities, test developers need to recognize their complementarity. We would thus argue that test developers need to find an appropriate balance among these qualities, and that this will vary from one testing situation to another. This is because what constitutes an appropriate balance can be determined only by considering the different qualities in combination as they affect the overall usefulness of a particular test.

Our notion of usefulness can be expressed as in Figure 2.1.

Usefulness = Reliability + Construct validity +
Authenticity + Interactiveness + Impact + Practicality

Figure 2.1:   Usefulness

This is a representation of our view that test usefulness can be described as a function of several different qualities, all of which contribute in unique but interrelated ways to the overall usefulness of a given test.[1] We believe that a basis for operationalizing this view of usefulness in the development and use of language tests is provided by the three principles that follow. (We provide detailed discussions of how these principles can be operationalized in test design and development in Chapters 7 and 9.)

Principle 1 It is the overall usefulness of the test that is to be maximized, rather than the individual qualities that affect usefulness.

Principle 2 The individual test qualities cannot be evaluated independently, but must be evaluated in terms of their combined effect on the overall usefulness of the test.

Principle 3 Test usefulness and the appropriate balance among the different qualities cannot be prescribed in general, but must be determined for each specific testing situation.

These principles reflect our belief that, in order to be useful, any given language test must be developed with a specific purpose, a particular group of test takers and a specific language use domain (i.e. situation or context in which the test taker will be using the language outside of the test itself) in mind. (We will refer to this domain as a 'target language use', or TLU, domain, and the tasks in the TLU domain as 'TLU tasks'. This is discussed in greater detail on pages 44–5 in Chapter 3.) Usefulness thus cannot be evaluated in the abstract, for all tests. We can describe the notion of test usefulness in terms of the six test qualities, and outline general considerations and procedures for assessing these. We cannot, however, offer general prescriptions about either what the appropriate balance among the different qualities should be or what are minimum acceptable levels. This can only be done for a given test and testing situation.

Evaluating the overall usefulness of a given test is essentially subjective, since this involves value judgments on the part of the test developer. In a large-scale test that will be used for making important decisions about large numbers of individuals, for example, the test developer may want to design the test and test tasks so as to achieve the highest possible levels of reliability and validity. In a classroom test, on the other hand, the teacher may want to utilize test tasks that will provide higher degrees of authenticity, interactiveness, and impact.

Test qualities

In considering the specific qualities that determine the overall usefulness of a given test, we believe it is essential to take a systemic view, considering tests as part of a larger societal or educational context. In this discussion, we will focus on the use of tests in educational programs, which will include many components, such as teaching materials and learning activities, as well as tests. The main difference between tests and other components of an instructional program, in our view, is in their purpose. While the primary purpose of other components is to promote learning, the primary purpose of tests is to measure. Tests can serve pedagogical purposes, to be sure, but this is not their *primary* function. Four of the qualities that we will discuss with respect to tests are shared by other components of a learning program. Thus, we can consider the authenticity of a particular language sample that may be used for instruction, the interactiveness of a particular learning task, the impact of a given learning activity, or the practicality of a particular teaching approach for a given situation. Two of the qualities—reliability and validity—are, however, critical for tests, and are sometimes referred to as essential *measurement* qualities. This is because these are the qualities that provide the major justification for using test scores—numbers—as a basis for making inferences or decisions.

Reliability

Reliability is often defined as consistency of measurement. A reliable test score will be consistent across different characteristics of the testing situation. Thus, reliability can be considered to be a function of the consistency of scores from one set of tests and test tasks to another. If we think of test tasks as sets of task characteristics, as described in the next chapter, then reliability can be considered to be a function of consistencies across different sets of test task characteristics. (Test task characteristics are discussed in Chapter 3.) This can be represented as in Figure 2.2.

Figure 2.2:   Reliability

In this figure, the double-headed arrow is used to indicate a correspondence between two sets of task characteristics (A and A') which differ only in incidental ways. For example, if the same test were to be administered to the same group of individuals on two different occasions, in two different settings, it should not make any difference to a particular test taker whether she takes the test on one occasion and setting or the other. Or suppose, for example, we had developed two forms of a test that were intended to be used interchangeably, it should not make any difference to a particular test taker which form of the test she takes; she should obtain the same score on either form. Thus, in a test designed to rank order individuals from highest to lowest, if the scores obtained on the different forms do not rank individuals in essentially the same order, then these scores are not very consistent, and would be considered to be unreliable indicators of the ability we want to measure. Similarly, in a test designed to distinguish individuals who are at or above a particular mastery level of ability from those who are below it, if the scores obtained from the two forms do not identify the same individuals as 'masters' and 'non-masters', then this test would be unreliable for making such classification decisions. Another example would be if we used several different raters to rate a large number of compositions. In this case, a given composition should receive the same score irrespective of which particular rater scored it. If some raters rate more severely than others, then the ratings of different raters are not consistent, and the scores obtained could not be considered to be reliable.

Reliability is clearly an essential quality of test scores, for unless test scores are relatively consistent, they cannot provide us with any information at all about the ability we want to measure. At the same time, we need to recognize that it is not possible to eliminate inconsistencies entirely. What we can do, however, is try to minimize the effects of those potential sources of inconsistency that are under our control, through test design. Of the many factors that can affect test performance, the characteristics of the test tasks are at least partly under our control. Thus, in designing and developing language tests, we try to minimize variations in the test task characteristics that do not correspond to variations in TLU tasks. In Chapters 7 and 9 we discuss ways in which we can take reliability considerations into account in order to reduce inconsistencies across test tasks, as we design a test and evaluate its potential usefulness.

In addition to using test design to minimize variations in test task characteristics, we need to estimate their effects on test scores, so as to determine how successful we have been. (Procedures for investigating and demonstrating reliability are discussed in the Suggested Readings at the end of this chapter.)

Construct validity

Construct validity pertains to the meaningfulness and appropriateness of the *interpretations* that we make on the basis of test scores. When we interpret scores from language tests as indicators of test takers' language ability, a crucial question is, 'To what extent can we justify these interpretations?' The clear implication of this question is that as test developers and test users we must be able to provide adequate justification for any interpretation we make of a given test score.[2] That is, we need to demonstrate, or justify, the validity of the interpretations we make of test scores, and not simply assert or argue that they are valid.

In order to justify a particular score interpretation, we need to provide evidence that the test score reflects the area(s) of language ability we want to measure, and very little else. In order to provide such evidence, we must define the construct we want to measure. For our purposes, we can consider a *construct* to be the specific definition of an ability that provides the basis for a given test or test task and for interpreting scores derived from this task. The term *construct validity* is therefore used to refer to the extent to which we can interpret a given test score as an indicator of the ability(ies), or construct(s), we want to measure. Construct validity also has to do with the domain of generalization to which our score interpretations generalize. The domain of generalization is the set of tasks in the TLU domain to which the test tasks correspond. At the very least we want our interpretations about language ability to generalize beyond the testing situation itself to a particular TLU domain. These two aspects of the construct validity of score interpretations are represented visually in Figure 2.3.

This figure indicates that test scores are to be interpreted appropriately as indicators of the ability we intend to measure *with respect to a specific domain of generalization*. Thus, when we consider the construct validity of a score interpretation, we need to consider both the construct definition and the characteristics of the test task. We need to consider the characteristics of the test task for two reasons. First we need to determine the extent to which the test task corresponds to tasks in the TLU domain, or the domain of generalization. (This correspondence is discussed below as

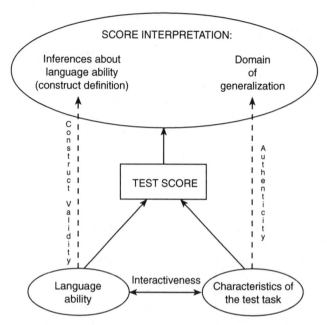

Figure 2.3:   Construct validity of score interpretations

'authenticity'.) A second reason is to determine the degree to which the test task engages the test taker's areas of language ability (discussed below under 'interactiveness').

Construct validation is the on-going process of demonstrating that a particular interpretation of test scores is justified, and involves, essentially, building a logical case in support of a particular interpretation and providing evidence justifying that interpretation.[3] Several types of evidence (for example, content relevance and coverage, concurrent criterion relatedness, predictive utility) can be provided in support of a particular score interpretation, as part of the validation process, and these are discussed in the Suggested Readings at the end of this chapter. In Chapters 7 and 9 we discuss ways in which we can logically take validity considerations into account as we design a test and evaluate its potential usefulness.

It is important for test developers and users to realize that test validation is an on-going process and that the interpretations we make of test scores can never be considered absolutely valid. Justifying the interpretations we make on the basis of language test scores begins with test design and continues with the gathering of evidence to support our intended interpretations. However, even when we have provided evidence in support of a particular set of interpretations, we need to recognize that these must be viewed as tenuous. For this reason, we should not give the impression that a given interpretation is 'valid' or 'has been validated'.

Summary of reliability and construct validity

The primary purpose of a language test is to provide a *measure* that we can interpret as an indicator of an individual's language ability. The two measurement qualities, reliability and construct validity, are thus essential to the usefulness of any language test. Reliability is a necessary condition for construct validity, and hence for usefulness. However, reliability is not a sufficient condition for either construct validity or usefulness. Suppose, for example, that we needed a test for placing individuals into different levels in an academic writing course. A multiple-choice test of grammatical knowledge might yield very consistent or reliable scores, but this would not be sufficient to justify using this test as a placement test for a writing course. This is because grammatical knowledge is only one aspect of the ability to use language to perform academic writing tasks. In this case, defining the construct to include only one area of language knowledge is inappropriately narrow, since the construct involved in the TLU domain— ability to perform academic writing tasks—involves other areas of language knowledge, as well as metacognitive strategies, and may involve topical knowledge and affective responses as well.

Authenticity[4]

In Chapter 3 we argue that, in order to justify the use of language tests, we need to be able to demonstrate that performance on language tests corresponds to language use in specific domains other than the language test itself. One aspect of demonstrating this pertains to the correspondence between the characteristics of TLU tasks and those of the test task. It is this correspondence that is at the heart of authenticity, and we would describe a test task whose characteristics correspond to those of TLU tasks as relatively authentic. We define *authenticity* as the degree of correspondence of the characteristics of a given language test task to the features of a TLU task. This relationship is shown in Figure 2.4 (this corresponds to arrow 'B' in Figure 1.1 in Chapter 1).

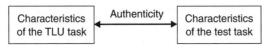

Figure 2.4: Authenticity

Authenticity as a critical quality of language tests has not generally been discussed in language testing textbooks, even though it has been debated among language testing researchers now for over a decade. We consider authenticity to be an important test quality because it relates the test task to the domain of generalization to which we want our score interpretations to generalize. Authenticity thus provides a means for investigating the extent to which score interpretations generalize beyond performance on the test to language use in the TLU domain, or to other similar nontest language use domains. This links authenticity to construct validity, since investigating the generalizability of score interpretations is an important part of construct validation.

Another reason for considering authenticity to be important is because of its potential effect on test takers' perceptions of the test and, hence, on their performance. One way in which test takers and test users tend to react to a language test is in terms of the perceived relevance, to a TLU domain, of the test's topical content and the types of tasks required. It is this relevance, as perceived by the test taker, that we believe helps promote a positive affective response to the test task and can thus help test takers perform at their best.

We believe that most language test developers implicitly consider authenticity in designing language tests. In developing a reading test, for example, we are likely to choose a passage whose topical content matches the kinds of topics and material we think the test taker may read outside of the testing situation. Or, if the TLU domain requires test takers to participate in conversations, then we will design a test task in which interaction and feedback are characteristics. What we are proposing, then, in defining authenticity in terms of task characteristics, is not a radical departure from current testing practice. Rather, we believe our approach provides a more precise way of building considerations of authenticity into the design and development of language tests.

In attempting to design an authentic test task, we first identify the critical features that define tasks in the TLU domain, using as a starting point a framework of task characteristics such as that described in the next chapter. We then either design test tasks or select sample tasks that have these critical features. In Chapters 6 and 9 we describe ways in which the task characteristics can be used to identify and define critical features of test tasks so as to permit us to assess their relative authenticity.

Because of the way in which we have defined TLU domain, our definition of authenticity can apply to a wide variety of domains, including language classrooms in which the teaching is 'communicative', or 'task-based'. This allows us to consider the relevance of test content and test tasks to classroom teaching and learning activities that are themselves related to a specific TLU domain. This definition also allows for possible different perceptions of authenticity. Different test takers may have different perceptions about their TLU domains. Similarly, test takers' perceptions of the relevance of the characteristics of a given test task to their TLU domains may be different from those of the test developers. For example, suppose you were applying for a position as sales clerk in a department store where English was spoken, and the personnel office required you to take an

English test as part of the screening process. What might be your reaction to a test that required you to summarize orally a letter to the editor of a newspaper on the subject of hazardous waste disposal? You would obviously question the content of the test. How relevant would either the topic or the rhetorical organization of this particular genre of English (summarization) be to the English you are likely to use on the job? You might perceive this particular aspect of language use to be largely irrelevant to your ability to carry out an interactive conversation with customers, even though the ability to describe something orally might be relevant to your job. Or suppose you were told that you needed to know enough vocabulary to talk about the items you would be selling and were given a test consisting of a written passage describing the types of merchandise the department store sells, in which various words had been deleted, and you were required to fill in the missing words. You might perceive the topical content of this test as relevant to your job, but the task of filling in missing words as irrelevant. What all of this implies is that authenticity must be assessed from a number of perspectives, and that these must all be taken into consideration in the development and use of language tests. In Chapters 7 and 9 we discuss ways in which we can take considerations of authenticity into account as we design a test and evaluate its potential usefulness.

Interactiveness

We define *interactiveness* as the extent and type of involvement of the test taker's individual characteristics in accomplishing a test task. The individual characteristics that are most relevant for language testing are the test taker's language ability (language knowledge and strategic competence, or metacognitive strategies), topical knowledge, and affective schemata. (These are described on pages 65–6 in Chapter 4.) The interactiveness of a given language test task can thus be characterized in terms of the ways in which the test taker's areas of language knowledge, metacognitive strategies, topical knowledge, and affective schemata are engaged by the test task. For example, a test task that requires a test taker to relate the topical content of the test input to her own topical knowledge is likely to be relatively more interactive than one that does not. We can represent interactiveness as in Figure 2.5.

In this figure, the double-headed arrows are intended to represent interactions between language ability, topical knowledge and affective schemata, and the characteristics of the test task. Unlike authenticity, which pertains to the correspondence between test tasks and TLU tasks, and must thus consider the characteristics of both kinds of tasks, interactiveness resides in the interaction between the individual (test taker or language user) and

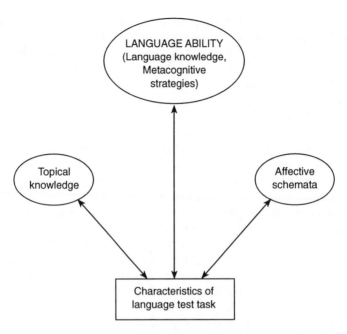

Figure 2.5:   Interactiveness

the task (test or TLU).[5] Interactiveness is thus a quality of any task, and both TLU tasks and test tasks can potentially vary in their interactiveness. It is for this reason that we distinguish interactiveness from authenticity.

In Chapter 4 we define language ability as including areas of language knowledge and strategic competence, or metacognitive strategies. Thus, in order for us to be able to make inferences about *language* ability, responding to the test task must involve the test taker's areas of language knowledge and her strategic competence. We can think of many types of test tasks, such as those involving mathematical calculation or responding to visual, non-verbal information, that might involve the test taker in a high level of interaction with the test input. However, unless this interaction requires the use of language knowledge, we would not be able to make inferences about language ability on the basis of the test taker's performance. For example, a geometry test task that requires the test taker to utilize graphic and numeric information in a diagram to solve the problem presented may be very engaging, but we would not attempt to interpret performance on this task as an indication of language ability. Interactiveness is thus a critical quality of language test tasks, since it is this quality that provides the vital link with construct validity. In Chapters 7 and 9 we discuss ways in which we can take considerations of interactiveness into account as we design a test and evaluate its potential usefulness.

Illustrative examples of authenticity and interactiveness in test tasks

In order to achieve a better understanding of what we mean by authenticity and interactiveness, we will present four examples of test tasks that differ in terms of these qualities. We believe this will help you to understand how actual test tasks differ in terms of their authenticity and interactiveness.

The first example (A) is from a hypothetical institution abroad in which some of the typists do not understand English very well, but have nevertheless developed a high level of ability to perform certain typing tasks in English. These typists find it difficult to engage in any sort of reciprocal language use in English, or to produce written text in English on their own. Nevertheless, they are excellent typists and produce high quality typescripts, even from handwritten documents, which is the only task required for their job. A screening test for new typists in this situation might involve simply asking job applicants to type from a handwritten document. If the applicants know that their on-the-job use of English will be limited to exactly this kind of typing, they will probably perceive the typing test as highly relevant to the job. Clearly, however, the test meets very few of the criteria for interactiveness, since it does not necessarily require the test takers to process the handwritten document as language. That is, a typist might be able simply to copy the letters and words, without processing the document as a piece of discourse. This example illustrates a test task which would be evaluated as highly authentic but low in terms of interactiveness. The 'A' in the upper left corner of the diagram in Figure 2.6 indicates where this example test falls in terms of authenticity and interactiveness.

We can use the same testing situation for a second example (B). Suppose that these same applicants were capable of carrying on 'small talk' conversations in English about food, the weather, clothing, and so forth, and suppose that we tested them by interviewing them in English. If the topics in the interview were of interest to them, the interview might actually involve the same types of interactions involved in non-test conversation. If the scores from this interview were used to select individuals whose sole

	Interactiveness	
	Low	High
Authenticity		
High	A	D
Low	C	B

Figure 2.6:   Authenticity and interactiveness

use of English was to type from handwritten documents, how would this example rate with respect to authenticity and interactiveness? This task would probably be judged to be relatively low in authenticity due to the lack of relevance of the test task to the TLU tasks. On the other hand, it would probably be rated relatively high in interactiveness, particularly if the interview format allowed the test taker a reasonable amount of control in selecting topics and influencing the structure of the interaction. The 'B' in the diagram in Figure 2.6 indicates where this example falls.

For our third example (C), suppose international students entering an American university were given a test of English vocabulary in which they were required to match words in one column with meanings in a second column. Scores from this test would be used to provide diagnostic information about students' ability to read academic texts in English. How does this rate in terms of authenticity and interactiveness? This task can be said to be relatively low in authenticity because there are very few (if any) language use domains in American universities that involve this sort of task. It is also relatively low in interactiveness because of the highly restricted involvement of language knowledge and the minimal involvement of the three metacognitive strategies. The 'C' in the diagram in Figure 2.6 shows where this example falls.

As a final example: suppose we used a role play in which a prospective salesperson was required to attempt to sell a product. The role play might involve a face-to-face oral conversation with an interlocutor who plays the role of a potential customer. The test taker might be required to engage the hypothetical customer in a conversation, decide upon what kind of approach to use in the selling task, and carry out the task. How authentic and interactive is this test task? It would be rated as relatively high in both authenticity and interactiveness. It is high in authenticity because of the correspondence between characteristics of the TLU domain and characteristics of the test task. It is high in interactiveness because of the involvement of assessment, goal-setting, and planning strategies, as well as the high level of involvement of all of the areas of language knowledge and the test taker's topical knowledge. The 'D' in the diagram in Figure 2.6 indicates where this test task falls.

Some things to remember about authenticity and interactiveness

Taken together, the concepts of authenticity and interactiveness have the following implications for how we design, develop, and use language tests.

1   Both authenticity and interactiveness are relative, so that we speak of 'relatively more' or 'relatively less' authentic or interactive, rather than 'authentic' and 'inauthentic,' or 'interactive' and 'non-interactive'.

2   We cannot determine the relative authenticity or interactiveness of a

test task just by looking at it; we must consider three sets of characteristics: those of the test takers, of the TLU task, and of the test task.

3   Certain test tasks may be relatively useful for their intended purposes,
even though they are low in either authenticity or interactiveness.

4   In either designing new tests or analyzing existing tests, our estimates
of authenticity and interactiveness are only guesses. We can do our best
to design test tasks that we believe will be authentic and interactive for
a given group of test takers, but we need to realize that different test
takers may process the same test task in different ways, often in ways
we may not anticipate.

5   The minimum acceptable levels that we specify for authenticity and
interactiveness will depend on the specific testing situation. We have
argued that these qualities must be considered essential to language tests
if these are to reflect current views about the nature of language use,
language learning, and language teaching. At the same time, however,
the minimum acceptable levels for authenticity and interactiveness must
be balanced with those for the other test qualities.

Authenticity, interactiveness, and construct validity

Authenticity, interactiveness, and construct validity all depend upon how
we define the construct 'language ability' for a given test situation. Authenticity has to do with the relevance of the test task to the TLU domain, and
is thus related to the traditional notion of content validity.[6] This also provides a basis for specifying the domain to which we want our score interpretations to generalize and hence, for investigating this aspect of construct
validity. The relationship between interactiveness and construct validity is
a function of the relative involvement of areas of language knowledge, strategic competence, or metacognitive strategies, and topical knowledge. That
is, the extent to which high interactiveness corresponds to construct validity
will depend on how we have defined the construct and on the characteristics of the test takers. Thus, it is possible for a test task not to provide a
valid measure of a given construct, even though it is relatively interactive
for a given group of test takers. A test task that requires the processing of
a great deal of non-verbal visual input in the form of graphs and charts,
for example, might be quite interactive, in that it involves the test taker's
metacognitive strategies and topical knowledge. However, if it requires very
little involvement of areas of language knowledge, it may not provide a
valid measure of language knowledge.

Impact

Another quality of tests is their impact on society and educational systems
and upon the individuals within those systems. The impact of test use operates at two levels: a micro level, in terms of the individuals who are affected

Figure 2.7:   Impact

by the particular test use, and a macro level, in terms of the educational system or society. Impact can be represented as in Figure 2.7.

The very acts of administering and taking a test imply certain values and goals, and have consequences. Similarly, the uses we make of test scores imply values and goals, and these uses have consequences. As Bachman (1990) points out, 'tests are not developed and used in a value-free psycho-metric test-tube; they are virtually always intended to serve the needs of an educational system or of society at large' (p. 279). What values and goals are implied, for example, when we choose to give a test rather than seeking information from a different source, such as a teacher who knows the potential test takers, or by reviewing the test takers' records? What are the consequences for society, the educational system, and the individuals involved, of basing our decisions on test scores, rather than on some other criterion such as seniority or personal connections? Thus, whenever we use tests, we do so in the context of specific values and goals, and our choice will have specific consequences for, or impact on, both the individuals and the system involved.

Washback

An aspect of impact that has been of particular interest to both language testing researchers and practitioners is what is referred to as 'washback', and most discussions of this have focused on processes (learning and instruction).[7] These processes take place in and are implemented by individuals, as well as educational and societal systems, and they have effects on individuals, educational systems, and society at large. We thus feel washback can best be considered within the scope of impact, and this is the perspective we will present here.[8]

Washback has been discussed in language testing largely as the direct impact of testing on individuals, and it is widely assumed to exist. Hughes, for example, defines washback as 'the effect of testing on teaching and learning' (1989: 1), and asserts that testing can have either a beneficial or a harmful effect on teaching and learning. Cohen discusses the effects of washback more broadly, in terms of 'how assessment instruments affect educational practices and beliefs' (1994: 41). Wall and Alderson (1993), on the other hand, argue convincingly, on the basis of extensive empirical research, that test developers and test users cannot simply assume that tests will have an impact on teaching and learning, but must actually investigate the specific areas (such as content of teaching, teaching methodology, ways of assessing achievement), direction (positive, negative), and extent of the presumed impact. Their work also makes it clear that washback has potential for affecting not only individuals, but the educational system as well, which implies that language testers need to investigate this aspect of washback also. Thus, in investigating washback, one must be prepared to find that it is far more complex and thorny than simply the effect of testing on teaching.

Impact on individuals

A variety of individuals will be affected by and thus have an interest, or hold a 'stake', in the use of a given test in any particular situation. 'Stakeholders' that are directly affected include the test takers and the test users, or decision makers. In addition, a large number of individuals (e.g. test takers' future classmates or co-workers, future employers) will be indirectly affected. Finally, to the extent that it has an impact on the societal or educational system at large, it can be argued that virtually every member of the system is indirectly affected by the use of the test. Rather than attempting to discuss the general systemic effect of test use or the potential indirect impact on individuals, we will focus our attention here on the impact on those individuals who are most directly affected by test use: test takers and teachers.

Impact on test takers

Test takers can be affected by three aspects of the testing procedure:

1 the experience of taking and, in some cases, of preparing for the test,
2 the feedback they receive about their performance on the test, and
3 the decisions that may be made about them on the basis of their test scores.

The experiences of preparing for and taking the test have the potential for affecting those characteristics of test takers that are discussed in our model of language use in Chapter 4. In high-stakes tests such as public examinations or standardized tests for nationally or internationally recognized qualifications, test takers may spend several weeks preparing individually for the test. In some countries, where high-stakes nation-wide public examinations are used for selection and placement into higher levels of the school system or into universities, teaching may be focused on the syllabus of the test for up to several years before the actual test, and the techniques needed in the test will be practiced in class.

The experience of taking the test itself can also have an impact on test takers. The test taker's topical knowledge, for example, can be affected if the test provides topical or cultural information that is new. We thus need to ask whether the topical content of the test task informs or misinforms the test taker. The test taker's perception of the TLU domain may be affected by the test, particularly in cases where the TLU domain may be unfamiliar (for example, an international student planning to enroll in a program of study at an American college or university). We thus need to ask whether the test informs or misleads the test taker as to various aspects of the TLU domain. Test takers' areas of language knowledge may also be affected by the test. For many test takers, the test can provide some confirmation or disconfirmation of their own perceptions of their language ability, and may affect their areas of language knowledge. For example, if something is presented as grammatically correct in the input, but is actually ungrammatical, this can be misleading. Conversely, the test taker may improve her language knowledge either while taking the test or from feedback received. Finally, the test taker's use of strategies may be affected by the characteristics of the test task, particularly with tasks that are highly interactive. We would suggest that one way to promote the potential for positive impact is through involving test takers in the design and development of the test, as well as collecting information from them about their perceptions of the test and test tasks. If test takers are involved in this way, we would hypothesize that the test tasks are likely to be perceived as more authentic and interactive, and that test takers will have a more positive perception of the test, be more highly motivated, and probably perform better.

The types of feedback test takers receive about their test performance are likely to affect them directly. We thus need to consider how to make feedback as relevant, complete, and meaningful to the test taker as possible. Feedback is almost always in the form of some sort of score, and so we need to make sure that the scores we report are meaningful to test takers. We also need to consider additional types of feedback, such as verbal descriptions to help interpret test scores, as well as verbal descriptions of the actual test tasks and the test taker's performance. The provision of rich verbal description, especially if given in a personal debriefing with the appropriate test administrator, can be very effective in developing a positive affective response toward the test on the part of test takers.[9]

Finally, the decisions that may be made about the test takers on the basis of their test scores may directly affect them in a number of ways. Acceptance or non-acceptance into an instructional program, advancement or non-advancement from one course to another, or in a career, employment or non-employment, are all decisions that can have serious consequences for test takers. We thus need to consider the fairness of the decisions to be made. *Fair decisions* are those that are equally appropriate, regardless of individual test takers' group membership. We need to ask whether the decision procedures and criteria are applied uniformly to all groups of test takers. *Fair test use* also has to do with the relevance and appropriateness of the test score to the decision. We need to consider the various kinds of information, including scores from the test, that could be used in making the decisions, as well as their relative importance and the criteria that will be used. Is it fair, for example, to make a life-affecting decision solely on the basis of a test score? Finally, fair test use has to do with whether and by what means test takers are fully informed about how the decision will be made and whether decisions are actually made in the way described to them. For example, if test takers are told that acceptance into a program will be based on their test scores and grades, but acceptance is actually based primarily on letters of reference, we might question the fairness of the decision procedure.

Impact on teachers

The second group of individuals who are directly affected by tests are test users, and in an instructional program the test users that are most directly affected by test use are teachers. As noted above, impact on the program of instruction, as implemented by classroom teachers, has been referred to by language testers as washback. Most teachers are familiar with the amount of influence testing can have on their instruction. Despite the fact that teachers may personally prefer to teach certain material in a specific way, if they find that they have to use a specified test they may find 'teaching to the test' almost unavoidable. The term 'teaching to the test' implies doing something in teaching that may not be compatible with teachers' own values and goals, or with the values and goals of the instructional program. The notion of teaching to the test can be related to authenticity, discussed earlier, if we consider the instructional setting to be the TLU domain. From this perspective, if teachers feel that what they teach is not relevant to the test (or vice versa), this must be seen as an instance of low test authenticity, in which the test may have harmful washback, or negative impact on instruction. One way to minimize the potential for negative impact on instruction is to change the way we test so that the characteristics of the test and test tasks correspond more closely to the characteristics of the instructional program.

The opposite situation is where those responsible for the instructional program are not satisfied with the quality of that program and the results it produces. This dissatisfaction is often based on the results of tests, but it may also arise because various aspects of the program (for instance, curriculum, materials, types of learning activities) may be out of touch with what teachers currently believe promotes effective learning. A number of language testers have argued that, in situations such as this, one way to bring instructional practice in line with current thinking in the field is to develop a testing procedure that reflects this thinking. That is, in this situation the hypothesis is that we should be able bring about improvement in instructional practice through the use of tests that incorporate or are compatible with what we believe to be principles of effective teaching and learning. However, we would reinforce Wall and Alderson's (1993) point that we cannot simply assume that imposing an 'enlightened' test will automatically have an effect on instructional practice. Indeed, as their research has demonstrated, the impact of testing on instruction varies with respect to the particular aspects of instruction that are affected, and the extent of the impact can range from virtually nothing to quite a lot, and can be both positive and negative.

Impact on society and education systems

As test developers and test users we must always consider the societal and educational value systems that inform our test use. The consideration of values and goals is particularly complex in the context of second or foreign language testing, since this situation inevitably leads us to the realization that the values and goals that inform test use may vary from one culture to the next. For example, one culture may place great value on individual effort and achievement, while in another culture group cooperation and respect for authority may be highly valued. Values and goals also change over time, so that issues such as secrecy and access to information, privacy and confidentiality, which are now considered by many to be basic rights of test takers, were at one time not even a matter of consideration.

We must also consider the consequences of our actions, realizing that the use of a language test is likely to have consequences not only for the individual stake holders, as discussed above, but also for the educational system and society. This is of particular concern with high-stakes tests, which are used to make major decisions about large numbers of individuals. Consider, for example, the potential impact on the language teaching practice and language programs in a given country of using a particular type of test task, such as the multiple-choice item or a specific type of oral interview, in widely used high-stakes tests on a national level. Similarly, we need to consider the potential impact on societal values and goals of using language tests for particular purposes. For example, what might be the impact on society of using language tests for purposes of grouping school children into different instructional programs, or for screening individuals applying for immigration, or as part of the licensing procedure for professionals? If test use reflects the values and goals of only a small segment of society, to what extent might this use exert a positive or a negative influence on the values and goals of the society as a whole?

We thus need to think through carefully what might happen as a result of our using a test for a particular purpose. We can organize our assessment of potential consequences as follows:

1   list, as completely and in as much detail as we can, the intended uses of the test;
2   list the potential consequences, both positive and negative, of using the test in these ways;
3   rank these possible outcomes in terms of the desirability or undesirability of their occurring;
4   collect information to determine how likely each of the various outcomes is.

This analysis of the possible consequences of using the test should be complemented by a consideration of the consequences of using alternatives to testing to achieve the same purpose.

In summary, the impact of test use needs to be considered within the values and goals of society and the educational program in which it takes place, and according to the potential consequences of such use. In assessing the impact of test use, we must consider the characteristics of the particular testing situation (purpose, TLU domain, test takers, construct definition) in terms of the values and goals of the individuals affected and of the educational system and society, and of the potential consequences for the individuals, the educational system, and society. The notion of washback in language testing can be characterized in terms of impact, and includes the potential impact on test takers and their characteristics, on teaching and learning activities, and on educational systems and society. In Chapters 7 and 9 we discuss specific considerations for assessing the potential impact of test use and for taking these into account in the design and development of tests. We illustrate how this can be done through the projects that are presented in Part Three.

Practicality

The last test quality that needs to be considered is practicality, which is different in nature from the other five qualities. While those qualities pertain to the *uses* that are made of test scores, practicality pertains primarily to the ways in which the test will be implemented, and, to a large degree, whether it will be developed and used at all. That is, for any given situation, if the resources required for implementing the test exceed the resources available, the test will be impractical, and will not be used unless resources can be allocated more efficiently, or unless additional resources can be allocated. Although the consideration of practicality logically follows the consideration of the other qualities, this does not imply that practicality is any less important than the other qualities of usefulness. On the contrary, in the test development process the determination of usefulness is cyclical, so that considerations of practicality are likely to affect our decisions at every stage along the way, and may lead us to reconsider and perhaps revise some of our earlier specifications.

In designing and developing a test, we try to achieve the optimum balance among the qualities of reliability, construct validity, authenticity, interactiveness, and impact for our particular testing situation. In addition, we must determine the resources required to achieve this balance, in relationship to the resources that are available. Thus, determining the practicality of a given test involves the consideration of (1) the resources that will be required to develop an operational test that has the balance of qualities we want, and (2) the allocation and management of the resources that are available. This is discussed and illustrated in detail in Chapter 8. In this chapter we will simply define practicality and introduce the primary aspects of practicality that need to be considered.

We can define *practicality* as the relationship between the resources that will be required in the design, development, and use of the test and the resources that will be available for these activities. This relationship can be represented as in Figure 2.8.

$$\text{Practicality} = \frac{\text{Available resources}}{\text{Required resources}}$$

If practicality ≥ 1, the test development and use is practical.
If practicality < 1, the test development and use is not practical.

Figure 2.8:   Practicality

Practicality is a matter of the extent to which the demands of the particular test specifications can be met within the limits of existing resources. We believe this view of practicality is useful because it enables us to define a 'threshold level' for practicality in any given testing situation. If the resource demands of the test specifications do not exceed the available resources at any stage in test development, then the test is practical and development and test use can proceed. If available resources are exceeded, then the test is not practical and the developer must either modify the specifications to reduce the resources required, or increase the available resources or reallocate them so that they can be utilized more efficiently. Thus, a practical test is one whose design, development, and use do not require more resources than are available.

Types of resources

In order to assess practicality, we need to specify what we mean by resources, which we can classify into three general types. *Human resources* include, for example, test writers, scorers or raters, and test administrators, as well as clerical and technical support personnel. *Material resources* include space (such as rooms for test development and test administration), equipment (such as typewriters, word processors, tape and video recorders, computers) and materials (such as paper, pictures, library resources). *Time* consists of development time (time from the beginning of the test development process to the reporting of scores from the first operational administration) and time for specific tasks (for example, designing, writing, administering, scoring, analyzing). In considering the different types of resources, it is also essential to estimate the specific monetary costs that may be associated with each, since in many testing situations the total amount of resources available is essentially a function of budget. These different types of resources are listed in Figure 2.9.

---

1 Human resources
   (e.g. test writers, scorers or raters, test administrators, and clerical support)

2 Material resources
   Space (e.g. rooms for test development and test administration)
   Equipment (e.g. typewriters, word processors, tape and video recorders, computers)
   Materials (e.g. paper, pictures, library resources)

3 Time
   Development time (time from the beginning of the test development process to the reporting of scores from the first operational administration)
   Time for specific tasks (e.g. designing, writing, administering, scoring, analyzing)

Figure 2.9: Types of resources

Different types of resources, and their associated costs, will be required in varying degrees at different stages of test development and use. Furthermore, the specific types and amounts of resources required will vary according to the design of the specific test, and available resources will differ from one situation to another. For these reasons, practicality can only be determined for a specific testing situation; a test specification that is practical in one situation may not be practical in another. It thus makes little sense to say that a given test or test task is more or less practical than another, in general. What we can probably say, however, is that some tests or test tasks are relatively more or less demanding of different types of resources, or at different stages in the testing process. We discuss resource allocation and management in detail in Chapter 8.

Conclusion

We believe the approach to defining test usefulness developed here makes a contribution to the field of language testing for two reasons. First, it provides a principled basis for considering the relative importance of all the qualities that contribute to usefulness, and enables us to consider how these interact with each other. Second, it ties the notion of usefulness to the specific testing situation. That is, it links considerations of reliability, validity, authenticity, interactiveness, impact, and practicality to the specific purpose of the test, to a specific TLU domain, to specific groups of test takers and test users, and to specific local conditions with respect to the availability and allocation of resources. This approach to test usefulness thus makes two requirements of test developers. First, we must consider these qualities with respect to specific tests, and not solely in terms of abstract theories and statistical formulae. Second, we must consider these qualities from the very beginning of the test planning and development process, and rather than relying solely on *ex post facto* analyses.

Summary

The most important consideration in designing a language test is its usefulness, and this can be defined in terms of six test qualities: reliability, validity, authenticity, interactiveness, impact, and practicality. These six test qualities all contribute to test usefulness, so that they cannot be evaluated independently of each other. Furthermore, the relative importance of these different qualities will vary from one testing situation to another, so that test usefulness can only be evaluated for specific testing situations. Similarly, the appropriate balance of these qualities cannot be prescribed in the abstract, but can only be determined for a given test. The most important consideration to keep in mind is not to ignore any one quality at the expense of others. Rather, we need to strive to achieve an appropriate balance, given the purpose of the test, the characteristics of the TLU domain and the test takers, and the way we have defined the construct to be measured.

Reliability can be defined as consistency of measurement; inconsistency is variation in test scores that is due to factors other than the construct we want to measure. Of the many factors that can affect test performance, the ones over which we have some control are the characteristics of test tasks. Thus, in designing and developing language tests, we try to minimize variations in the test task characteristics that are not motivated by the way in which we have defined the construct and TLU tasks. In addition to attempting to minimize such unmotivated variations through design, we need to estimate their effects on test scores, to determine how successful we have been in minimizing them as sources of inconsistency of measurement.

Construct validity pertains to the meaningfulness and appropriateness of the interpretations that we make on the basis of test scores. The validity of these interpretations cannot simply be asserted, but must be demonstrated. Test validation is the ongoing process of demonstrating that a particular interpretation of test scores is justified, and involves providing evidence justifying that interpretation. The justification that we need to provide is evidence of *construct validity*, or evidence that the test score reflects the area of language ability we want to measure, and very little else.

Authenticity is an important quality for language tests for two reasons:

1   it provides a link between test performance and the TLU tasks and domain to which we want to generalize, and
2   the way test takers perceive the relative authenticity of test tasks can, potentially, facilitate their test performance.

We define authenticity as the degree of correspondence of the characteristics of a given language test task to the characteristics of a TLU task.

Interactiveness is an important test quality because it pertains to the degree to which the constructs we want to assess are critically involved in accomplishing the test task. Interactiveness is also important because it is at the heart of many current views of language teaching and language learning. Interactiveness is a function of the extent and type of involvement of the test taker's language ability (language knowledge plus metacognitive strategies), topical knowledge, and affective schemata in accomplishing a test task.

Both authenticity and interactiveness are relative, so that we speak of 'relatively more' or 'relatively less' authentic and interactive, rather than 'authentic' and 'inauthentic', or 'interactive' and 'non-interactive'. Furthermore, we cannot determine the relative authenticity or interactiveness of a test task just by looking at it; we must also consider the characteristics of the test takers, the TLU domain, and the test task.

Impact can be defined broadly in terms of the various ways in which test use affects society, an education system, and the individuals within these. As test developers and test users we must always consider the societal, educational, and individual value systems that inform our test use. We also need to think through carefully what might happen as a result of our using a test for a particular purpose. Impact operates at two levels: a macro level, in terms of the societal or educational system in general, and a micro level, in terms of the individuals who are affected by the particular test use. The notion of washback, or backwash, which has been of considerable concern in language testing, can be viewed in terms of various aspects of impact.

Unlike the other five qualities, which pertain to the uses that are made of test scores, *practicality* pertains to the ways in which the test will be implemented in a given situation, or whether the test will be used at all. We can define practicality as the relationship between the resources that will be required in the design, development, and use of the test and the resources that will be available for these activities. A practical test is one whose design, development, and use do not require more resources than are available. Several *types of resources* can be identified: human resources, material resources, and time. The specific resources required will vary from one situation to another, as will the resources that are available. Thus, practicality can only be determined for a specific testing situation, and it makes little sense to say that a given test or test task is more or less practical than another, in general. Considerations of practicality are likely to affect our decisions at every stage in the process of test development and use, and these may lead us to reconsider and perhaps revise some of our earlier specifications. In designing and developing a test, we try to achieve the optimum balance among the qualities of reliability, construct validity, authenticity, interactiveness, and impact, for our particular testing situation. In addition, we must determine the resources required to achieve this balance, in relationship to the resources that are available.

Exercises

1   What was your conception of test usefulness prior to reading this chapter? How has your conception changed now that you have read the chapter? How might your procedure in developing a test now differ from the procedures you might have followed in the past?

2   Interview someone who is currently using a language test, but who is not familiar with the framework of usefulness presented in this chapter. Ask this person to consider the usefulness of the test. To what extent has the person taken into account the various qualities of usefulness described in this chapter?

3   Think of a situation for which you might need to develop a test. Work with other members of your class in two small groups, each of which comes up with a proposal for a test for use in this situation. Then compare and evaluate the two proposals in terms of the potential usefulness of each proposal.

4   Suppose someone were to propose that the test task for Project 3 in Part Three be used for the purpose described in Project 4 in Part Three. In what specific ways would the various qualities of usefulness be reduced?

5   Reflect on a language test you once took or administered and its overall usefulness. Are there any aspects of its apparent usefulness that cannot be captured in the six qualities described in this chapter? If so, how might you modify or add to the qualities of usefulness to capture the additional qualities you came up with?

Suggested readings

1   *Standards for Educational and Psychological Testing* (APA 1985) provides an extensive and authoritative discussion of reliability and valid-

ity, as well as standards for test use. The standards described in this publication are widely accepted by the measurement profession, as well as by test developers and test users.

2 Bachman (1990) discusses reliability and validity in Chapters 6 and 7 respectively. Messick (1989) provides an extensive theoretical framework for considering validity of score use.

3 Discussions of test qualities in the context of educational performance assessment can be found in Linn, Baker, and Dunbar (1991), Moss (1992), Baker, O'Neil, and Linn (1993), Linn (1994), Messick (1994), and Wiggins (1994).

4 Widdowson (1978, 1983) discusses authenticity in language teaching materials and exercises.

5 Bachman (1990) Chapter 8 provides an extensive discussion of authenticity in language tests.

6 Canale (1988) discusses the importance of providing rich feedback to test takers.

7 Swain (1985) speaks of designing test tasks that 'bias for the best', or that provide test takers with opportunities to perform at their highest level of ability.

8 Wall and Alderson (1993) and Alderson and Wall (1993) discuss their recent research into washback. Hughes (1989), Weir (1990), and Cohen (1994) provide general discussions of washback.

Notes

1 Many of these qualities are discussed in *Standards for Educational and Psychological Testing* (APA 1985).

2 Current measurement theorists generally include, as considerations in the validity of test use, score interpretations and the consequences of the decisions that are made on the basis of test scores (see, for example, Messick 1989). While we understand the logic of this view, we prefer to consider consequences of decisions separately, under the quality of impact.

3 Another kind of justification that needs to be provided pertains to the consequences, or impact, of the particular decisions that will be made on the basis of test scores, or what can be called the consequential aspect of validity. This involves demonstrating that the consequences of making particular decisions about individuals and of using test scores to inform these decisions are consistent with the values, goals, and objectives of the situation—societal and educational—in which the test is being used. Because of the importance language testers accord to impact, we will discuss this test quality in a separate section below.

4 Authenticity, interactiveness, and impact are three qualities that many measurement specialists consider to be part of validity. We agree that

authenticity and interactiveness are related to construct validity and that impact is part of the consequential basis of test use. However, we believe that these qualities are important enough to the development and use of language tests to warrant separate consideration, and will discuss them as separate qualities.

5   Our definition of interactiveness is essentially an extension of Bachman's (1990) 'interactional/ability' approach to defining authenticity. The definitions of authenticity and interactiveness that we present here thus represent what Bachman (1990) has characterized as the 'real-life' and 'interactional/ability' approaches to defining authenticity, and recognize the value and usefulness of each in characterizing test tasks.

6   Authenticity is also related to the notion of 'face validity', a term which has largely been rejected by both language testers and specialists in educational measurement. Face validity is the appearance of validity, or the extent to which the test appeals to test takers and test users. We would argue that the notion of 'test appeal' is essentially a function of authenticity and interactiveness, and thus do not consider 'face validity' or 'test appeal' to be a separate quality of tests. See Bachman (1990 pages 285–9) for an extensive discussion of the problems with the term 'face validity'.

7   Another term that has also been used is 'backwash' (for example, Hughes 1989; Weir 1990). The term 'washback', however, seems to be more prevalent in both language testing and applied linguistics, and so we will use this latter term.

8   Considering washback within the scope of impact appears to be consistent with current research in language testing, such as that by Wall and Alderson (1993), who use the term 'impact study' to refer to their research into washback.

9   Canale (1988) discusses the need to 'humanize' the experience of testing, and includes the provision of rich feedback about performance in this.

3 Describing tasks: Language use in language tests

Introduction

As indicated in Chapter 1, the ability to describe the characteristics of language use tasks and test tasks is critical in order to demonstrate how performance on a given language test is related to language use in specific situations *other than* the language test itself. The characteristics of tasks are of interest for several reasons. First, these characteristics provide the link between tasks in different domains—the domain of test tasks and the domain of non-test tasks—and permit us to select or design test tasks that correspond in specific ways to language use tasks. Second, the characteristics of the test task will help determine the extent and ways in which the test taker's language ability is engaged. Third, the degree of correspondence between the characteristics of a given test task and of a particular language use task will determine, to a large extent, the authenticity of the test task, the validity of inferences made, and the domain to which those inferences will generalize. Finally, the characteristics of the test task can potentially be controlled by the way language tests are designed and developed.

In this chapter we present a framework that we believe can be used for describing both language use tasks and test tasks. The material in this chapter operationalizes the concepts presented in Chapter 5 of *Fundamental Considerations in Language Testing* (Bachman 1990). In the chapters in Part Two, and in the projects in Part Three, we provide extensive discussions, along with examples, of how this framework can be applied to practical problems in designing and developing useful tests of language ability.

Language use tasks

In order to utilize the notion of language use task in the design and development of language tests, we need to describe what we mean by this term. We can begin our discussion of language use tasks with a definition of *task* given by the psychologist, John B. Carroll (1993) in discussing cognitive abilities: 'a task [is] any activity in which a person engages, given an appropriate setting, in order to achieve a specifiable class of objectives' (Carroll

1992: 8). Carroll emphasizes two aspects of tasks that are relevant to both language use and language testing:

1 the individual must understand what sort of result is to be achieved, and
2 the individual needs to have some idea of the criteria by which performance will be assessed.

Applied linguists have discussed language tasks extensively, and there seems to be general agreement that these are (1) closely associated with, or situated in specific situations, (2) goal-oriented, and (3) involve the active participation of language users. (See the references in Suggested Readings.) Following these definitions, we define a *language use task* as an activity that involves individuals in using language for the purpose of achieving a particular goal or objective in a particular situation. We would note that this definition of language use task thus includes both the specific activity and the situation in which it takes place.

Target language use (TLU) domain

Because language use, by its very nature, is embedded in particular situations, each of which may vary in numerous ways, each instance of language use is virtually unique, making it impossible to list all the possible instances. We believe it is possible, however, to identify certain distinguishing characteristics of language use tasks and to use these characteristics to describe a language use domain. In language testing, our primary purpose is to make inferences about test takers' language ability, and in most cases we are not interested in generalizing to just any, or all language use domains. Rather, we want to make inferences that generalize to those specific domains in which the test takers are likely to need to use language. In other words, we want to be able to make inferences about test takers' ability to use language in a target language use domain. For our purposes, then, we define a *target language use domain* as a set of specific language use tasks that the test taker is likely to encounter outside of the test itself, and to which we want our inferences about language ability to generalize. There are two general types of target language use domains that are of particular interest to the development of language tests. One type of domain consists of so-called 'real-life' domains, in which language is used essentially for purposes of communication. From now on, we will refer to these as *real-life domains*. The other type of domain consists of situations in which language is used for the purpose of teaching and learning of language. We will refer to this type as a *language instruction domain*.[1] If a language use task is within a specific target language use domain, then we will call it a *target language use task*.

An example may help clarify these notions. For the purpose of developing a given language test we might initially identify the TLU domain as 'English for business communication', and within this TLU domain we might identify a number of different language use settings, such as managing and operating an office, negotiating with clients and customers, and promoting products or services. Within each of these settings, it is possible to identify a number of specific language use tasks. In the office setting, for example, the language use tasks might include writing memos, preparing reports, answering and taking messages on the phone, and giving and following directions. Language use tasks involved in negotiating with clients, on the other hand, might include reading potential clients' financial statements and annual reports, writing proposals, responding to written offers, and oral interactions, both face-to-face and over the telephone. All of these tasks, which are within our defined TLU domain, are thus TLU tasks. At some point in the test development process, we may discover that for the purposes of our test, the TLU domain has been defined too broadly, and decide that the focus should be narrowed to that of the office setting. In this case, the TLU domain is redefined to include only those language use tasks that are involved in managing and operating an office, and these then become the set TLU tasks.

Language use tasks can be thought of informally as constituting the elemental activities and situations of language use. That is, language use can be viewed as the performance of a set of interrelated language use tasks. A language test can be thought of as a procedure for eliciting instances of language use from which inferences can be made about an individual's language ability. It therefore follows that in order for such inferences to be made, a language test should consist of language use tasks. We thus believe that the key to designing tests that will be useful for their intended purposes is to include, in the test, tasks whose distinguishing characteristics correspond to those of TLU tasks. In order to accomplish this, we need a framework of task characteristics that will enable us to describe both the TLU tasks and the tasks to be included in the test. We describe such a framework in the next section of this chapter.

Characteristics of test tasks

Effect of task characteristics on test performance

Language teachers intuitively realize that the types of tasks that are included in language tests are important. Frequently one of the first questions asked in our testing classes is about our opinions of the 'best' way to test a particular area of language ability. These teachers may not yet have refined their thinking as to what specific characteristics might make one test task more appropriate for a given purpose than another. However, they are clearly aware that the way they test language ability affects how their students perform on language tests and hence the quality of the information obtained from their tests.

There is also considerable research in language testing that demonstrates the effects of test method on test performance. (See, for example, the Suggested Readings for this chapter.) This research and language teachers' intuitions both lead to the same conclusion: the characteristics of the tasks used are always likely to affect test scores to some degree, so that there is virtually no test that yields only information about the ability we want to measure. The implication of this conclusion for the design, development, and use of language tests is equally clear: since we cannot totally eliminate the effects of task characteristics, we must learn to understand them and to control them so as to insure that the tests we use will have the qualities we desire and are appropriate for the uses for which they are intended.

Precision in characterizing different test tasks

When we think about the different types of tasks that are commonly used for language tests, we realize that they are not single wholes, but rather collections of characteristics. Consider, for example, the *multiple-choice* item, which has often been used as a kind of test task: multiple-choice test items vary in a number of ways, such as in their length, syntactic complexity, level of vocabulary, topical content, and type of response required, to name but a few. Similarly, the 'composition' task type encompasses a wide variety of prompts that can differ in characteristics such as the intended audience, purpose, and specific organizational pattern requested. It is thus clear that we cannot characterize test tasks precisely if we think of them only as holistic types. Therefore we need a descriptive framework of task characteristics.

In this section we provide a framework for describing the characteristics of test tasks in a way that we believe enables test developers and test users to investigate the degree of correspondence between TLU tasks and test tasks. Our position is, however, that it is neither feasible nor necessary, for the purpose of developing language test tasks and tests, to provide an exhaustive discourse analysis of language use. This reflects the need to focus our specifications on those features that are critical to the kinds of inferences we want to make and the specific domains to which we want these inferences to generalize. Thus, rather than providing a 'testing-motivated discourse analysis', we regard our approach to specifying the characteristics of a language use setting as 'discourse-motivated test design and analysis'.

This framework also enables test developers to better understand which specific characteristics can be varied, and to suggest ways in which these can be varied, thus providing a valuable tool for tailoring tests appropriately for specific groups of test takers, and so enabling them to perform at their best. Of the many factors that can affect test performance (for example, unexpected disturbances during the test administration, individual characteristics of test takers, or temporary changes in their physical or mental condition), the characteristics of the test task are the only factors directly under our control as test developers. We therefore believe that attempting to control the test task characteristics by design provides the most useful and practical means for maximizing the usefulness of our tests for their intended purposes.

A framework of language task characteristics

The framework of task characteristics that we describe below builds on that proposed by Bachman (1990), and consists of a set of features for describing five aspects of tasks: setting, test rubric, input, expected response, and relationship between input and response.[2] We would emphasize that the purpose of this framework is to provide a basis for language test development and use. This involves three activities:

1 describing TLU tasks as a basis for designing language test tasks,
2 describing different test tasks in order to insure their comparability, and as a means for assessing reliability, and
3 comparing the characteristics of TLU and test tasks to assess authenticity.

In our own experience in test development, as well as in teaching courses in language testing, and consulting on test development projects, we have found that these characteristics are useful for describing not only the characteristics of test tasks, but also the characteristics of TLU tasks that are relevant to the design and development of test tasks. Thus, in the discussion below, we will use the term 'task' to refer to both TLU tasks and test tasks.

We would hasten to point out that it is not our purpose to prescribe any particular types of test tasks or combination of test task characteristics. On the contrary, we view this framework as a tool for achieving greater flexibility or adaptability in test development, rather than as a recipe for developing tests in one particular way. In addition, it is not our purpose to insist on this particular set of characteristics for all test development situations. Indeed, we have found that, in many test development situations, test developers need to make some modifications in the specific characteristics they include for their own purposes, and we illustrate this in some of the projects in Part Three. Furthermore, the order in which the test task characteristics are specified in a given test development project will not necessarily follow the order in which they are described in this framework. It is because of its adaptability that we believe the framework presented below provides a valuable tool for learning the process of analyzing tasks for purposes of test development and a starting place for task analysis in many practical test development projects.

Our framework of test task characteristics is presented in Table 3.1.

Characteristics of the setting

Characteristics of the *setting* comprise the physical circumstances under which either language use or testing takes place. These characteristics include

1   physical setting,
2   participants, and
3   time of task.

Physical characteristics

These characteristics include the location, the noise level, temperature, humidity, seating conditions, and lighting. Also included are the degree of familiarity of the materials and equipment to the test takers or language users. In a testing situation, materials and equipment may be fairly specialized (for instance, pencils, paper, word processors, audio-visual equipment, props, etc.). In a TLU setting, such as in an office, for example, familiarity with files, a voice-mail system, or a computer system will clearly affect an individual's use of language.

Participants

These are the people who are involved in the task. In a testing situation, the participants include not only the test takers, but also those who are involved in administering the test. What is their status and their relationship to the test takers? How familiar are they to the test takers? In some TLU tasks, such as a conversation, two or more participants actively engage with each other in the negotiation of meaning. In other tasks, such as reading a book, the participants may have quite different roles, with one (the reader) interpreting the discourse without the possibility of actively engaging the other (the writer) in the negotiation of meaning.

Time of task

This is the time at which the test is administered or at which the TLU task takes place. Is the test administered when the test takers are fresh or fatigued? This characteristic is probably of the greatest use in assessing the degree to which the time of testing influences the test takers' ability to perform at their best.

Task characteristics

Characteristics of the setting

Physical characteristics
Participants
Time of task

Characteristics of the test rubrics

Instructions

Language (native, target)
Channel (aural, visual)
Specification of procedures and tasks

Structure

Number of parts/tasks
Salience of parts/tasks
Sequence of parts/tasks
Relative importance of parts/tasks
Number of tasks/items per part

Time allotment
Scoring method

Criteria for correctness
Procedures for scoring the response
Explicitness of criteria and procedures

Characteristics of the input

Format

Channel (aural, visual)
Form (language, non-language, both)
Language (native, target, both)
Length
Type (item, prompt)
Degree of speededness
Vehicle ('live', 'reproduced', both)

Language of input

Language characteristics
Organizational characteristics

Grammatical (vocabulary, syntax, phonology, graphology)
Textual (cohesion, rhetorical/conversational organization)

Pragmatic characteristics

Functional (ideational, manipulative, heuristic, imaginative)
Sociolinguistic (dialect/variety, register, naturalness, cultural references and
figurative language)

Topical characteristics

Characteristics of the expected response

Format

   Channel (aural, visual)
   Form (language, non-language, both)
   Language (native, target, both)
   Length
   Type (selected, limited production, extended production)
   Degree of speededness

Language of expected response

   Language characteristics
      Organizational characteristics
         Grammatical (vocabulary, syntax, phonology, graphology)
         Textual (cohesion, rhetorical/conversational organization)
      Pragmatic characteristics
         Functional (ideational, manipulative, heuristic, imaginative)
         Sociolinguistic (dialect/variety, register, naturalness, cultural references, and
           figurative language)
      Topical Characteristics

Relationship between input and response

   Reactivity (reciprocal, non-reciprocal, adaptive)
   Scope of relationship (broad, narrow)
   Directness of relationship (direct, indirect)

Table 3.1:   Task characteristics

Characteristics of the test rubric

The test rubric includes those characteristics of the test that provide the structure for particular test tasks and that indicate how test takers are to proceed in accomplishing the tasks. In a test task these need to be made as explicit and clear as possible, while in language use these characteristics are generally implicit. For this reason, rubric may be a characteristic for which there is relatively little correspondence between language use tasks and test tasks. The characteristics of rubric include:

1   the structure of the test, that is, how the test itself is organized,
2   instructions,
3   the duration of the test as a whole and of the individual tasks, and
4   how the language that is used will be evaluated, or scored.

Instructions

With test tasks, instructions need to be explicit, because of the need to make inferences on the basis of test performance. In a language test, instructions are the means by which the test takers are informed about the procedures for taking the test, how it will be scored, and how the results will be used. (Instructions are discussed in detail in Chapter 10.)

Language: the language in which the instructions are presented: test takers' native language, the target language, or both.

Channel: the channel in which the instructions are presented: aural, visual, or both.

Specification of procedures and tasks: the manner and extent to which procedures and tasks are clearly and explicitly specified for test takers: lengthy or brief; with or without examples; provided one at a time, linked to particular parts of the test, or provided entirely in one location.

Structure

This is how the parts of the test are put together and presented to the test takers.

Number of parts/tasks: the number of parts or tasks in the test as a whole, or in the discourse.

Salience of parts/tasks: the extent to which the different parts of the test are clearly distinguished from one another: a single task or a clearly defined number of separate tasks.

Sequence of parts/tasks: the order of the parts of the test or test tasks: fixed or variable sequence of response by test takers.

Relative importance of parts/tasks: whether or not and how the parts or tasks of the test differ in importance.

Number of tasks/items per part: how many different tasks are included in each part of the test.

Time allotment

Time allotment is the amount of time allotted for individual test tasks, for the parts, and for the entire test. Is the test designed to be *speeded* (so short that not all test takers are expected to be able to attempt to complete each task), or is it a *power test* (in which enough time is allowed to permit every test taker to attempt every task)?

Scoring method

Because the purpose of a language test task is to measure the test taker's language ability, the evaluation of test takers' responses will take the form of a scoring method, which specifies how numbers will be assigned to test takers' performance. (Scoring methods are discussed in detail in Chapter 11.)

Criteria for correctness: how the correctness of the response is determined: by means of an objective scoring key, multiple value rating scales, judgments of correct/incorrect, etc.

Procedures for scoring the response: the steps involved in scoring the tests: scored in a particular sequence, all rated by the same raters, etc.

Explicitness of criteria and procedures: the extent to which the test takers are informed about the nature of the scoring criteria and procedures: information on how the test will be scored given, omitted, or left deliberately vague.

Characteristics of the input

Input consists of the material contained in a given test task or TLU task, which the test takers or language users are expected to process in some way and to which they are expected to respond. This material is described in terms of format and language characteristics.

Format has to do with the way in which the input is presented, and includes the following characteristics: channel, form, language, length, type, degree of speededness, and vehicle.

Channel: aural, visual, or both.

Form: language, non-language (pictures, gestures, actions, etc.), or both.

Language (if *form* is language): native, target, or both. Input presented in the native language will generally be easier to interpret than input in the target language.

Length: single words, phrases, sentences, paragraphs, extended discourse. The length of the input influences the amount of interpretation required. Input can be presented in very short chunks and thus require limited interpretation, or it can be presented in extended discourse requiring more extensive interpretation.

Type of input (if *form* is language): Item or prompt:
An *item* consists of a highly focused chunk of language or non-language information. In a language test, the purpose of an item is to elicit either a selected or a limited production response. (See 'Type of response' below.) The input in many test tasks, such as the familiar multiple-choice or completion questions for testing discrete areas of language knowledge, consists of items. In real-life language use, the input in a telephone conversation in which we listen to short utterances and provide short, limited responses (e.g. 'yes', 'ummm', 'really?') could be characterized as a series of items.

A *prompt* is input in the form of a directive, the purpose of which is to elicit an extended production response. (See 'Type of response' below.)

A test task such as a directive to write a composition contains input of this type. In real-life language use, for example, the request from a department head to describe the most effective plan for increasing student enrollments in first-year language classes is, in effect, a prompt, since the purpose of the request is to elicit a specific, extended response.

Degree of speededness: the rate at which the test taker or language user has to process the information in the input.

Vehicle: the means by which input is delivered: 'live', 'reproduced', or both. For example, input consisting of a lecture for use in a listening comprehension test could be presented live or reproduced (via audio or videotape).

Language of input

In tasks in which the form of the input is language, these characteristics relate to the nature of the language that is used. They correspond to the areas of language knowledge and topical knowledge, which are discussed in the next chapter. We will simply list them here.

Language characteristics include organizational and pragmatic characteristics.

Organizational characteristics include grammatical characteristics (vocabulary, morphology, syntax, phonology, graphology) and textual characteristics (cohesion, rhetorical or conversational organization).

Pragmatic characteristics include functional characteristics (ideational, manipulative, heuristic, and imaginative) and sociolinguistic characteristics (dialect/variety, register, naturalness, cultural references, and figurative language).

Topical characteristics refer to the type of information, such as personal, cultural, academic, or technical, that is in the input.

Characteristics of the expected response

In any language use situation, the participants will have certain expectations about the characteristics of their respective responses as the discourse evolves. In a language test, the expected response consists of the language use or, perhaps, the physical response we are attempting to elicit by the way the instructions have been written, the task designed, and by the kind of input provided. Because test takers do not always understand instructions, or may choose not to respond in the way intended, we distinguish the expected response, which is part of the test design, from the actual response, which may or may not be what was intended or expected.

Format: the way in which the response is produced. The format of the response can be described in terms of channel, form, language, length, type, and degree of speededness, as discussed above under input format.

Type of response: selected, limited production, and extended production.

Measurement specialists traditionally distinguish two kinds of responses: a selected response in which the test taker must select one response from among several given choices, and a constructed response in which the test taker actually has to produce or construct a response. However, since constructed responses may vary considerably in length, we believe it is useful to distinguish two types of constructed response, based on the notion of a sentence or utterance. Using the sentence or utterance as a means of distinguishing different types of constructed responses is not entirely arbitrary, since it is with texts consisting of multiple sentences or utterances that a wider range of areas of language knowledge, including knowledge of cohesion and rhetorical organization, comes into play.

Selected response: In a selected response, typified by multiple-choice tasks, the test taker must select one response from among two or more that are provided.

Limited production response: A limited production response consists of a single word or phrase, and may be as long as a single sentence or utterance. This response type is typical of what are sometimes called short completion items.

Extended production response: An extended production response is one that is longer than a single sentence or utterance, and can range from two sentences or utterances to virtually free composition, either oral or written.

Degree of speededness: The amount of time that the test taker or language user has to plan and execute a response. If the score on the test task depends primarily upon how quickly the test taker responds, the task is speeded.

Language of expected response

When the response type is either a limited or an extended production and the form of the response is language, we need to describe the language of the expected response. This can be done using essentially the same characteristics as for the language of the input, as discussed above.

Relationship between input and response

In addition to describing the characteristics of the input and response separately, we can describe how they are related to each other, in terms of the reactivity, scope, and directness of the relationship.

Reactivity: The extent to which the input or the response directly affects subsequent input and responses.

Reciprocal tasks are those in which the test taker or language user engages in language use with another interlocutor. In reciprocal tasks, the test taker or language user receives feedback on the relevance and correctness of the response, and the response in turn affects the input that is subsequently provided by the interlocutor. The feedback may be either explicit or implicit in the reactions (verbal, physical) of the interlocutor. Reciprocal language use and test tasks thus have two distinguishing features: (1) the presence of feedback, and (2) interaction between the two interlocutors, so that the language used by the participants at any given point in the communicative exchange affects subsequent language use. A typical example of a reciprocal test task would be the give-and-take that occurs in a face-to-face oral interview.

Non-reciprocal: In non-reciprocal language use there is neither feedback nor interaction between language users. Reading is an example of non-reciprocal language use since the language user's internal or external response to what is read does not change the form of subsequent material in the text. Typical examples of non-reciprocal test tasks are taking a dictation and writing a composition.

Adaptive: A recent development in measurement is the use of adaptive tests, in which the particular tasks presented to the test taker are determined by the responses to previous tasks. The first task presented in an adaptively administered test is typically of medium difficulty. If this task is performed correctly, the next task presented will be slightly more difficult. If that task is missed, the next one will be slightly easier, and so on. In most adaptive tests, test takers do not receive feedback on the correctness of their responses, and may not know that their responses determine which tasks will be presented subsequently. Adaptive test tasks thus do not involve the feedback that characterizes reciprocal language use, but they do involve an aspect of interaction, in the sense that their responses affect subsequent input. Some language use tasks may be adaptive as well, as for example in situations in which one simplifies, uses paraphrase, or slows down in order to accommodate and repair breakdowns in communication. The person to whom one is talking may not be aware that what is said is being tailored so as to make the input more understandable and hence, facilitate the response. (See Snow and Ferguson 1977 for discussions of this.) The differences among reciprocal, non-reciprocal, and adaptive input and response are summarized in Table 3.2 overleaf, from Bachman (1990).

Scope of relationship: The amount or range of input that must be processed in order for the test taker or language user to respond as expected.

Broad scope: Tasks that require the test taker or language user to process

Relationship between input and response	Feedback: knowledge of relevance or correctness of response	Interaction: response affects subsequent input
Reciprocal	+ (present)	+ (present)
Adaptive	– (absent)	+ (present)
Non-reciprocal	– (absent)	– (absent)

Table 3.2:   Distinguishing features of reactivity between input and response (after Bachman 1990: 151)

a lot of input can be characterized as *broad scope*. An example of a broad scope test task is a 'main idea' reading comprehension question that deals with the content of an entire passage. A broad scope language use task might be listening to a conversation in a foreign language with the idea of getting the gist, without paying attention to specific details.

Narrow scope: Tasks that require the processing of only a limited amount of input can be characterized as *narrow scope*. An example of a narrow scope test task is a short stand-alone multiple-choice grammar item, since the response is to be made on the basis of a relatively limited amount of input. Another example would be a reading comprehension question that focuses on a specific detail or a limited part of the reading passage. An example of a narrow scope language use task might be scanning the sale ads in the newspaper for a particular piece of furniture.

Directness of relationship: the degree to which the expected response can be based primarily on information in the input, or whether the test taker or language user must also rely on information in the context or in his own topical knowledge.

Direct: the response includes primarily information supplied in the input. An example of a relatively direct test task would be a speaking test in which the test taker describes the content of a picture.

Indirect: the response includes information not supplied in the input. An example of a relatively indirect test task would be a speaking test in which the test taker gives his opinion of a recent event.

It is fairly common for certain types of test tasks to include a direct relationship between input and response. A task that requires the test taker to read a piece of discourse and then answer comprehension questions that request information explicitly stated in the passage, for example, involves such a direct relationship. Many, if not most, language use tasks, on the other hand, involve an indirect relationship between input and response. In a conversation, for example, the language users expect each other to respond with new, rather than given information, the new information being supplied by the language users.

Applications of the task characteristics framework

The task characteristics framework can be used in a variety of ways. Two of the most important are creating a template for describing and comparing characteristics of TLU tasks and of test tasks, in order to determine the degree of match between the two, and manipulating the task characteristics to create completely new methods. These applications are illustrated in the examples that follow.

1 Using a task characteristics checklist for comparing characteristics of target language use tasks and test tasks

As already indicated, the task characteristics are useful for describing both TLU tasks and test tasks that have been designed with a particular TLU domain in mind. A convenient way to determine the extent to which the characteristics of the test task correspond to those of the TLU task is to create a checklist that places descriptions of the two tasks side by side.

In Project 8 in Part Three we use the checklist to compare the characteristics of a TLU task, 'Ordering a Meal', with the characteristics of an achievement test task patterned after it. For example, in the TLU task the vehicle of the oral input is 'live', whereas in the achievement test it is 'reproduced'; the reactivity of the relationship between input and response in the TLU task is 'reciprocal', whereas in the test task it is 'non-reciprocal'.

2 Using a task characteristics checklist to create completely new test task types

The task characteristics framework can also be used to help modify existing task types to create new task types that might be more useful for the given purpose of the test or for the particular group of test takers. The task characteristic framework can stimulate thinking and direct attention to characteristics which might not otherwise be considered. The basic technique is to use the task characteristics to describe the tasks currently in use, and then consider how different combinations of task characteristics might create a more useful task. While some combinations might appear incompatible with one another, other combinations might appear quite plausible and lead to the development of new task types.

A number of years ago, one of the authors had just such an experience of modifying an existing test task type so that it would be more appropriate for a particular testing situation. The language ability to be measured was the ability to comprehend spoken input, and the TLU situation was that of test takers happening upon a conversation already in progress and trying to pick up on the gist of the conversation as quickly as possible. The tasks that were commonly used to test listening comprehension at the time involved recorded input for interpretation (one or two sentences long) followed by short stand-alone tasks requiring selected (multiple-choice) responses. In these tasks, the input was generally non-speeded and the scope of the relationship between input and response was fairly narrow, with crucial details in the input presented only once, and little irrelevant information included.

Stimulated by Upshur's work with experimental speaking tests involving speeded responses and timed scoring procedures (Upshur 1969), one of the authors speculated that it might be possible to measure listening comprehension by scoring test takers on the amount of time it took them to respond by making a specific inference on the basis of spoken input. He also wanted to simulate a conversational listening task by distributing crucial information in the input over a fairly long stretch of recorded material. The main point was repeated in the input several times in different forms and at different levels of difficulty. The resulting tasks differed from the more commonly used listening comprehension test tasks in only two characteristics—speededness of input and response and scope of the relationship between input and response. Nevertheless, the new test tasks looked quite different from commonly used tasks and also apparently measured different abilities from those commonly measured in listening comprehension tests (Palmer 1972). This development process illustrates the power of imagining what new tasks might look like if just one or two characteristics of an existing task were changed.

Summary

In order to use scores from language tests to make inferences about language ability or to make decisions about individuals, we must be able to demonstrate how test performance corresponds to non-test language use. This can be done by developing a framework of language use that enables us to consider the language used on language tests as a specific instance of language use, a test taker as a language user in the context of a language test, and a language test as a specific language use situation.

Since the purpose of language testing is to enable us to make inferences about test takers' ability to use language to perform tasks in a particular domain, two essential notions for the design, development, and use of language tests are those of language use task and target language use domain. A *language use task* is an activity that involves individuals in using language for the purpose of achieving a particular goal or objective in a particular situation or setting. A *target language use (TLU) domain* is a set of specific tasks and their attendant settings that the test taker is likely to encounter outside of the test itself and that require language use.

Because of the complexity and variety of language use, we cannot make a list of all instances of language use, but must instead identify certain distinguishing characteristics to describe a language use domain. We present a framework of characteristics for describing language use tasks and test tasks. Task characteristics are broken down into characteristics of the *setting*, the *test rubric*, the *input*, the *expected response*, and the *relationship between input and response*. Two important uses of the task characteristics framework are (1) creating a template for describing both a TLU situation and a test task in order to evaluate the degree to which these two tasks correspond to each other, and (2) varying certain test method characteristics in order to create new testing methods.

Exercises

1   Read the outlined description of the tasks in the TLU domain for Project 1 in Part Three. Create a table like the one in the project (or like the example template in Chapter 6), and fill it in with the characteristics of a task or tasks in another TLU domain of interest to you.

2   Read the description of Project 2 in Part Three. Make a list of specific test task characteristics that would appear to contribute to its validity, authenticity, and interactiveness.

3   Obtain a copy of a test with which you are familiar. Using the task characteristics, try to identify and describe some of the types of test tasks, including the characteristics of the test rubric itself. To what extent was this possible? What problems did you run into, if any?

4   Obtain a copy of a test with which you are familiar. Describe one type of test task using the task characteristics. Then experiment by changing one or more of the task characteristics and note how the form of the test task would change. How do you think this change would affect the *usefulness* of the test in the situation for which it was developed? Are there other testing situations for which this modified task might become particularly useful? Why?

5   Think of a situation in which language is taught communicatively, with a specific TLU domain in mind. Describe one type of teaching task in the instructional TLU domain using the task characteristics. Then describe the characteristics of a comparable task in the real-life TLU domain. What are the similarities and differences between the characteristics of the two types of tasks?

6   Think of a situation in which language is taught communicatively at a beginning level. Describe the characteristics of an instructional task.

Then list a number of tasks in the non-instructional TLU domain. Which of those tasks have characteristics which are most compatible with the characteristics of the instructional task?

Suggested readings

1   *Language use and discourse*: Brown and Yule (1983), Widdowson (1978), and van Dijk (1977) provide extensive discussions of language use and discourse.
2   *Features of language use context*: Hymes' (1972) description of the features of a speech event is still considered by many to be the most useful analysis to date.
3   *Tasks and task characteristics*: The following research studies illustrate the effects of various aspects of test methods on test performance: Bachman and Palmer 1982; Shohamy 1984; Alderson and Urquhart 1985. A detailed theoretical discussion of 'test method facets' can be found in Bachman (1990): Chapter 5. Carroll (1993) provides a discussion of tasks from the perspective of cognitive psychology. A discussion of tasks in language learning can be found in a collection of articles edited by Crookes and Gass (1993a). Of particular relevance for language testing are the articles in this collection by Crookes and Gass, Pica et al., and Duff.
4   *Adaptive input and responses*: A series of papers on the phenomena of baby talk and other simplified registers is contained in a collection of articles edited by Snow and Ferguson (1977).

Notes

1   These two domains are not necessarily distinct, since much of the research and thinking in language teaching methodology for at least the past twenty years has been aimed at creating teaching and learning tasks in which the purpose for using language is to communicate, and not simply to learn.
2   Bachman (1990) uses the terms 'test method' and 'facets' to refer to what we call here 'task' and 'characteristics'. We prefer the term 'task' for two reasons. First, this refers directly to what the test taker is actually presented with in a language test, rather than to an abstract entity. Second, the term 'task' is more general, and relates more directly to the notion of task as it is currently used in the contexts of language acquisition and language teaching. We have found that the term 'facets' is perceived by many practitioners as highly technical and inaccessible, while the term 'characteristics' is much less of a problem.

4 Describing language ability: language use in language tests

Introduction

As indicated in Chapter 1, our approach to the design and development of language tests is based on the premise that if we want to use the scores from a language test to make decisions about individuals or inferences about their language ability, we must be able to demonstrate how performance on that language test is related to language use in specific settings other than the language test itself. We argued that in order to demonstrate this correspondence we need a conceptual framework that includes two sets of characteristics:

1 those of language use tasks and test tasks, and
2 those of language users or test takers.

In Chapter 3 we presented a framework for describing the characteristics of tasks, while in this chapter we present a model for describing the characteristics of the language users, or potential test takers.

The characteristic of individuals that is of primary interest in language testing is language ability, since this is what we want to make inferences about. Other individual characteristics that we also need to consider are personal characteristics, topical knowledge, and affective schemata. We include these in our discussion for two reasons. First, we believe that these characteristics can have important influences on both language use and test performance. Second, we believe that it is possible and desirable to design language tests so that these characteristics facilitate rather than impede test takers' performance.

Language use

In the past twenty years language use has been discussed from a number of different perspectives that emphasize its interactional nature. (See, for example, the references in Suggested Readings for this chapter.) In general, *language use* can be defined as the creation or interpretation of intended meanings in discourse by an individual, or as the dynamic and interactive negotiation of intended meanings between two or more individuals in a particular situation. In using language to express, interpret, or negotiate intended meanings, language users create discourse. This discourse derives meaning not only from utterances or texts themselves, but, more importantly, from the ways in which utterances and texts relate to the characteristics of a particular language use situation. For example, the sentence, 'How many times have you tried to fix that lock yourself?' might be interpreted as either a question or a complaint, depending on the situation in which it is used and the knowledge or perceptions of each other that the language users share.

Language use involves complex and multiple interactions among the various individual characteristics of language users, on the one hand, and between these characteristics and the characteristics of the language use or testing situation, on the other. Because of the complexity of these interactions, we believe that language ability must be considered within an interactional framework of language use. The view of language use we present here thus focuses on the interactions among areas of language ability (language knowledge and strategic competence, or metacognitive strategies), topical knowledge, and affective schemata, on the one hand, and how these interact with the characteristics of the language use situation, or test task, on the other. Our view of language use and performance on language tests is presented as a visual metaphor in Figure 4.1.

This figure is our attempt to express visually some of the major interactions that we assume to be involved in language use. We would note that we conceive of this not as a working model of language processing, but rather as a conceptual basis for organizing our thinking about the test development process. The components that are within the smaller, bold circle ('topical knowledge', 'language knowledge', 'personal characteristics', 'strategic competence', and 'affect') represent characteristics of individual language users, while the outer circle includes characteristics in the task or setting with which the language user interacts. The double-headed arrows indicate interactions. The figure indicates that strategic competence is the component that links other components within the individual, as well as providing the cognitive link with the characteristics of the language use task and setting.

This figure can be used to help keep track of and recall important abilities or attributes that influence the usefulness of language tests. For example, in evaluating a test's interactiveness (see Chapters 2 and 7) we need to keep in mind the involvement of topical knowledge, language knowledge, affect, and strategic competence in carrying out the test task. All four of these are represented prominently in this figure. And in describing the construct to be measured (see discussion in Chapter 6) we can choose to include one or more of the following components in the construct definition: language knowledge, possibly topical knowledge, and possibly strategic competence.

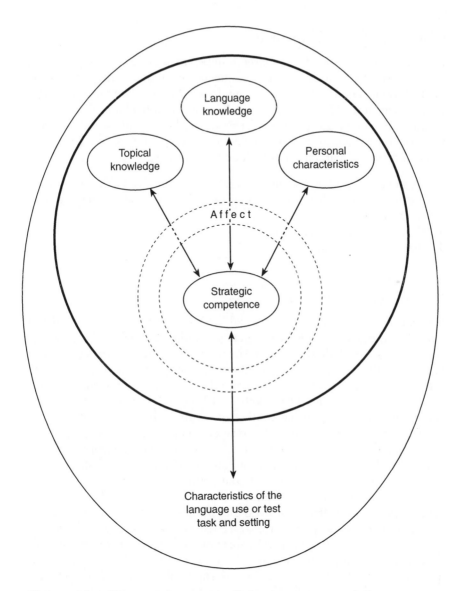

Figure 4.1: Some components of language use and language test performance

Thus, we have found this figure to be a useful aid to teaching and remembering the material presented in this chapter. In the rest of this chapter we describe in detail what we believe are the characteristics of language users that are most relevant to the development and use of language tests.

Characteristics of individuals

Language use is affected by a large number of individual characteristics, many of which, such as fatigue or unexpected mood shifts, are largely unpredictable, and there is little we can do to accommodate these in designing language tests. However, there are four sets of individual characteristics whose effects on language test performance are better understood, and that we need to consider in the way we design, develop, and use language tests. These individual characteristics include the following:

1   personal characteristics, such as age, sex, and native language,
2   the topical knowledge that test takers bring to the language testing situation,
3   their affective schemata, and
4   their language ability.

Personal characteristics

Personal characteristics are individual attributes that are not part of test takers' language ability but which may still influence their performance on language tests. A wide range of personal test taker characteristics could be relevant to the decisions we make about test design and development, and extended discussions of these as they relate to second language learning and teaching can be found in Skehan (1989) and Brown (1994). Cohen (1994) discusses these in the context of language testing, and provides a list of test taker characteristics that includes age, foreign language aptitude, socio-psychological factors, personality, cognitive style, language use strategies, ethnolinguistic factors, and multilingual ability (1994: 74).

In any test development project, the developer will need to develop a specific list of personal characteristics that have to be considered in terms of their potential contribution to the usefulness of the test. For example, information on some personal characteristics, such as 'age', 'native languages', 'level and type of general education', or 'type and amount of prior experience with a given test', may have an obvious influence on all the qualities of usefulness, and collecting information on these personal characteristics may be quite valuable in designing test tasks to optimize these qualities. The effect of other test taker characteristics, such as 'cognitive style', on the development of test tasks may be somewhat less obvious. Moreover, collecting information on these characteristics may be less practical. Therefore the more problematic characteristics might not be included. Since the number of personal characteristics that could potentially affect the test performance of any given test taker is very large, it is virtually impossible for us to provide a complete listing of all the characteristics that should be considered. Thus the following list of characteristics is not intended to be exhaustive, but may provide a starting place for describing the characteristics of test takers. We discuss the specification of test takers' characteristics in Chapter 6.

1   Age
2   Sex
3   Nationality
4   Resident status
5   Native language
6   Level and type of general education
7   Type and amount of preparation or prior experience with a given test

Topical knowledge

What we will call topical knowledge (sometimes referred to as knowledge schemata or real-world knowledge) can be loosely thought of as knowledge structures in long-term memory. Individuals' topical knowledge needs to be considered in a description of language use because this provides the information base that enables them to use language with reference to the world in which they live, and hence is involved in all language use. Certain test tasks that presuppose cultural or topical knowledge on the part of test takers may be easier for those who have that knowledge and more difficult for those who do not. For example, we might expect students of economics or finance to bring relevant topical knowledge to a writing task that requests them to discuss the advantages and disadvantages of a liberal fiscal policy. By the same token, a reading passage that included a great deal of information specific to a particular culture might be more difficult for individuals who do not possess the relevant cultural knowledge than for those who do.

Affective schemata

Affective schemata can be thought of as the affective or emotional correlates of topical knowledge. These affective schemata provide the basis on which language users assess, consciously or unconsciously, the characteristics of the language use task and its setting in terms of past emotional experiences in similar contexts. The affective schemata, in combination with the characteristics of the particular task, determine, to a large extent, the language user's affective response to the task, and can either facilitate or limit the flexibility with which he responds in a given context. The affective responses of language users may thus influence not only whether they even attempt to use language in a given situation, but also how flexible they are in adapting their language use to variations in the setting.

In a language test, test takers' affective schemata may influence the ways in which they process and attempt to complete the test tasks. If we ask test takers to deal with an emotionally charged topic, such as abortion, gun control, or national sovereignty, their affective responses to this topic may limit their ability to utilize the full range of language knowledge and meta-cognitive strategies available to them. This is not to say that we should avoid emotionally charged topics in language tests, but simply to point out that we need to be aware that test takers' performance on tasks that include such topics may be affected as much by their affective schemata as by their language ability. Emotional responses can also facilitate language use. We need to recognize that controversial topics may stimulate some individuals to perform at a high level, precisely because they feel strongly about the topic. Similarly, individuals who have positive feelings about interacting conversationally with others are likely to perform very well in a face-to-face oral interview. Test performance can thus be facilitated or inhibited by positive or negative affective responses, both to the topical content of test tasks and to a particular type of test task.

A number of language testers have indicated that we should attempt to design our tests to elicit test takers' best performance.[1] We believe that one way to do this is to design the characteristics of the test task so as to promote feelings of comfort or safety in test takers that will in turn facilitate flexibility of response on their part. However, there needs to be a balance between what the test taker feels comfortable with and what we want to measure. For example, we may want to use a one-on-one oral interview because this most closely corresponds to a task in the TLU domain, even though we realize that some test takers may feel threatened by a face-to-face interaction. Realizing this, we could try to minimize this threat by building into the interview a warm-up phase, conducted at a level of language with which the test taker feels comfortable, and designed to put the test taker at ease.

Language ability

If we are to make inferences about language ability on the basis of performance on language tests, we need to define this ability in sufficiently precise terms to distinguish it from other individual characteristics that can affect test performance. We also need to define language ability in a way that is appropriate for each particular testing situation, that is, for a specific purpose, group of test takers, and TLU domain. For example, we may want to focus on test takers' knowledge of how to organize utterances to form texts for one particular testing situation, while in another we may be more interested in their knowledge of appropriate politeness markers. The way we define language ability for a particular testing situation, then, becomes the basis for the kinds of inferences we can make from the test performance. When we define an ability this way, for purposes of measurement, we are defining what we called, in Chapter 2, a 'construct'. In designing, developing, and using language tests, we can define our construct from a number of perspectives, including everything from the content of a particular part of a language course to a theoretical model of language ability. In Chapter 6 we discuss the procedures and considerations involved in defining constructs. Here we will present a theoretical model of language ability that we believe provides a valuable framework for guiding the definition of constructs for any language testing development situation. We would hasten to point out that it is not our intention to suggest that all language testing should be based on all, or even specific parts of this particular model. At the same time, however, we believe very strongly that the consideration of language ability in its totality needs to inform the development and use of any language test.

The model of language ability that we adopt in this book is essentially that proposed by Bachman (1990), who defines language ability as involving two components: language competence, or what we will call *language knowledge*, and *strategic competence*, which we will describe as a set of metacognitive strategies. It is this combination of language knowledge and metacognitive strategies that provides language users with the ability, or capacity, to create and interpret discourse, either in responding to tasks on language tests or in non-test language use.[2]

Language knowledge

Language knowledge can be thought of as a domain of information in memory that is available for use by the metacognitive strategies in creating and interpreting discourse in language use. Language knowledge includes two broad categories: organizational knowledge and pragmatic knowledge. We recognize that many of the language tests we develop will focus on only one or a few of these areas of language knowledge. Nevertheless, we believe that there is a need to be aware of the full range of components of language ability as we design and develop language tests and interpret language test scores. For example, even though we may only be interested in measuring an individual's knowledge of vocabulary, the kinds of test items, tasks, or texts used need to be selected with an awareness of what other components of language knowledge they may evoke. We believe, therefore, that the design of every language test, no matter how narrow its focus, should be informed by a broad view of language ability. The areas of language knowledge are summarized in Table 4.1.

Organizational knowledge

Organizational knowledge is involved in controlling the formal structure of language for producing or comprehending grammatically acceptable utterances or sentences, and for organizing these to form texts, both oral

---

Organizational knowledge
(how utterances or sentences and texts are organized)

Grammatical knowledge
(how individual utterances or sentences are organized)

Knowledge of vocabulary
Knowledge of syntax
Knowledge of phonology/graphology

Textual knowledge
(how utterances or sentences are organized to form texts)

Knowledge of cohesion
Knowledge of rhetorical or conversational organization

Pragmatic knowledge
(how utterances or sentences and texts are related to the communicative goals of the language user and to the features of the language use setting)

Functional knowledge
(how utterances or sentences and texts are related to the communicative goals of language users)

Knowledge of ideational functions
Knowledge of manipulative functions
Knowledge of heuristic functions
Knowledge of imaginative functions

Sociolinguistic knowledge
(how utterances or sentences and texts are related to features of the language use setting)

Knowledge of dialects/varieties
Knowledge of registers
Knowledge of natural or idiomatic expressions
Knowledge of cultural references and figures of speech

Table 4.1:   Areas of language knowledge

and written.[3] There are two areas of organizational knowledge: grammatical knowledge and textual knowledge.

Grammatical knowledge is involved in producing or comprehending formally accurate utterances or sentences.[4] This includes knowledge of vocabulary, syntax, phonology, and graphology.

Textual knowledge is involved in producing or comprehending texts, which are units of language—*spoken or written*—that consist of two or more utterances or sentences. There are two areas of textual knowledge: knowledge of cohesion and knowledge of rhetorical or conversational organization.

Knowledge of cohesion is involved in producing or comprehending the explicitly marked relationships among sentences in written texts or among utterances in conversations

Knowledge of rhetorical or conversational organization is involved in producing or comprehending organizational development in written texts or in conversations.

Pragmatic knowledge

Pragmatic knowledge enables us to create or interpret discourse by relating utterances or sentences and texts to their meanings, to the intentions of language users, and to relevant characteristics of the language use setting. There are two areas of pragmatic knowledge: functional knowledge and sociolinguistic knowledge.

Functional knowledge, or what Bachman (1990) calls 'illocutionary competence', enables us to interpret relationships between utterances or sentences and texts and the intentions of language users. The utterance 'Could you tell me how to get to the post office?', for example, most likely functions as a request for directions rather than as a request for a 'yes' or 'no' answer. The most appropriate responses are likely to be either a set of directions or, if the speaker does not know how to get to the post office, a statement to this effect. A verbal response such as 'Yes, I could', while accurate in terms of the literal meaning of the question, is inappropriate, since it misinterprets the function of the question as a request for information. Quite frequently the appropriate interpretation of a given utterance also involves the language users' prior knowledge of the language use setting, including the characteristics of the participants. For example, to determine whether the comment, 'How many times have you tried to fix this lock yourself?' should be interpreted as a request or as a criticism, we need to know whether or not the person who has tried to fix the lock is generally successful in completing tasks such as this, and whether the person making the remark is prone to indirect criticism. Functional knowledge includes knowledge of four categories of language functions: ideational, manipulative, instrumental, and imaginative.

Knowledge of ideational functions enables us to express or interpret meaning in terms of our experience of the real world. These functions include the use of language to express or exchange information about ideas, knowledge, or feelings. Descriptions, classifications, explanations, and expressions of sorrow or anger are examples of utterances that perform ideational functions.

Knowledge of manipulative functions enables us to use language to affect the world around us. This includes knowledge of the following:

1 *instrumental functions*, which are performed to get other people to do things for us (examples include requests, suggestions, commands, and warnings);
2 *regulatory functions*, which are used to control what other people do (examples include rules, regulations, and laws); and

3 *interpersonal functions*, which are used to establish, maintain, and change interpersonal relationships (examples include greetings and leave-takings, compliments, insults, and apologies).

Knowledge of heuristic functions enables us to use language to extend our knowledge of the world around us, such as when we use language for teaching and learning, for problem-solving, and for the retention of information.

Knowledge of imaginative functions enables us to use language to create an imaginary world or extend the world around us for humorous or esthetic purposes; examples include jokes and the use of figurative language and poetry.

Although we have grouped functions into four general categories, these are by no means mutually exclusive. Furthermore, functions do not normally occur only in individual, isolated utterances. On the contrary, the majority of language use involves the performance of multiple functions in connected discourse.

Sociolinguistic knowledge enables us to create or interpret language that is appropriate to a particular language use setting. This includes knowledge of the conventions that determine the appropriate use of dialects or varieties, registers, natural or idiomatic, expressions, cultural references, and figures of speech. When we use different registers appropriately for delivering a classroom lecture and conversing with our children, sociolinguistic knowledge is involved. Similarly, when we use cultural references, such as 'beyond the pale', or figures of speech, such as 'Don't push my buttons', to convey our intended meaning appropriately, we are using sociolinguistic knowledge.

Strategic competence

We conceive of strategic competence as a set of metacognitive components, or strategies, which can be thought of as higher order executive processes that provide a cognitive management function in language use, as well as in other cognitive activities.[5] Using language involves the language user's topical knowledge and affective schemata, as well as all the areas of language knowledge discussed above. What makes language use possible is the integration of all of these components as language users create and interpret discourse in situationally appropriate ways. With respect to language testing, this conceptualization of strategic competence as metacognitive components provides an essential basis both for designing and developing potentially interactive test tasks and for evaluating the interactiveness of the test tasks we use. (See the discussion in Chapter 2.) We identify three general areas in which metacognitive components operate: goal-setting, assessment, and planning. The three areas of metacognitive strategy use are illustrated in Table 4.2 and Figure 4.2.

Goal setting
(deciding what one is going to do)

Identifying the test tasks
Choosing one or more tasks from a set of possible tasks (sometimes by default, if only one task is understandable)
Deciding whether or not to attempt to complete the task(s) selected

Assessment
(taking stock of what is needed, what one has to work with, and how well one has done)

Assessing the characteristics of the test task to determine the desirability and feasibility of successfully completing it and what is needed to complete it
Assessing our own knowledge (topical, language) components to see if relevant areas of knowledge are available for successfully completing the test task
Assessing the correctness or appropriateness of the response to the test task

Planning
(deciding how to use what one has)

Selecting elements from the areas of topical knowledge and language knowledge for successfully completing the test task
Formulating one or more plans for implementing these elements in a response to the test task
Selecting one plan for initial implementation as a response to the test task

Table 4.2: Areas of metacognitive strategy use

Goal setting (deciding what one is going to do)

Goal setting involves:

1 identifying the language use tasks or test tasks,
2 choosing, where given a choice, one or more tasks from a set of possible tasks, and
3 deciding whether or not to attempt to complete the task(s).

Since the purpose of a language test is to elicit a specific sample of language use, tests typically present the test taker with a limited range of tasks, so that the test taker's flexibility in setting goals for performance on test tasks is generally not as great as that enjoyed by language users in non-test language use.

Assessment (taking stock of what is needed, what one has to work with, and how well one has done)

Assessment provides a means by which the individual relates her topical knowledge and language knowledge to the language use setting and tasks or to the testing situation and tasks. Assessment also takes into consideration the individual's affective responses in the application of assessment strategies.

Assessing the characteristics of the language use or test task involves

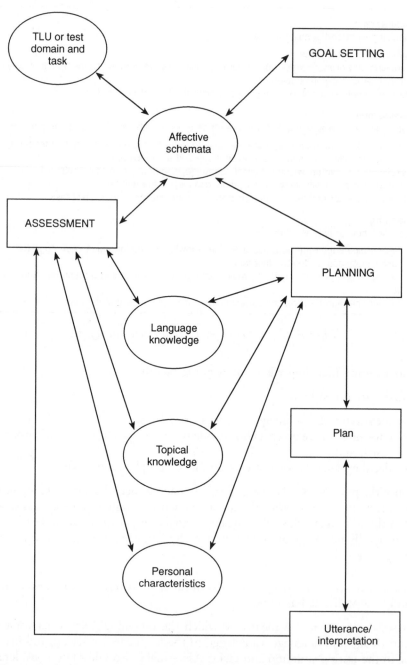

Figure 4.2:   Metacognitive strategies in language use and language test performance

identifying the characteristics of the language use task or test task, in order to determine

1 the desirability and feasibility of successfully completing the task, and
2 what elements of topical knowledge and language knowledge this is likely to require.

Assessing the individual's own topical knowledge and language knowledge involves determining the extent to which relevant topical knowledge and areas of language knowledge are available, and if available, which ones might be utilized for successfully completing the task. This aspect of assessment also considers the individual's available affective schemata for coping with the demands of the task.

Assessing the correctness or appropriateness of the response to the test task involves evaluating the individual's response to the task with respect to the perceived criteria for correctness or appropriateness. The relevant criteria pertain to the grammatical, textual, functional, and sociolinguistic characteristics of the response, as well as its topical content. In the event the response appears to be incorrect or inappropriate. This aspect of assessment enables the individual to diagnose the possible causes of the problem, which might lead to changing the communicative goal, the plan for implementing that goal, or both, depending on the situation. Affective schemata are involved in determining the extent to which failure was due to inadequate effort, to the difficulty of the task, or to random sources of interference.

Planning (deciding how to use what one has)

Planning involves deciding how to utilize language knowledge, topical knowledge, and affective schemata to complete the test task successfully. Assuming that the assessment strategies have determined which of these components are available for use, planning involves three aspects:

1 selecting a set of specific elements from topical knowledge and language knowledge (for example, concepts, words, structures, functions) that will be used in a plan,
2 formulating one or more plans whose realization will be a response (interpretation, utterance) to the task, and
3 selecting one plan for implementation as a response to the task.

Formulating a plan may involve an internal prioritization among the various elements that have been selected, as well as the consideration of how these can be most effectively combined to form a response. The plan thus specifies how the various elements will be combined and ordered when realized as a response. The product of the planning strategy, then, is a plan whose realization is a response to the task.

The following example illustrates the interactions among the goal-setting, assessment, and planning strategies. Palmer (1972, 1981) has described a test in which the test taker must describe a picture as quickly as possible so that the examiner can distinguish this picture from three other similar pictures in a set of four pictures. Each of the four pictures in a given set includes a stick figure of a person doing something, and each picture in the set differs from the other three by a single characteristic. One set of four pictures is reproduced in Figure 4.3.

Figure 4.3:   Example pictures from Experimental Speaking Test
(after Palmer 1981: 44)

Palmer reports that in responding to these tasks test takers appeared to have made different assessments of what was required for accomplishing this task. We would further speculate that as a result of these different assessments, test takers set different goals and utilized different types of plans for formulating their utterances. Some test takers, for example, may have set a goal of describing the entire picture, and of responding in complete sentences. These test takers formulated plans that were realized in grammatically accurate utterances that provided a great deal of descriptive information about the pictures. Other test takers may have set a goal of conveying only the critical information that was unique to the particular picture to be described, and formulated plans that were realized in responses that were often single words or short phrases. Still other test takers, whose lexical knowledge may not have included the words needed to describe the features of the objects in the particular picture, may have set as their goal describing the physical characteristics of the picture itself. These test takers formulated plans for responses that did not refer to the topical content of the pictures at all, but that described the pictures in terms of their placement on the page (for example, 'the one on the right') or their non-verbal visual information (e.g. lines and shapes, different shades of black and gray).

Language 'skills'

Language ability has traditionally been considered, by language teachers and language testers alike, to consist of four skills: listening, reading, speaking, and writing. Indeed, a model of language proficiency that has been very influential in language testing during the second half of this century describes language ability in terms of the four skills and several components (for example, grammar, vocabulary, and pronunciation).[6] These four skills have traditionally been distinguished in terms of channel (audio, visual) and mode (productive, receptive). Thus, listening and speaking involve the audio channel, and receptive and productive modes, respectively, while reading and writing are in the visual channel, and receptive and productive modes, respectively. However, is it adequate to distinguish the four skills simply in terms of channel and mode? If it is, then all language use that involves the audio channel and the productive mode could be considered speaking, while any language use in the visual channel and receptive mode would be reading.

We believe that it takes very little reflection to discover the inadequacies of this approach. First, it would classify widely divergent language use tasks or activities together under a single 'skill'. Consider, for example, how different are activities such as participating in a face-to-face conversation and listening to a radio newscast, even though both involve listening. Similarly, engaging in an electronic mail discussion probably has more in common with an oral conversation than with reading a newspaper, even though both the e-mail discussion and reading a newspaper involve the visual channel. Second, this approach fails to take into consideration the fact that language use is not simply a general phenomenon that takes place in a vacuum. We do not just 'read'; we read about something specific, for some particular purpose, in a particular setting. That is, language use takes place, or is realized, in the performance of specific situated language use tasks.

It is this conception of language use as the performance of specific situated language use tasks that provides, we believe, a much more useful means for characterizing what have traditionally been called language skills. We would thus not consider language skills to be part of language ability at all, but to be the contextualized realization of the ability to use language in the performance of specific language use tasks. We would therefore argue that it is not useful to think in terms of 'skills', but to think in terms of specific activities or tasks in which language is used purposefully. Thus, rather than attempting to define 'speaking' as an abstract skill, we believe it is more useful to identify a specific language use task that involves the activity of speaking, and describe it in terms of its task characteristics and the areas of language ability it engages. Thus, we would argue that the concept that has been called 'skill' can be much more usefully seen as a specific combination of language ability and task characteristics.[7] Furthermore, if we are to find this concept of 'ability-task' to be useful in the design, development, and use of language tests, then we must define specific instances of it in terms of their task characteristics (setting, input, expected response, and relationship between input and response) and the areas of language ability and topical knowledge these tasks engage.

Language ability: A test design and analysis checklist

As with the framework of task characteristics presented in the previous chapter, we believe that our model of language ability can be used in the design and development of language tests. To facilitate this, we have found that it is useful to work with a checklist, and this is illustrated in the examples below, as well as in the exercises at the end of this chapter. The use of this checklist in the design and development of language tests is also described in detail in Chapter 6.

Examples

1   Using a language ability checklist to help define the construct we want to measure

We can use the model of language knowledge to create a checklist such as the one in Table 4.3.

This checklist can be used to help us define the construct that we want to measure in a given language test, as part of the test design process. To illustrate how this might be done, turn to Project 1 in Part Three (pages 253–84) and read the parts of the specifications that describe the purpose of the test, the tasks in the TLU domain, and the characteristics of the test takers. Based on this information only, try to fill in the 'comments' column of the checklist in Table 4.3 for this testing situation. Your comments should indicate the degree to which you feel the particular component is of interest, and ought to be measured, given the specifications. After you have made your comments, read the definition of the construct to be measured (page 260) and the proposed scoring procedures (pages 280–4)

Component of language ability	Comments
GRAM: Vocabulary	
GRAM: Syntax	
GRAM: Phonological/ Graphological	
TEXT: Cohesion	
TEXT: Rhetorical organization	
FUNCT: Ideational	
FUNCT: Manipulative	
FUNCT: Heuristic	
FUNCT: Imaginative	
SOCIO: Dialect	
SOCIO: Register	
SOCIO: Naturalness	
SOCIO: Cultural references and figurative language	
META: Goal setting	
META: Assessment	
META: Planning	

Table 4.3:   Components of language ability: A test design and analysis checklist

to see how well your perceptions matched those of the test developer of Project 1.

2   Using a language ability checklist to help select an existing test

This checklist can also be used as a guide in selecting an existing test for a particular language testing situation. It can be used to judge the degree to which components of language ability are involved in a given test or test task. To illustrate how this might be done, turn to Project 2 in Part Three and read the prompt (pages 279–80). Based on your reading of the prompt only, try to fill in the 'comments' column of the checklist in Table 4.3 for this testing situation. This time your comments should indicate the degree to which you believe the various components are involved in or required for the successful completion of the task. If you feel the component is irrelevant, you might write 'not required', 'very limited involvement', or 'somewhat involved'. If you feel that the component is required for successful completion of the task, you might write 'required', or 'critical'. After making your comments, list the components that you feel will be measured by this task.

Summary

In order to use scores from language tests to make inferences about language ability or to make decisions about individuals, we must be able to demonstrate how test performance corresponds to non-test language use. This can be done by developing a framework of language use that enables us to consider test performance as a specific instance of language use, a test taker as a language user in the context of a language test, and a language test as a specific language use setting.

We believe that for language testing purposes we must consider language ability within an interactional framework of language use. We present a view of language use that focuses on the interactions among areas of language ability, topical knowledge, and affective schemata, on the one hand, and how these interact with characteristics of the language use setting, or test task, on the other. We present this view not as a working model of language processing, but as a basis for understanding how to design and develop language tests and how to use their results appropriately.

The characteristics of individuals—language users or test takers—include *personal characteristics, topical knowledge, affective schemata*, and *language ability*. Language ability consists of *language knowledge* and *strategic competence*, or metacognitive strategies. Language knowledge, which is information specific to language use that is stored in memory, includes both *organizational knowledge* and *pragmatic knowledge*. Organizational knowledge, which includes *grammatical knowledge* and *textual knowledge*, enables language users to create and interpret utterances or sentences that are grammatically accurate, and to combine these to form texts, either oral or written, that are cohesive and rhetorically or conversationally organized. Pragmatic knowledge, which includes *functional knowledge* and *socio-linguistic knowledge*, enables language users to relate words, utterances, and texts to concepts, communicative goals, and the features of the language use setting.

Strategic competence consists of *metacognitive strategies*, which are executive processes that enable language users to engage in *goal setting*, *assessment*, and *planning*. Goal setting involves:

1 identifying the language use tasks or test tasks,
2 choosing, where given a choice, one or more tasks from a set of possible tasks, and
3 deciding whether or not to attempt to complete the task(s).

Assessment involves three aspects:

1 assessing the characteristics of the language use task to determine the desirability and feasibility of accomplishing it,
2 assessing the elements of topical and language knowledge to determine whether the necessary elements are available, and
3 monitoring and evaluating the correctness and appropriateness of response—utterance or interpretation—in accomplishing the chosen task.

Planning involves the formulation of one or more plans for implementation as a response to the task. Plans are implemented through the performance of language use tasks, involving interpreting and producing utterances or sentences in discourse. This model of language ability can be used both in the design of new language tests and in the selection of an existing test for a particular language testing situation. (These applications are illustrated in the exercises at the end of the chapter.)

The notion of language 'skills' as abstract modalities in which language is realized is felt not to be useful for language testing, since attempts to characterize the four language skills (listening, speaking, reading, and writing) in terms of channel (audio, visual) and mode (receptive, productive) are inadequate on two counts. First, these features fail to capture important differences among language use activities that are within the same 'skill' (for instance, engaging in an oral conversation and listening to a radio newscast). Second, this approach to distinguishing the four skills treats them as abstract aspects of language ability, ignoring the fact that language use is realized in specific situated language use tasks. Thus, rather than attempting to distinguish among four abstract skills, we find it more useful to identify specific language use tasks and to describe these in terms of their task characteristics and the areas of language ability they engage. If we are to find the concept 'skill' useful in the design, development, and use of language tests, then we must define specific 'skills' in terms of their task characteristics (setting, input, expected response, and relationship between input and response) and the areas of language ability and topical knowledge these tasks engage.

Exercises

1   Try to put yourself in the mind of a person who is taking the test described in Project 2 of Part Three. Discuss how the metacognitive strategies might be involved as you read through the instructions and the prompt, and as you write the formal letter and the informal memo.

2   Try to recall and describe the involvement of metacognitive strategies as you read through this chapter for the first time. In what ways would they be involved differently if you were to read the chapter a second time?

3   Use the language ability checklist (Table 4.3) to describe the areas of language knowledge and metacognitive strategies that would be involved in your discussing Exercise 2 and arriving at an answer together with a friend or fellow student.

4   Use the language ability checklist to describe the areas of language knowledge that might be useful to measure for placing students into different courses in a language program with which you are familiar.

5   Using the components of language ability in Figure 4.1, explain how language use in responding to a minimal pair listening test task (a task in which the test takers listen to one of two words that differ by a single phoneme and decide which word has been pronounced) would differ from language use in a test task involving listening to and understanding an academic lecture. How would the test takers' topical knowledge, areas of language knowledge, and use of the metacognitive strategies be involved differently in the two tasks?

6   Think of a particular test or testing situation relevant to your testing experience or testing needs. Starting with the list of test taker characteristics provided in Project 1, modify this list as would be appropriate to help you maximize the usefulness of the test for your testing situation.

7   Imagine the following two testing situations: (a) an entrance test to measure the ability of college-bound international students to read and understand the vocabulary and sentence structure in textbooks used in an introductory course in American History, and (b) an entrance test to measure the ability of immigrant elementary school students to read and understand the vocabulary and sentence structure in textbooks used in an introductory course in American History. Prepare a list of possible test taker characteristics for each group of students. Then use the differences in the test taker characteristics to explain why test tasks that would be authentic, interactive, and have positive impact for one group of test takers might not be interactive and might have negative impact for the other group.

Suggested Readings

1 *Language use and discourse*: Widdowson (1978) and Brown and Yule (1983) provide extensive discussions of language use and discourse.
2 *Personal characteristics*: A detailed discussion of individual characteristics in the context of second language acquisition can be found in Skehan (1989: Chapters 3–6). Brown (1994: Chapters 4–7) provides an extensive discussion of these within the context of language learning and teaching. Cohen (1994: Chapter 3) discusses a number of test taker characteristics that he suggests may help explain differences in performance on language tests. Christison (1995) discusses the issue of test taker characteristics from the perspective of individual variation in multiple intelligences.
3 *Language ability/communicative competence*: A detailed theoretical discussion of 'communicative language ability' can be found in Bachman (1990: Chapter 4). Canale and Swain (1980), Canale (1983), and Savignon (1983) present earlier views of language ability as communicative competence. Widdowson (1983) provides a useful discussion of what he calls 'communicative capacity'.
4 *Strategies*: Discussions of strategies in language use can be found in Widdowson (1983) and Bialystok (1990). O'Malley and Chamot (1990), Oxford (1990), and Wenden (1991) discuss language learning strategies. Sternberg (1985, 1988) discusses metacognitive strategies in intelligence.

Notes

1 Swain (1985) refers to this principle as 'bias for the best'.
2 This view of language ability is consistent with what Widdowson (1983) has called 'communicative capacity', as well as with research in applied linguistics that has increasingly come to view language ability as consisting of two components: (1) language knowledge, sometimes referred to as 'competence' and (2) cognitive processes, or strategies, which implement that knowledge in language use (see, for example, Widdowson 1983; Bachman 1990; Bialystok 1990). It is also consistent with information processing, or cognitive models of mental abilities, which also distinguish processes or heuristics from domains of knowledge (see, for example, Sternberg 1985, 1988).
3 Organizational knowledge includes those components that enable individuals to produce or comprehend instances of what Widdowson (1978) calls 'usage'.
4 We will follow Brown and Yule's (1983) distinction between 'utterances', which are spoken, and 'sentences', which are written. However, since we hypothesize that the areas of language knowledge are involved

in both oral and written language use, we will use both terms, 'utterance' and 'sentence', in our discussion, unless we intend to specify either oral or written language.

5   The view of metacognitive strategies we present here is derived largely from Sternberg's description of the metacomponents in his model of intelligence (see, for example, Sternberg 1985, 1988). These metacomponents are involved in planning, monitoring, and evaluating individuals' problem solving. We would thus hypothesize that the metacognitive strategies we discuss here are involved not only in language use, but in virtually all cognitive activity.

6   Lado (1961) and Carroll (1961, 1968) provide examples of such 'skills and components' models.

7   This concept that the activities of listening, speaking, reading, writing are realizations of the interaction between language ability and the characteristics of language use or test tasks is consistent with the measurement concept that test items can best be seen as combinations of constructs, or traits, and test methods. This view of test items as trait method units provides the conceptual basis for one approach to construct validation. (See the discussion and references in Bachman 1990: Chapter 7.)

PART TWO

Language test development

UNIT 10
Language and development

5 Overview of test development

Introduction: Stages and activities in test development

We now turn from our discussion of frameworks that can be used in test development to a specific set of procedures for developing useful language tests. This chapter serves as a pre-organizer for the remainder of the book, which will explain how to carry out each step in test development and provide extensive examples. The chapters in Part Two are organized, in a very general way, according to the process of test development. Since numerous exercises will be provided for the specific steps in the test development process in the chapters that follow, there are no exercises for this chapter. We would note again that although we list, in Stage 3, a number of activities that will involve statistical analyses, these activities and analyses will not be discussed in this book. We have, instead, provided references to relevant readings in Chapters 3 and 11, as well as at the end of this chapter.

Readers might want to read this chapter now as a general preview of material to come and then review it prior to reading each of the remaining chapters in order to re-acquaint themselves with the whole test development process before considering the details of each activity.

Test development is the entire process of creating and using a test, beginning with its initial conceptualization and design, and culminating in one or more archived tests and the results of their use. The amount of time and effort we put into developing language tests will, of course, vary depending upon the situation. At one extreme, with low-stakes tests, the processes might be quite informal, as might be the case if one teacher were preparing a short test to be used as one of a series of weekly quizzes to assign grades. At the other extreme, with high-stakes tests, the processes might be highly complex, perhaps involving extensive trialing and revision, as well as coordinating the efforts of a large test development team. This might be necessary if a test were to be used to make important decisions affecting a large number of people. We would again point out that although the amount of time and effort that goes into test development may vary, depending on the use for which the test is intended, the qualities of usefulness need to be carefully considered and this consideration should not be sacrificed in either low-stakes or high-stakes situations.

Whatever the situation might be, we strongly believe that careful planning of the test development process in all language testing situations is crucial, for three reasons. First, and most importantly, we believe that careful planning provides the best means for assuring that the test will be useful for its intended purpose. Second, careful planning tends to increase accountability: the ability to say what was done and why. As teachers we must expect that test users (students, parents, and administrators) will be interested in the quality of our tests. Careful planning should make it easier to provide evidence that the test was prepared carefully and with forethought. Third, we favor careful planning because it increases the amount of satisfaction we experience. When we have a plan to do something that we value, and complete it, we feel rewarded. The more careful the plan (the more individual steps it contains) the more opportunities we create to feel rewarded. The less careful the plan, the fewer the rewards. At the extreme—no plan at all except the completion of the test—there is only one reward: the completed test.

We organize test development conceptually into three stages: design, operationalization, and administration. We say 'conceptually' because the test development process is not strictly sequential in its implementation. In practice, although test development is generally linear, with development progressing from one stage to the next, the process is also an iterative one, in which the decisions that are made and the activities completed at one stage may lead us to reconsider and revise decisions, and repeat activities, that have been done at another stage. While there are many ways to organize the test development process, we have discovered over the years that this type of organization gives a better chance of monitoring the usefulness of the test throughout the development process and hence producing a useful test. The test development process is illustrated in Figure 5.1. We have included 'considerations of qualities of usefulness' in order to emphasize that all decisions and activities involved in test development are made in order to maximize the overall usefulness of the test.

Stage 1: Design

In the design stage we describe in detail the components of the test design that will enable us to insure that performance on the test tasks will correspond as closely as possible to language use, and that the test scores will be maximally useful for their intended purposes. Design is in general a linear process, but in some cases some activities are iterative, that is, will need to be repeated a number of times. For example, there are certain parts of the process, such as considering qualities of usefulness and resource allocation and management, that are recurrent and will need to be considered and thought about throughout the process.

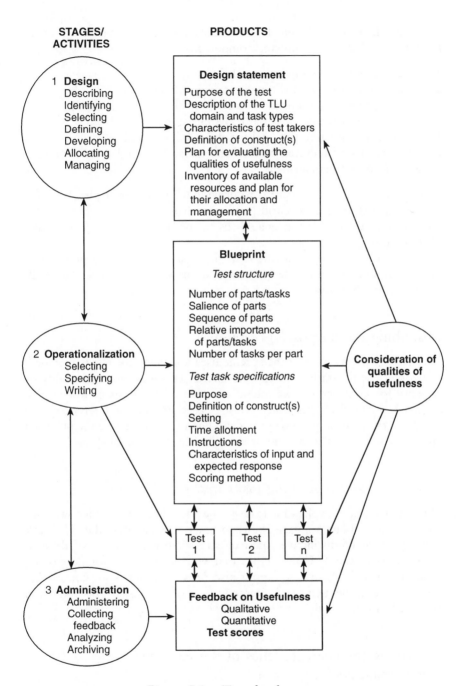

Figure 5.1:   Test development

The product of the design stage is a design statement, which is a document that includes the following components:

1   a description of the purpose(s) of the test,
2   a description of the TLU domain and task types,
3   a description of the test takers for whom the test is intended,
4   a definition of the construct(s) to be measured,
5   a plan for evaluating the qualities of usefulness, and
6   an inventory of required and available resources and a plan for their allocation and management.

The purpose of this document is to provide us with a principled basis for developing test tasks, a blueprint, and tests. It is important to prepare this document carefully, for this enables us to monitor the subsequent stages of development.

There are six activities involved in the design stage, corresponding to the six components of the design statement, as indicated above. These are described briefly below.

Describing the purpose(s) of the test

This activity makes explicit the specific uses for which the test is intended. It involves clearly stating the specific inferences about language ability or capacity for language use we intend to make on the basis of test results, and any specific decisions which will be based upon these inferences. The resulting statement of purpose provides a basis for considering the potential impact of test use. This activity is discussed in detail in Chapter 6.

Identifying and describing tasks in the TLU domain

This activity makes explicit the tasks in the TLU domain to which we want our inferences about language ability to generalize, and describes TLU task types in terms of distinctive characteristics. It provides a set of detailed descriptions of the TLU task types that will be the basis for developing actual test tasks. These descriptions also provide a means for considering the potential authenticity and interactiveness of test tasks. This activity is discussed in Chapter 6.

Describing the characteristics of the language users/test takers

This activity makes explicit the nature of the population of potential test takers for whom the test is being designed. The resulting description provides another basis for considering the potential impact of test use. This activity is discussed in Chapter 6.

Defining the construct to be measured

This activity makes explicit the precise nature of the ability we want to measure, by defining it abstractly. The product of this activity is a *theoretical definition* of the construct, which provides the basis for considering and investigating the construct validity of the interpretations we make of test scores. This theoretical definition also provides a basis for the development, in the operationalization stage, of test tasks. In language testing, our theoretical construct definitions can be derived from a theory of language ability, a syllabus specification, or both. This activity is discussed in Chapter 6.

Developing a plan for evaluating the qualities of usefulness

The plan for evaluating usefulness includes activities that are part of every stage of the test development process. A plan for assessing the qualities of usefulness will include an initial consideration of the appropriate balance among the six qualities of usefulness and setting minimum acceptable levels for each, and a checklist of questions that we will ask about each test task we develop. These are discussed in Chapter 7. Assessing usefulness in pretesting and administering will include collecting feedback. This will deal with a range of information, both quantitative, such as test scores and scores on individual test tasks, and qualitative, such as observers' descriptions and verbal self-reports from students on the test taking process. Finally, the plan will include procedures for analyzing the information we have collected. This will include procedures such as the descriptive analysis of test scores, estimates of reliability, and appropriate analyses of the qualitative data.

Identifying resources and developing a plan for their allocation and management

This activity makes explicit the resources (human, material, time) that will be required and that will be available for various activities during test development, and provides a plan for how to allocate and manage them throughout the development process. This activity further provides a basis for considering the potential practicality of the test, and for monitoring this throughout the test development process. This activity is discussed in Chapter 8.

Stage 2: Operationalization

Operationalization involves developing *test task specifications* for the types of test tasks to be included in the test, and a *blueprint* that describes how test tasks will be organized to form actual tests. Operationalization also involves developing and writing the actual test tasks, writing instructions, and specifying the procedures for scoring the test. By specifying the conditions under which language use will be elicited and the method for scoring responses to these tasks, we are providing the *operational definition* of the construct.

Developing test tasks and a blueprint

In developing test tasks, we begin with the descriptions of the TLU task types provided in the design statement, and modify these, again taking into consideration the qualities of usefulness, to produce test task specifications. These comprise a detailed description of the relevant task characteristics, and provide the basis for writing actual test tasks. We would note that the particular task characteristics that are included and the order in which they are arranged in the test task specifications are likely to vary somewhat from one testing situation to another, and hence will not necessarily correspond exactly to either the theoretical framework of task characteristics presented in Chapter 3 or the way in which they are presented in Figure 5.1.

A blueprint consists of characteristics pertaining to the structure, or overall organization, of the test, along with test task specifications for each task type to be included in the test. The blueprint differs from the design statement primarily in terms of the narrowness of the focus and the amount of detail included. A design statement describes the general parameters for the design of a test, including its purpose, the TLU domain for which it is designed, the individuals who will be taking the test, what the test is intended to measure, and so forth. A blueprint, on the other hand, describes how actual test tasks are to be constructed, and how these tasks are to be arranged to form the test. Procedures for developing test task specifications and a blueprint are discussed in Chapter 9.

Writing instructions

Writing instructions involves describing fully and explicitly the structure of the test, the nature of the tasks the test takers will be presented, and how they are expected to respond. Some instructions are very general and apply to the test as a whole. Other instructions are closely linked with specific test tasks. Considerations and procedures for writing instructions are discussed in Chapter 10.

Specifying the scoring method

Specifying the scoring method involves two steps:

1 defining the criteria by which the quality of the test takers' responses will be evaluated and
2 determining the procedures that will be followed to arrive at a score.

Scoring methods are discussed in Chapter 11.

Stage 3: Test administration

The test administration stage of test development involves giving the test to a group of individuals, collecting information, and analyzing this information, for two purposes:

1 assessing the usefulness of the test, and
2 making the inferences or decisions for which the test is intended.

Administration typically takes place in two phases: try-out and operational testing.

Try-out involves administering the test for the purpose of collecting information about the usefulness of the test itself, and for the improvement of the test and testing procedures.[1] The revisions made on the basis of feedback obtained from a tryout might be fairly local, and might consist of minor editing. Or the analysis of the results of the try-out might indicate that a more global revision is required, perhaps involving returning to the design stage and rethinking some of the components in the design statement. In major testing efforts, tests or test tasks are almost always tried out before they are actually used. In classroom testing, try-outs are often omitted, although we strongly recommend giving the test to selected students or fellow teachers in advance, since this can provide the test developer with information that can be useful in improving the test and test tasks before operational test use.

Operational test use involves administering the test primarily in order to accomplish the specified use/purpose of the test, but also for collecting information about test usefulness. In all cases of test development, we administer and score the test and then analyze the results, as appropriate to the demands of the situation.

Procedures for administering tests and collecting feedback

Administering a test involves preparing the testing environment, collecting test materials, training examiners, and actually giving the test. Administrative procedures need to be developed for use in both try-out and operational test use. Collecting feedback involves obtaining qualitative and quantitative information on usefulness from test takers and test users. Feedback is collected first during tryouts and later during operational test use. These activities are discussed in Chapter 12.

Procedures for analyzing test scores

Although we do not discuss these procedures in this book, we feel that listing them here will be helpful for understanding the entire test development process. References to sources that describe these procedures are provided in Chapter 2 and at the end of this chapter.

Describing test scores: using descriptive statistics to characterize the quantitative characteristics of test scores.

Reporting test scores: using statistical procedures for determining how to report test scores most effectively both to test takers and other test users.

Item analysis: using various statistical procedures for analyzing and improving the quality of individual test tasks, or items.

Estimating reliability of test scores: using a number of statistical procedures for estimating the consistency of test scores across different specific conditions of test use.

Investigating the validity of test use: includes a number of logical considerations and empirical procedures, both quantitative and qualitative, for investigating the validity of inferences made from test scores under specific conditions of test use. In this book we discuss a number of qualitative procedures that are relevant to investigating construct validity, but do not discuss any quantitative procedures for this.

Archiving

Archiving involves building up a large pool, or bank, of test tasks so as to facilitate the development of subsequent tests. Archiving makes it possible to make the test potentially more adaptable or appropriate to specific kinds of test takers. Typically, archiving procedures are designed to allow easy retrieval of tasks and important information about the task. Archiving also facilitates the maintaining of test security. Finally, archiving procedures may be used to facilitate the selection of tasks with particular characteristics. As with procedures for test analysis, we do not discuss archiving in this book, but provide some references at the end of this chapter.

Summary

Test development is the entire process of creating and using a test. The process is organized into three stages: design, operationalization, and administration. While test development is generally linear, with development progressing from one stage to the next, the process is also an iterative one, in which the decisions that are made and activities that are completed at any stage may lead us to reconsider and revise decisions and repeat activities that have been performed at another stage.

In the *design stage* we describe in detail the components of the test design that will enable us to insure that performance on the test tasks will correspond as closely as possible to language use, and that the test scores will be maximally useful for their intended purposes. The *operationalization stage* involves developing *test task specifications* for the types of test tasks to be included in the test, and a *blueprint* that describes how test tasks will be organized to form actual tests. Operationalization also involves developing and writing the actual test tasks, writing instructions, and specifying the procedures for scoring the test. The *administration stage* of test development involves giving the test to a group of individuals, collecting information, and analyzing this information. Organizing test development in this way helps us monitor the usefulness of the test throughout the development process and produce a useful test.

Suggested readings

Cronbach (1989), Guilford and Fruchter (1978), and Gronlund and Linn (1990) provide detailed discussions about procedures for describing and reporting test scores, for conducting item analysis, for estimating reliability, and for investigating validity.

Note

1   Other terms that are used more or less synonymously with 'try-out' include 'pre-test' and 'trial'.

6 Describing, identifying, and defining: test purposes, tasks in the TLU domain, characteristics of test takers, and the construct to be measured[1]

SECTION 1:
Describing the specific purposes of the test

Introduction

The primary use of language tests is to make inferences about language ability. In many situations the results of language tests are also used to provide information for making decisions about individuals. Indeed, because tests are used so extensively as a basis for making decisions, this is often seen as their primary purpose. However, unless we can demonstrate that the inferences we make on the basis of language tests are valid, we have no justification for using test scores for making decisions about individuals. For this reason it is crucial that we clearly specify the inferences that we need to make on the basis of test scores, and, in those situations where we need to use test scores for making decisions, we must demonstrate that these inferences are appropriate for the decisions we need to make.

Making inferences

In Chapter 4 we defined language ability as the capacity for creating and interpreting discourse. This involves the interaction of the language user's language knowledge and topical knowledge with the context (the language use task), mediated by the metacognitive strategies and facilitated by positive affect. In most situations in which we may want to develop a language test, inferences are likely to be about various components of language ability. However, there are situations in which the test developer may wish or be asked to make broader inferences pertaining to individuals' future performance on tasks or in jobs that may involve language use. That is, the language test developer may be asked to provide predictions, on the basis of a language test, about individuals' capability to successfully perform future tasks or jobs that involve language use.[2]

McNamara (1996) makes a useful distinction between two types of inferences that might be made from scores on language tests:

1 inferences about an individual's capability to perform future tasks or jobs that require the use of language, and
2 inferences only about an individual's ability to use *language* in future tasks or jobs.[3]

McNamara argues that language testers should generally avoid developing language tests whose purpose is to infer how well an individual is likely to be able to perform job-related tasks. This is because performance on such tasks will undoubtedly require, in addition to language ability, job-related topical knowledge, skills, and personality characteristics that are essentially unrelated to language ability. In testing situations in which it is either desirable or necessary to develop a test whose purpose is to make inferences about individuals' future performance in tasks or jobs that require language ability, we believe it is essential for the test developer to determine which individual characteristics, in addition to language ability, are to be assessed, and what specific inferences, if any, are to be made about these. This will directly influence how the construct to be measured will be defined. (This is discussed in Section 4.) In making this determination, and in defining the construct in such situations, it is essential to engage the expertise of a subject matter specialist in the design and development of the language test. We would also highly recommend combining a test of job-related skills and knowledge with the language test.

Once we have made inferences about language ability, we may use these inferences for a variety of secondary purposes, which include making decisions of various sorts, as well as for use in research. The specific kinds of decisions we want to make will directly affect subsequent steps in test development, in particular how we define the construct to be measured (discussed below in this chapter), and how we develop our scoring procedures (discussed in Chapter 11).

Making decisions

The most common secondary purpose for developing tests is to help us make decisions. These decisions will vary in terms of the seriousness of their impact on individuals and the numbers of individuals they will affect. The decisions that are most commonly made on the basis of language test scores are about the test takers, teachers, and programs. The decision makers will typically include a wide range of individuals such as test takers, teachers, administrators, and employers, as well as various groups of individuals, such as district school boards, state boards of education, and the boards of directors of companies.

High- and low-stakes decisions

High-stakes decisions are those that are likely to have a major impact on the lives of large numbers of individuals, or on large programs. Examples of high-stakes decisions about individuals include decisions about admission to academic programs, the awarding of scholarships, and the employment and retention of teachers. An example of a high-stakes decision about programs is the allocation of resources—teachers, funds, and materials—to schools in a given state or district. In addition to having a major impact on large numbers of individuals or large programs, high-stakes decisions are not easily reversed, so that decision errors cannot be easily corrected. For example, if an applicant performs poorly on a job interview because of nervousness or lack of specific preparation, he may not be offered a job, even though he is well qualified for it. And once the job is filled, there may not be another opening for a long time. Similarly, if a language program is eliminated from a school system, it may be extremely difficult to reinstate it at a later time.

Low-stakes decisions are those that have relatively minor impact on the lives of relatively small numbers of individuals, or on small programs, and can generally be reversed quite easily. For example, a teacher might use a test to diagnose students' strengths and weaknesses in order to assign them to specific learning activities. If the teacher misdiagnoses some students' areas of weakness and then assigns them to inappropriate learning activities, relatively few individuals are affected, and the errors can be quickly and easily corrected. Similarly, if the teacher uses a classroom quiz to help gather feedback on the effectiveness of a particular unit of materials or set of learning activities, and then decides, on the basis of scores on the quiz, to continue with these materials and activities, he can easily change this if he finds that the materials and activities really are not working effectively.

Decisions about test takers

Decisions about test takers include selection, placement, diagnosis, progress, and grading.

Selection

Selection decisions involve determining which individuals should be admitted to a particular educational program or offered a particular job. For example, teachers or administrators may need to decide which international students are most likely to succeed in a college-level program, and may want to use performance on language tests to help make these admission decisions. In other situations, employers may want to use a language test as part of a procedure for hiring an applicant for a job.

Placement

Placement decisions involve determining in which of several different levels of instruction it would be most appropriate to place the test taker. For example, if high school students who have studied a foreign language wish to be considered for placement into advanced level foreign language courses in college, they might be required to take a language test to determine the appropriate level of course. Based on the results of this test, the language department head and teachers will decide which applicants to accept.

Diagnosis

Diagnosis involves identifying specific areas of strength or weakness in language ability so as to assign students to specific courses or learning activities. For example, if a language program included three different courses, one focused on the editing of sentence level grammar and punctuation errors, a second focused on revising the organization of essays, and a third focused on logic of argumentation in writing, a teacher might use a test that included all these different language use activities as a basis for deciding which course would be most appropriate for students to take.

Progress and grading

In most instructional programs, both students and teachers are interested in receiving feedback on students' progress. Information from language tests can be useful for the purpose of *formative evaluation*, to help students guide their own subsequent learning, or for helping teachers modify their teaching methods and materials so as to make them more appropriate for their students' needs, interests, and capabilities. Language tests can also provide useful information for *summative evaluation* of students' achievement or progress at the end of a course of study. This evaluation is typically reported in the form of grades, and these are frequently arrived at on the basis of test scores.

Decisions about teachers or administrators

Inferences about students' language ability can be used to assess the effectiveness of teachers and administrators, and this assessment might subsequently be used as a basis for making decisions about hiring, salaries, retention, and promotion.

Decisions about programs

Finally, inferences about students' language ability can be used to make decisions about programs. For example, a teacher, a school principal, or a state board of education might use students' language test scores to determine the effectiveness of various levels of instructional programs in meeting their objectives. Such decisions could be used further to determine whether to continue a given program as it is, to modify it, or to eliminate it.

Relationship between decisions to be made and amount of resources that are allocated to test development

In every testing situation, the chances of making the correct or most appropriate decision will depend heavily on the quality of the information upon which it is based. Thus, if we use test scores as a basis for making decisions, it is our responsibility as test developers and users to insure that these scores are of as high a quality or as useful as we can possibly make them. The amount of resources allocated during the test development process for insuring that our tests are useful will clearly depend on the level of decision to be made. In general, the higher the stakes, the greater the resources that need to be allocated. The need to allocate resources to test development activities is understandable in the case of high-stakes decisions. What many classroom teachers fail to appreciate, however, is that even in relatively low-stakes classroom tests the decisions they make about their students and about their teaching are very important. We believe that it is in such situations that our approach to language test development is particularly applicable, since it provides a principled basis for test development and a set of clear criteria, the qualities of usefulness, for guiding test development and for evaluating the tests we develop. Moreover, this approach encourages teachers to put their often very limited resources into developing a smaller number of high quality tests that can be used a number of times.

Research uses

In addition to using performance on language tests to make decisions, we can use test scores to describe levels or profiles of language ability for a variety of research purposes. Research into the nature of first or second language acquisition, for example, might require information about the rate and order of acquisition of particular areas of language knowledge, and a language test might be one way to obtain this information. Another use of language tests involves research into the nature of language ability itself, including the effects of different test taker characteristics on language test performance, the relationships among tests of different areas of language ability, and the relationship between test task characteristics and performance on language tests.

Multiple uses of test scores

The scores from a given language can be used for multiple as well as single purposes. For example, a test such as that described in Project 1 can be used not only to select students for entrance into the program or to exempt students from study in program, but also to determine the level at which they would be placed within a series of courses in the program. And if administered both before and after instruction, the test could also be used to make decisions about the effectiveness of instruction. Brown (1980) provides a discussion of an actual example of a similar multi-use test in the context of a university writing program.

Due to the cost of developing and administering language tests, it makes good sense to make as much use of the scores as is appropriate. However, what constitutes an 'appropriate' use of scores from a language test needs to be clearly demonstrated as part of the process of test validation, as discussed in Chapter 2. That is, each use that is made of a given test score needs to be justified with appropriate evidence. It is therefore important for the test developer to consider carefully whether the resources saved through multiple uses offset the additional resources required for validating those additional uses.

Exercises for Section 1

1   Project 1 in Part Three provides a detailed example of a statement specifying the purpose of a test. Read the introduction to the project and the specification of the purpose of the test, and then consider the following:

   a   Why do you think the test developer has decided to make inferences only about language ability, and not about capability for performing tasks in the TLU domain?

   b   What considerations do you think led the test developer to identify this as a 'relatively high-stakes' decision? What programmatic procedures might be implemented to lower the impact of the decisions to be made on the basis of the test?

   c   Discuss the decisions that will be made on the basis of the test scores. How appropriate do you feel these decisions are for this situation? What additional kinds of decisions might need to be made in other, similar, situations?

   d   Do you think a test is necessary for making these decisions? How adequate or appropriate do you think a single test might be for making these decisions? What other kinds of information might be useful for making these decisions?

2   Read the description of the purpose of the test in Project 2 in Part Three. Then discuss the following questions:

   a   What kinds of inferences will be made on the basis of the test scores?

b What kinds of decisions will be made on the basis of the test scores?

c Do you think these decisions are high- or low-stakes? Why?

3 Think of a test you need to develop. Then answer the following questions:

a What kinds of inferences will be made on the basis of the test scores?

b What kinds of decisions will be made on the basis of the test scores?

c Do you think these decisions are high- or low-stakes? Why?

Suggested readings for Section 1

1 Extensive discussions of the uses of language tests are provided in Bachman (1990) Chapter 3, and McNamara (forthcoming).

2 An example of the use of a language test for multiple purposes (placement and research) is provided in Brown (1980).

3 A discussion of decision making is provided in Carroll and Hall (1985) Chapter 10.

SECTION 2:
Identifying, selecting, and describing tasks in the TLU domain

Introduction

As was noted in Chapter 1, we believe that for a language test to be useful, the language used, both in the test tasks themselves and in the test taker's response to these test tasks, must correspond in demonstrable ways to language use in a specific target language use (TLU) domain. To establish this correspondence, we need to identify the TLU tasks in the relevant domain and describe these tasks in terms of their task characteristics, using a framework such as that presented in Chapter 3. These sets of characteristics provide the basis for developing test tasks whose characteristics correspond to those of TLU tasks. This correspondence between TLU tasks and test tasks is also the basis for determining the domain of generalization for the interpretations about ability that we intend to make on the basis of test results.

In this section we discuss how to identify, select, and describe TLU tasks for purposes of test development. Although we describe these activities in this order, we would emphasize that they will not necessarily be implemented in a linear sequence, but are interactive, and will generally be happening simultaneously. The more explicit and detailed we can be in our descriptions of the TLU tasks, the more guidance we will have in developing test tasks whose characteristics correspond to those of the TLU tasks. In addition, a precise description of the TLU tasks will facilitate our evaluation of the usefulness of our test and test tasks for their intended purpose. We discuss considerations and procedures for developing test tasks in Chapter 9.

Identifying tasks in the TLU domain

In order to identify tasks in a particular domain, we will use a variety of sources and kinds of information.[4] Depending on how familiar we, as test developers, are with the relevant domain, we may initially be able to identify tasks informally with 'best guesses', using our own knowledge, talking with other individuals who are familiar with the domain, and so forth. However, even in cases where the test developer is quite familiar with the domain, we believe it is essential to refine these best guesses with a more systematic approach to identifying the tasks. This is particularly critical in cases where the test developer is not at all familiar with the relevant domain.[5]

As a general approach to identifying tasks in the relevant domain, we recommend needs analysis, which is commonly used in language curriculum development. In general, needs analysis, or needs assessment, involves the systematic gathering of specific information about the language needs of learners and the analysis of this information for purposes of language syllabus design. The procedures of needs analysis can be adapted to the activity of identifying tasks, and might involve the following steps:

1   identify the stakeholders who are familiar with relevant language use situations, who can help identify the relevant domain and tasks;
2   identify or develop procedures for gathering information about tasks;
3   gather information on the domain and tasks in collaboration with stakeholders;
4   analyze the tasks in terms of their task characteristics; and
5   make an initial grouping of tasks into categories of tasks with similar characteristics.

There are a number of different philosophical perspectives and a multitude of methodological approaches to designing and conducting needs analysis, as well as a wide range of methods for collecting relevant information. Discussions of these issues can be found in the Suggested Readings at the end of this section.

The amount of time and effort expended in identifying tasks will be influenced by the demands of the particular testing situation. For example, when designing a high stakes test for use with a wide variety of test takers, it might be important to conduct a very detailed needs analysis and prepare an extensive list of tasks consistent with this analysis. On the other hand, when designing a low-stakes classroom test for use with a single group of students, we may already have in mind some specific tasks to be used as the basis for designing test tasks, so the process might be much less involved.

In some cases it may be essential for language users to be able to carry out certain tasks with a specific level of accuracy and appropriateness of language use. In such cases we may want to insure these critical tasks are included in our task analysis. Suppose, for example, non-native English speaking immigrant midwives were applying to be licensed to work as midwives in the United States, and we needed to test their ability in English. Suppose that a needs analysis indicated that one of the critical tasks that midwives had to perform was translating prescriptions verbatim from the language of immigrants into English. In this case, because this TLU task is critical, we would want to design and develop test tasks whose characteristics closely resembled those of the critical TLU task, as well as insuring that the accuracy and appropriateness of language use required in the test task were consistent with the levels required in the related TLU task.

Two types of TLU domains: Real-life and language instructional

In Chapter 3 we described two general types of TLU domains that are of particular relevance to the design and development of language tests: real-life domains and language instructional domains. While the general procedures for identifying tasks for potential development as test tasks are essentially the same for these two domains, the considerations with respect to usefulness are somewhat different. That is, in the case of language instructional domains there may be a trade-off, in terms of qualities of usefulness, between basing the development of test tasks on the characteristics of tasks in a real-life domain versus those of tasks in the language instructional domain. For this reason we discuss these two domains separately.

Real-life domains

In many situations we may be designing a test to be used in making decisions that are directly relevant to the test taker's performance on tasks in a real-life domain.[6] For example, we may be asked to test applicants for a job in order to make hiring decisions. In this case, the relevant domain is independent of language teaching considerations, and such considerations will not influence test development, so that we would proceed directly with the identification and description of real-life tasks. Real-life tasks are appropriate bases for designing language test tasks when there is a clear basis for knowing under what real-life conditions the test taker will be using the language being tested. For example, if test takers are being tested so as to determine whether they are prepared to use a second language to serve as bilingual tour guides, it would make sense to use this domain as the basis of test development.

An additional consideration in using real-life tasks as a basis for developing language test tasks, is that the test takers' language ability is at a high enough level and broad enough for it to be reasonable to ask them to perform test tasks based on real-life tasks.

Language instructional domains

When characteristics of language instructional tasks closely match characteristics of real life tasks

Where the test takers are students in a language course, it is frequently necessary to develop a test that will provide feedback on how well students have learned the content of the course. This is the case for a classroom quiz or achievement test. A major consideration here is to determine the domain on which to base our test tasks. If the tasks in the language instructional domain correspond closely to those in an appropriate real-life domain, then the test developer can use tasks in either domain or both as a basis for developing test tasks. For example, in the case of classroom achievement tests for a course in 'survival English' for immigrants, where the teaching and learning tasks include practicing dialogs based upon a real-life domain—'survival' situations in the community—the characteristics of test tasks patterned after characteristics of the instructional dialog tasks could also closely resemble the characteristics of the real-life tasks.

When characteristics of language instructional tasks do not match characteristics of clearly identifiable real-life tasks

A more problematic type of situation is where there is a lack of correspondence between the characteristics of the teaching and learning tasks and those of a real-life domain. Suppose, for example, that you were asked to develop an achievement test for a course in which instructional tasks are not patterned after tasks in a real-life domain, but it was clear what an appropriate domain might be. In this case, you might describe tasks in the real-life domain in order to determine whether the characteristics of any of these tasks could be incorporated into test tasks without creating an unfair discrepancy between the test task characteristics and those of the instructional tasks. In effect you would be increasing the relevance of the test tasks to a real-life domain. One reason for doing this might be to have a positive impact on instruction by suggesting that if test tasks can be made more authentic (made to resemble real-life tasks), then instructional tasks could also be made more authentic.

When it is difficult to determine what the appropriate real-life domain might be

In other achievement testing situations it might be very difficult to determine what an appropriate real-life domain might be. This is commonly the case where students are learning a foreign language that they do not use at all outside the language class, and may be doing so for any of a wide variety of reasons or for no obvious reason except to fulfill an educational requirement. In this case it would probably not be useful to make up a real-life domain, base test tasks on tasks in this, and run the risk of creating a negative impact on test takers and test users. It might be better to base test tasks exclusively on instructional tasks. At the same time, it might be useful to ask why it is so difficult to determine what an appropriate real-life domain might be and, perhaps, lead teachers and course developers to re-evaluate the nature of the curriculum.

In situations where there is clearly a *mismatch* between the characteristics of instructional tasks and of the tasks in an obviously relevant real-life domain, it will be necessary to try to find a balance between the qualities of authenticity and impact. On the one hand the test developer could choose to maximize fairness, an aspect of impact on test takers, by designing test tasks whose characteristics correspond to those of the language teaching tasks. To do so, however, may sacrifice authenticity and promote a negative impact on instruction, if there is, in fact, a relevant real-life domain upon which test tasks could be based, and an obvious mismatch between the characteristics of instructional and real-life tasks. On the other hand, the test developer could choose to maximize authenticity and, potentially, positive impact on instruction, by developing test tasks whose characteristics correspond to those of real-life tasks. To choose this route may be at the expense of fairness to the students, depending on the degree of mismatch between instructional and real-life tasks.

It is our view that rather than automatically using language instructional tasks as the starting point for developing language test tasks, we must first determine the degree to which the instructional tasks correspond to the real-life tasks that the students will encounter after leaving the instructional setting. In cases where there is a close correspondence between the two, we can use either or both as a basis for developing test tasks. In cases where there is no obvious real-life domain, or where there is a lack of correspondence between real-life tasks and instructional tasks, the test developer must attempt to design the test tasks in such a way as to balance the qualities of authenticity and impact. Projects 1, 5, 6, 7, 8 and 9 illustrate variations in the process of identifying the tasks in a relevant TLU domain for the purpose of subsequent test task development.

Selecting TLU tasks for consideration as test tasks

Not all TLU tasks will be appropriate for use as a basis for developing test tasks. This is because they may not meet all our criteria for usefulness and hence are not likely to be useful as test tasks. For example, there may be tasks in the TLU domain that can be carried out with little use of the areas of language ability that we want to measure. To illustrate this, consider the following case. One of the authors was recently involved in helping a large multinational company develop a test to assess the capacity of individuals for using Chinese and English accurately and appropriately to function effectively as a bilingual receptionist in one of their Asian offices. This test would be used as part of the selection procedure for hiring a new receptionist. In this situation, the client clearly wanted an individual who could use both languages accurately and appropriately, so both grammatical knowledge and sociolinguistic knowledge (essentially knowledge of appropriate registers and forms of address) were included in the construct definition. A needs analysis indicated that one of the task types in the TLU domain involved the employee's answering the phone and transferring the call to another employee. This particular task could be accomplished by means of a couple of short formulaic utterances, such as (in English) 'Hello, this is B-P Enterprises. How may I direct your call?' and 'Just a moment, please, and I'll transfer your call.' The client was interested in being able to make valid inferences about the test takers' grammatical and sociolinguistic knowledge, and this task type would not be adequate for making inferences about these areas of language ability, since it might require little more than the knowledge of prefabricated patterns. That is, using this TLU task as a test task might limit the validity of the inferences we want to make.

Another situation in which we might need to exclude certain TLU tasks from consideration would be when those tasks are not appropriate for all of the test takers. This may occur when the TLU domain is broadly defined, such as when we need to develop a language test for use, along with other kinds of information, in selecting students for entrance into a university. The domain in this case involves using English in a university setting, and includes a wide range of tasks that are likely to vary in a number of ways, including the areas and levels of specific topical knowledge required to perform them. The test takers will most likely be a diverse group with relatively general topical knowledge, who will eventually choose different majors. If we include test tasks that correspond, in level and areas of topical content, to tasks in the TLU domain, this might have a negative impact. That is, tasks such as these could be considered unfair to test takers who do not already have the levels of specialized knowledge such tasks require. We might attempt to minimize this by excluding the tasks that require more specialized topical knowledge and trying to include test tasks whose characteristics are common to the TLU tasks of all of the test takers.

Describing TLU task types

In order to select TLU tasks for use as possible test tasks, we will need to analyze and describe these TLU tasks in terms of those characteristics that are common to a particular set of TLU tasks and that distinguish these tasks from other sets of TLU tasks. We will refer to this set of characteristics as *distinctive task characteristics*. These sets of distinctive task characteristics define, in effect, task 'types' which provide the templates for developing actual test tasks.

In some cases the test developer may find the framework for describing task characteristics described in Chapter 3 satisfactory for describing TLU tasks. In other cases he may want to modify the framework. This may involve omitting certain characteristics which do not seem relevant or adding others. This is illustrated in Project 10. The main point that we are advocating is that some sort of task characteristics framework and systematic analysis is useful in bringing precision to the description of the characteristics of TLU tasks.

Using a checklist to describe tasks

As a means for systematically describing TLU tasks, we can use checklists such as that shown in Table 6.1, or those used in syllabus-based Project 1, in Part Three. We will describe Project 1 briefly here, to illustrate the use of checklists for describing TLU tasks in both real-life and language instructional domains, as well as for comparing the characteristics of tasks in these two domains. We also use this project as a means of summarizing the activities of identifying, selecting, and describing TLU tasks for possible use as test tasks. These activities are illustrated in Figure 6.1 overleaf.

In Project 1 our needs analysis identified a variety of writing tasks that students might perform, many of which, such as writing letters to friends and short notes to instructors regarding a change in a grade, were not directly related to the purpose of the test of academic writing ability and were thus not considered for possible development as test tasks. In Tables 1 and 2 we initially described the characteristics of four tasks that we felt were directly relevant to the purpose of the test. On the basis of our analysis of the similarities and differences in tasks, we grouped Tasks 1 and 2 into a single task type, 'term paper' (labeled 'TLU Task Type A' in Figure 6.1). The resulting three tasks types, 'term paper', 'essay exam', and 'proposal'

	TLU task
Characteristics of the setting: Physical setting	
Participants	
Time of task	
Characteristics of input: Format	
Channel	
Form	
Language	
Type	
Characteristics of expected response: Format	
Channel	
Form	
Language	
Type	
Relationship between input and response	
Reactivity	
Scope	
Directness	

Table 6.1:   TLU task checklist

are found in both the instructional domain (the ESL writing program) and in the real-life domain (the writing that the students will be doing outside of their ESL writing classes). We then re-evaluated the characteristics of all three of these TLU tasks in terms of their potential contribution to the usefulness of the test. We determined that many of the characteristics the proposal task overlapped with important characteristics of the other two tasks in the two TLU domains. Moreover, some of the characteristics of

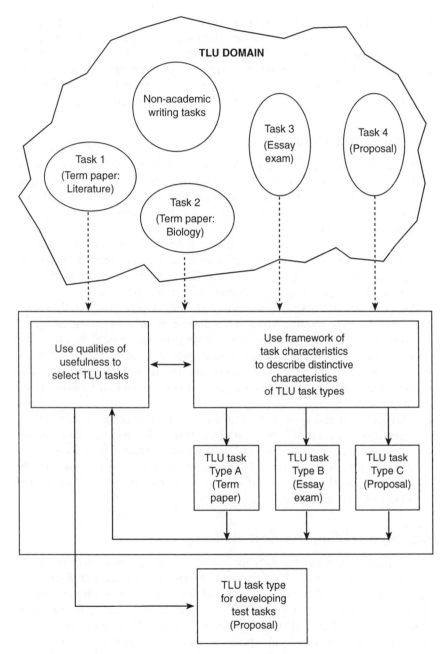

Figure 6.1: Selecting and describing TLU task types

the proposal task were of critical importance to the test. For example, the length of the input and response for the proposal (relatively shorter than for the term paper task) would allow us to develop a practical test task. We therefore decided to use the characteristics of the proposal task (labeled TLU Task 4 in Table P1.2 on page 258) as the basis for describing the TLU task type that would guide our development of test tasks.

Exercises for Section 2

1   Read over the list of the four TLU tasks (responding to complaints on the phone or in writing, writing memos to co-workers, writing business letters, problem solving via correspondence) listed for Project 2 in Part Three. Describe these tasks as well as you can using a table of task characteristics like that provided in Table 6.1.

2   Think of a testing situation with which you are familiar and make a list of possible TLU tasks. Then describe the characteristics of several of these tasks. See if you can characterize this particular set of tasks in terms of a common set of important characteristics.

3   Suppose you are asked to develop a test for a very traditional, audio-lingual language course which relies almost entirely on dialog memorization and structural pattern drills. What problems would this raise for you as a test developer? How would you respond to such a request? Are there any strategies you might use for developing authentic test tasks based on a real-life domain given or referred to in the instructional materials?

4   Make a list of task types for a TLU domain with which you are familiar. Then describe each task type using the task characteristics. Note which characteristics seem to be fixed and which characteristics seem to be variable for each task type. Does this exercise suggest how you might go about developing a *set* of specific test tasks based on each of the TLU task types? How?

Suggested readings for Section 2

Needs analysis/assessment: Extensive discussions of needs analysis methods for foreign language programs are given in the papers in Richterich and Chancerel (1980). Richterich (1983) provides case studies of exemplary needs analyses. An excellent discussion of different views of needs analysis is provided in Brindley (1989). Berwick (1989) discusses both theoretical orientations and different practical approaches to needs assessment. An extensive framework for conducting language needs analysis is described in Munby (1979). One of the most comprehensive discussions of needs analysis in education is that provided in Stufflebeam et al. (1985).

SECTION 3:
Describing the characteristics of the language users/test takers

Introduction

Throughout this book we have emphasized the need to keep in mind two kinds of correspondences: those between characteristics of TLU tasks and test tasks, and those between characteristics of language users and test takers. (See Chapter 1 Figure 1.1.) The first set of correspondences influences primarily the authenticity of the test tasks. The second set influences primarily the interactiveness of the test task. Both sets influence other aspects of usefulness as well, such as reliability (the test tasks need to be at appropriate levels for test takers in order to yield reliable scores) and impact (inappropriate test tasks are likely to create negative impact on test takers and instruction). Thus we need to manage the effects of these characteristics on test performance.

Describing the characteristics of test takers guides subsequent steps in test development by making explicit those test taker characteristics that may affect their test performance, and which we must, therefore, consider in determining the characteristics of the test tasks. As with the tasks in the TLU domain (see the discussion above), we need to describe the characteristics of the test takers as specifically as possible, and it is always important to base our description upon the best information available. We do not want to proceed on the basis of mere assumption.

As with the tasks in the TLU domain, we will base our description of test taker characteristics on a wide variety of sources and kinds of information. We may be able to form an initial description informally, using our own knowledge, talking with others who are familiar with the test takers, etc. However, even where the test developer is quite familiar with the test takers, we believe it is important to refine these initial informal approaches with a more systematic approach. This is even more important where the test developer is not at all familiar with the test takers. What we recommend is to use a combination of interviews, observations, self-reports, and questionnaires.

The characteristics of test takers that we believe are particularly relevant to test development can be divided into four categories:

1   personal characteristics,
2   topical knowledge,
3   general level and profile of language ability, and
4   predictions about test takers' potential affective responses to the test.

Personal characteristics of test takers

In Chapter 4 we described personal characteristics of test takers as individual attributes that are not part of test takers' language ability but which may still influence performance on language tests. Examples of these include age, sex, native language(s), level of general education, and amount and type of preparation for or prior experience with a given test. Clearly these characteristics will affect the usefulness of specific test tasks for the purposes for which we are designing the test.

As long as we have in mind a specific TLU domain and set of language users as well as a specific test language use domain and group of test takers when we start to develop our test, we are unlikely to get very far off track. Most inappropriate test tasks result from trying to develop a test without a specific TLU domain or specific test takers in mind. The number of personal characteristics that could potentially affect the test performance of any given test taker is very large. Thus, rather than attempting to provide an exhaustive list, we will list the personal characteristics we have included in our projects for illustrative purposes, namely those which have an obvious impact on our choice of test task characteristics in the context of the specific example project. The following list, taken from Project 1 in Part Three, provides an example of the kind of list that might be considered as a place to start in the description of personal characteristics, in any test development project.

1 Age: 18 and above, but mostly between 18 and 23
2 Sex: male and female
3 Nationalities: widely varied
4 Immigrant status: immigrants and international students
5 Native languages: widely varied
6 Level and type of general education: undergraduate transfer students with a minimum of one year's education in a North American junior college, college, or university,
7 Type and amount of preparation or prior experience with a given test: many test takers will be familiar with ESL proficiency tests such as the *Test of English as a Foreign Language* (TOEFL), the Cambridge *Certificate of Proficiency in English* (CPE), and the *Michigan Test of English Language Proficiency* (University of Michigan ND).

Topical knowledge of test takers

As noted in Chapter 2, all instances of language *use* involve topical knowledge. Although individual test takers vary and may be at many different levels, for purposes of test design we can group them into two general categories, in terms of the topical knowledge that we presuppose they bring to the test: those with homogeneous specific topical knowledge and those with widely varied topical knowledge.

Relatively homogeneous topical knowledge

A homogeneous group of test takers with specific topical knowledge can use that knowledge as the information base with which they can demonstrate their language ability. In designing a test for such a group of test takers, one possible source of information about their topical knowledge would be content area specialists. For example, if we were developing an English for academic purposes test for students intending to study English literature, we might ask literature teachers to help organize a description of relevant topical knowledge. Or suppose we wanted to assess the English-speaking ability of experienced automobile mechanics in order to make decisions about employing them for jobs involving interaction with English-speaking customers. (See Project 7 in Part Three.) Such test takers would, as a group, know a lot about auto repair and could be expected to talk about it. When designing a test for them, we might want to consult with automobile mechanics to develop a suitable description of their topical knowledge.

Relatively widely varied topical knowledge

In other testing situations, test takers as a group may not have a high level of control of a single area of topical knowledge *in common*. This might be the case if we were designing a test to develop language ability profiles of limited English proficiency elementary school children, or if we were designing a speaking test to be administered to a very diverse population of test takers. (See Project 4 in Part Three for an example.)

In cases such as these, we may need to look for and describe a number of different areas of these test takers' topical knowledge to guide our subsequent development of test tasks. We should not make the mistake of not requiring the test takers to use topical knowledge in responding to test tasks, for doing so will lower the usefulness of the test, particularly in areas of validity, authenticity, interactiveness, and impact.

Levels and profiles of language ability of test takers

In addition to describing the test takers' personal characteristics and topical knowledge, we also need to describe their general level of language ability in performing different types of language use tasks, such as listening to lectures, asking directions, reading newspapers, or writing business memos. All we need at this stage is a general description to help insure that the test will be at an appropriate level. This information will be useful in helping us tailor the test tasks to the test takers' specific levels of ability and types of language use tasks, thus maximizing the usefulness of the test.

We might also want to develop a preliminary profile of test takers' levels of language ability in specific areas, such as grammatical knowledge, textual knowledge, and sociolinguistic knowledge. Suppose, for example, that we wanted to develop an achievement test to measure students' mastery of specific grammatical structures taught in a class designed to prepare them for entrance into an American university. And suppose we knew that these students had a fairly high level of control of reading but were quite weak in listening. We might use this information to develop test tasks that relied primarily upon written input which would be comprehensible to the test takers and not compromise their ability to respond to the test task.

Potential affective responses to test tasks

As noted in Chapter 4, the test takers' affective responses to the characteristics of the test environment and tasks can potentially inhibit or facilitate optimum performance. For this reason, we need to consider carefully and describe as specifically as possible our expectations about how test takers are likely to feel about doing test tasks, given what we know about their personal characteristics, including their familiarity with the testing environment, their topical knowledge, and their level of language ability.

Test takers' familiarity with the test setting may determine, in part, their affective responses to the test tasks. When there is a high level of correspondence between characteristics of the TLU setting and tasks and the test setting and tasks, we may be able to assume that test takers will have a generally positive affective response to the test and test tasks. For example, suppose our TLU domain is that of a bilingual secretary in an employment agency in Montreal, Quebec. If we wanted to test applicants for this kind of job, we could ask the test takers to perform the same kinds of tasks that bilingual secretaries perform, and assume that they will react positively to such tasks.

The level and specificity of topical knowledge presupposed or required of test takers can also influence their affective responses to the test. We would generally expect that test takers who have the relevant topical knowledge will have positive affective responses to the test and test tasks, while those who do not may have negative affective responses. Suppose, for example, that we were testing applicants to a US college to determine whether they should be exempted from classes designed to prepare them for academic writing. Since students already enrolled in college classes are able to apply topical knowledge specific to a given course in completing academic writing tasks, tasks appropriate for these students might not be appropriate for students who are applying for admission. Including or presupposing highly specific topical content in the writing prompts in the test might therefore be expected to induce negative affective responses on the part of the test takers. (See Project 1 in Part Three.)

Finally, test takers' general levels and profiles of language ability can influence their affective responses. Test takers who have high levels of language ability are likely to feel positive about taking a language test, while less proficient test takers may feel threatened by the test.

Exercises for Section 3

1 Read the description of test takers for Project 1 in Part Three. Do you think this description is sufficiently complete for the purpose of test development? Are there any other characteristics of test takers that you might want to include? If so, what impact might these characteristics have on the design of test tasks?

2 Think of a specific testing situation and test with which you are familiar. Describe the characteristics of the test takers using the categories described in Section 3 above. Then compare your list of characteristics with those prepared by another student for a different set of test takers in a different testing situation.

3 Using the characteristics of test takers prepared in Exercise 2, evaluate the appropriateness of the test tasks for the test takers. Are there any characteristics of the test takers that might lead you to change some of the characteristics of the test tasks? Why? Justify your proposed changes in terms of their influence on specific qualities of usefulness.

4 Read the description of the test takers in Project 4, Part Three. Can you think of another testing situation you might face in which you had to deal with a similarly diverse group of test takers? What kinds of test tasks are used for the test takers in your situation? To what extent are these tasks designed to take into consideration the diverse characteristics of the test takers? What test task characteristics might you change to make them more adaptable to different test takers?

Suggested readings for Section 3

See the Suggested Readings in Chapter 4.

SECTION 4:
Defining the construct to be measured

Introduction

Another essential activity in the design stage is that of defining the construct to be measured. The way we do this will be determined, largely, by the kinds of inferences we want to make on the basis of scores from language tests, as discussed in Section 1 of this chapter. In this section, we discuss different approaches to defining the construct to be measured, corresponding to the different kinds of inferences we want to make.

In defining the construct, the test developer needs to make a conscious and deliberate choice to specify particular components of the ability or abilities to be measured in a way that is appropriate to a particular testing situation.[7] Specific definitions of the abilities, or constructs, are needed for three purposes:

1   to provide a basis for using test scores for their intended purpose(s),
2   to guide test development efforts, and
3   to enable the test developer and user to demonstrate the construct validity of these interpretations.

The test developer thus needs to decide what abilities to include and not include in the construct definition, based on the kinds of inferences that are to be made. Furthermore, in order to justify the use of test results, the test developer must include, in the design statement, a definition of the specific construct(s) to be measured. What this also means is that the test developer cannot simply accept, without question, the construct labels that other test developers have used, as either corresponding to the construct to be measured, or as being appropriate for this particular testing situation.

During the design stage of test development, we specify an abstract, *theoretical definition* of the construct we want to measure. In most situations this construct definition will include specific components of language knowledge. In addition, there are situations in which the test developer may want to make inferences about specific components of strategic competence, in which case these will also need to be specified in the construct definition. Finally, in some situations, particularly where we need to develop tests of language for specific purposes, the construct may be defined more broadly to include topical knowledge. Thus, the way in which the construct is defined for any given test development situation will need to be tailored to the needs of that particular situation.

It is important to keep in mind that irrespective of the particular approach we take to defining the construct, the way we do so will have clear implications for the scoring method to be used. Specifically, we need to keep in mind that whatever inference we want to make about a construct needs to be based on an observable 'product' or 'output', which usually consists of a score, but which can also be in the form of a verbal description. Thus, the more components we include in our construct definition, the more scores, or pieces of information we will need to derive from test performance and, potentially, to report to test users. We would hasten to point out that we are *not* suggesting that scoring procedures should determine how we define constructs. We are simply noting that the way we define the construct will have consequences, in terms of scoring.

Defining the construct, language ability

In Chapter 4, we defined language ability as including language knowledge and strategic competence, or metacognitive strategies. One consideration is thus to decide which specific components of language ability are to be included in the construct definition. In many testing situations the test user will want to make inferences about specific components of language ability, and may thus define the construct in terms of those components. This might be the case if the test is to be used in an instructional setting and its purpose is to diagnose areas of strength and weakness, or to assess the achievement of specific syllabus objectives. The test developer will then most likely base the construct definition on the specific components of language ability that are included in the course syllabus. In other cases, such as the use of tests for determining admission into an academic program, or for making decisions about employment, where there may not be an instructional syllabus, the test developer will most likely base the definition of the construct on the components described in a theory of language ability.

When we design test tasks that engage test takers in activities that generate a sample of language (spoken or written text), we have a product which we can analyze and use to tease out specific components of language ability. Not only can we do this, but we are very likely to do so, whether we are asked to or not. For example, if raters are given a composition to read and evaluate, or if they are given a recording of oral communication to score, they are likely to have some idea of what areas of language ability to focus on and how to weight them in the scoring. However, if raters are not told specifically what areas of language ability to focus on, they are likely to differ among themselves as to their scoring criteria. Thus, in order to provide for consistency of scoring of language samples, we feel it is important to define the construct componentially. If we need to arrive at a single score, we can later combine the scores on the various components to arrive at a single, 'composite' score. (For a discussion of this, see Chapter 11.)

In other situations the test developer may plan to develop test tasks that do not engage test takers in activities that generate extended samples of spoken or written text, yet may nonetheless yield responses that can be used to tease out specific components of language ability. For example, in Project 6 the test taker reads input consisting of a series of increasingly complex questions but responds with only single words or short phrases. Because the responses are too limited to analyze directly in terms of components of language ability, it might appear on the surface that the construct should be defined 'globally.' However, the characteristics of the input are described quite precisely and are, in fact, used to develop a definition of the components of the construct to be measured: knowledge of graphology, knowledge of work-experience related vocabulary, the grammar of questions, the grammar of phrases, the grammar of subordination, and the organization of paragraphs. The scores on the different questions are used to measure knowledge of different components of the construct.

Syllabus-based construct definitions

Syllabus-based construct definitions distinguish among the specific components of language ability that are included in an instructional syllabus. They are likely to be most useful when we need to obtain detailed information on students' mastery of specific areas of language ability. For example, suppose we were teaching a set of specific grammatical structures, and wanted to develop an achievement test to measure students' ability to use them, so as to provide feedback on mastery of these specific teaching points. We might prepare a definition of the construct 'ability to use grammatical structures accurately', which included a list of the structures we had taught, such as article usage, use of the past tense, subject-verb agreement, and so forth. (Projects 1, 3, 8, 9, and 10 in Part Three provide examples of syllabus-based construct definitions.)

Theory-based construct definitions

Theory-based construct definitions are different from syllabus-based definitions in that they are based on a theoretical model of language ability rather than the contents of a language teaching syllabus. For example, suppose we wanted to screen applicants for a bilingual secretary's job for which one requirement was the ability to produce letters and memos in the appropriate register. We might make a list of specific politeness formulae used for greetings, leave taking, introducing contradictions, introducing clarifications, and so forth, and use these as a basis for the construct definition. (See Projects 2, 4, 5, 6, and 7 in Part Three for examples using theory-based construct definitions.)

If we define the construct to include more than one specific area of language ability, we have the potential of providing several scores, or a profile of language ability. For example, if we define our construct broadly to include knowledge of grammatical organization, textual organization, functions, and sociolinguistic characteristics, for each test taker we could report a profile of scores in each of these areas of language ability. However, it is important to understand that just defining the components is not sufficient justification for making componential interpretations. We need to provide evidence of the construct validity of these interpretations—

evidence of the validity of the inferences about the different components of the construct definition—before reporting scores for the different components included in the construct definition. (Approaches to providing evidence relevant to construct validity are described in the references listed at the end of Chapter 2.)

Strategic competence

Strategic competence, or what in Chapter 4 we have called metacognitive strategies, is always involved in language use, even in tasks that are not very interactive. Thus the strategies are always implied in our construct definitions of language ability and can always be *assumed* to be part of the construct. However, in defining a construct for purposes of testing, we need to decide whether or not we want to make specific inferences about aspects of strategic competence.

Situations in which strategic competence is likely NOT *to be included in the construct definition*

In most language testing situations, we will probably not wish to make specific inferences about strategic competence, so we would not be likely to include this in our definition of the construct. The picture description test discussed in Chapter 4 (pages 74–5) illustrates this. In developing this experimental test, one of the authors noted that performance on the test seemed to be affected to a considerable extent by the strategies the test takers used. Recall that the test task required the test taker to describe one out of four similar pictures so that the examiner could identify which had been described. The test was scored on the basis of the amount of time taken to complete the task. Some test takers with very little language knowledge were able to complete the task very quickly by focusing only on the relevant differences among the pictures and then describing those differences using as simple language as possible. Other test takers with greater language knowledge took longer to complete the task because they didn't use that strategy.

Since the test developer wanted to use this test primarily as a test of language knowledge, he did not include strategic competence in the construct definition. In order to reduce the effect of differences in strategic competence on test performance and allow the scores to more accurately reflect differences in language knowledge, the test developer could have included instructions to the test takers to be sure to use complete, grammatically well-formed utterances in their responses.

Situations in which strategic competence IS *likely to be included in the construct definition*

In other testing situations, we may want to make specific inferences about strategic competence, and will need to include it in the construct definition. For example, if in the situation described above, the test developer had wanted to measure not only language knowledge but also the test takers' flexibility in adapting their language use to different situations, he could have included strategic competence in the construct definition, perhaps by defining it as 'ability to assess the content of the pictures and develop a plan for minimizing the amount and complexity of information to be described'. In this case, the test developer could have instructed the test takers to focus only on relevant differences among the pictures and to describe these in the simplest language possible, while still using language correctly. This might have served to increase the effect of differences in strategic competence on test performance and thus allowed the scores to more accurately reflect differences in both language knowledge and strategic competence.

When we include strategic competence in the construct *definition*, we need to decide upon the level of specificity with which this needs to be defined. If we wanted to assess competence in the use of specific strategies we would use a componential definition of language ability, as described above. In the model of strategic competence presented in Chapter 4, we indicated one componential breakdown, which included goal setting, assessment, and planning, so if we wanted to use this model, we might use one or more of these components in a componential definition of strategic competence. For example, suppose we wanted to test students' ability to use language in writing, and suppose the TLU situation was one in which the students would be writing a research paper. This task clearly involves to a considerable degree the students' ability to set goals, assess the context, and make plans. Therefore, we might include one or more of these components of strategic competence in the construct definition and develop scoring procedures that would allow us to make inferences about the operation of these specific strategies.[8]

The role of topical knowledge in construct definitions

In Chapter 4 we argued that the topical knowledge of language users is always involved in language use. It follows that if language test tasks are authentic and interactional, and elicit instances of language use, test takers' topical knowledge will always be a factor in their test performance. Historically, language testers have viewed topical knowledge almost exclusively as a potential source of test bias, or invalidity, and the traditional practice in developing language tests is to design test tasks that will minimize, or control, the effect of test takers' topical knowledge on test performance. We take a slightly different view and would argue that this is not appropriate for all situations. Although topical knowledge may, in many situations, be a potential source of bias, there are other situations in which it may, in fact, be part of the construct the test developer wants to measure. One question that needs to be asked, then, is 'When does the test developer consider topical knowledge a potential source of bias and when does he define it as part of the construct?' This question is addressed in Section 1 of this chapter, under 'Making inferences'. It is in such situations that the test developer is most likely to define topical knowledge as part of the construct to be measured. A more crucial question, we believe, has to do with how to go about defining the role of topical knowledge in the construct and what the possible consequences are of defining it in a particular way.

We believe that there are essentially three options for defining the construct to be measured, with respect to topical knowledge:

1 define the construct solely in terms of language ability, excluding topical knowledge from the construct definition,
2 include *both* topical knowledge and language ability in the construct definition, or
3 define topical knowledge and language ability as separate constructs.

Here we will discuss these three options for defining the construct, along with typical situations, intended inferences, potential problems, and possible solutions for each. We will list the considerations associated with each option in more or less outline form, and then provide an example for each option.

Option 1: Topical knowledge not included in the construct definition

Typical situations

Where test takers are expected to have relatively widely varied topical knowledge:

– language programs, where inferences about language ability are to be used to make decisions about individuals (e.g. selection, diagnosis, achievement)
– academic, professional, or vocational training programs, or for employment, where inferences about language ability will be one of several factors considered in the selection process
– research in which language ability is included as a construct.

It is important to remember that even if the test developer has decided not to include topical knowledge in the construct definition, it may still be involved in test takers' performance. For a particular testing situation, the test developer may simply choose to focus on language ability and not attempt to make inferences about topical knowledge.

Intended inference
Components of language ability only

Potential problem 1

Possible bias due to specific topical information in the task input; test takers who happen to have relevant topical knowledge may be favored.

Possible solutions

1   Include in the task input topical information that we expect none of the test takers to know. This is a widely used solution in language tests. *Potential problem*: this decontextualizes the test task, and thus probably biases the test against everyone to some extent.
2   Include in the task input topical information that we expect will be familiar to all of the test takers. *Potential advantage*: this contextualizes the task for everyone, and thus should facilitate optimum performance. *Potential problem*, particularly with tasks aimed at assessing comprehension: test takers may be able to answer the questions largely on the basis of topical knowledge.
3   Present test takers with several tasks, each with different topical content. There are two ways in which this solution might be implemented:
    a   have all test takers complete all tasks;
    b   give test takers a choice.
   We favor providing test takers with choices, since this is one way in which we can accommodate their specific interests.[9] In addition, we feel that this gives them a greater sense of involvement in the test taking process.

Potential problem 2

Possible ambiguous interpretation of low scores, and hence problem of questionable construct validity. Specifically, if test takers get low scores, this could be due either to low language ability or to low topical knowledge, or both.

Possible solutions

1   In test tasks that engage test takers in listening or reading activities, and that elicit selected or limited production responses, clearly specify the component(s) of language ability that each test task is designed to measure, and then design test tasks with this in mind.
2   In test tasks that engage test takers in speaking or writing activities that

elicit extended production responses, use analytic rating scales for rating components of language ability, or conduct qualitative analyses of the test takers' responses. The use of analytic rating scales enables us to focus on specific components of language ability.

Example 1

Suppose we wanted to measure the ability of international students applying to an American university to read 'academic' material in English for purposes of selecting them for admission. Bearing in mind the variety of disciplines in any given university, we might decide to develop a number of reading passages with different topical information and allow test takers to choose several to which to respond. We would need to design types of test tasks that focus on areas of language ability, and then write tasks for each of the different reading passages.

We would most likely be interested in the students' ability to control certain forms of written discourse and not the extent of their knowledge of the topic about which they happened to be reading. We would therefore not include topical knowledge in the construct definition, and would rate answers on the basis of components of language ability. (See Project 5 in Section Three, in which different test tasks are designed to measure different components of language ability.)

Example 2

Suppose we wanted to develop an achievement test for students of the Thai language to assess their ability to use the appropriate register with interlocutors of different relationships, ages, and social status in face-to-face oral interactions. We would most likely be interested in measuring their knowledge of the appropriate personal pronouns and politeness markers, and not the extent of their knowledge of any particular information that might be the topic of the interaction. We would therefore not include topical knowledge in the construct definition. We might develop a set of role plays that dealt only with topics with which we expected the students to be familiar. We might include role plays with a hypothetical superior, an office associate, a close friend, a hypothetical subordinate, and a young child. Test takers' responses to the role-play prompts and questions would be rated only in terms of the appropriateness of the register markers they used.

Option 2: Topical knowledge included in the construct definition

Typical situation

Where test takers are expected to have relatively homogeneous topical knowledge:

- language for specific purposes programs, where the language is being learned in conjunction with topical information related to specific academic disciplines, professions, or vocations, and where inferences from test scores are to be used to make decisions about individuals (for example, selection, diagnosis, achievement)
- selection for professional or vocational training programs, or for employment, where scores from the language test will be the major factor considered in the selection process. This involves using these inferences to make predictions about test takers' capability to perform future tasks or jobs that require the use of language.

Intended inference

Ability to process (interpret or express) specific topical information through language.

Potential problem 1

The test developer or user may mistakenly fail to attribute performance on test tasks to topical knowledge as well as to language ability. This problem of inference may be due to lack of clarity in the specification of test tasks and in the scoring of responses.

Potential problem 2

Test scores cannot provide specific feedback to the test user or to test takers, for diagnostic purposes.

Possible solution

Clear specification of construct definition for each test task and of criteria for scoring test takers' responses.

Example 1

Suppose we wanted to assess diplomats in the foreign service on their ability to read and understand descriptions of political activities associated with elections in the foreign country to which they are likely to be posted. We might design a set of tasks in which test takers are presented with a number of passages representing the types of discourse normally found in newspaper accounts. We might develop for each passage a set of multiple-choice items intended to measure the test takers' comprehension.

Example 2

Suppose we wanted to measure the ability of an international teaching assistant to give a short classroom lecture on the subject matter that she might be expected to teach, such as educational evaluation. We might design a test task that simulates a lecture, and define the construct as 'ability to give a well-organized lecture on the topic of validation'. (See the discussion of rating scales in Chapter 11.)

Comments

In Section 1 of this chapter, we discussed some of the considerations involved in attempting to make inferences and predictions about individuals' capability to perform tasks or jobs that require the use of language, and pointed out the demands this places on the test developer, who must clearly delineate the roles of individual characteristics, including topical knowledge, in the construct definition. In Chapter 11 we point out some of the problems involved in attempting to rate samples of spoken or written language with holistic rating scales. Because of these problems, as well as those of potential lack of clarity in test task specifications and lack of detailed feedback, we believe that the next option is preferable in most situations in which the test user wants to make inferences about both topical knowledge and language ability.

Option 3: Language ability and topical knowledge defined as separate constructs

Typical situation

Where the test developer may not know whether test takers have relatively homogeneous or relatively widely varied topical knowledge, and wants to measure both language ability and topical knowledge. (This is very similar to Option 2, with the differences that (1) the test developer has no expectations about test takers' topical knowledge and (2) the test user wants to be able to make inferences about both language ability and topical knowledge.):

– language for specific purposes programs, where the language is being learned in conjunction with topical knowledge related to specific academic disciplines, professions, or vocations
– selection for vocational training programs, or for employment, where scores from the language test will be the major factor considered in the selection process. These inferences will be used to make predictions about

test takers' capability to perform future tasks or jobs that require the use of language

– research in which language ability and topical knowledge are included as constructs.

Intended inferences

Components of language ability *and* areas of topical knowledge

Potential problem

Less practical than Option 2 because it requires the development of either two separate sets of test tasks, with separate scoring criteria, or two separate sets of rating scales, focusing on language ability and topical knowledge.

Example 1

Suppose we wanted to make inferences about elementary school students' ability to express, in writing, their knowledge of how to use a dictionary. We could present them with a writing prompt that requests them to explain to another student how to find the meaning of a word in the dictionary. We could use separate rating scales to score their language ability and topical knowledge. Thus, we could rate the composition in terms of areas of language ability, such as grammatical accuracy and knowledge/control of features of legible handwriting. In addition, we could rate it in terms of accuracy of content. This would potentially enable us to make separate inferences about students' control of areas of language ability in writing and of topical knowledge.

Example 2

Suppose we wanted to develop a screening/placement test in English and mathematics for immigrant children entering an elementary school. For part of this test, we may want to measure their ability to use English to understand written instructions, and include in the construct 'knowledge of the vocabulary of the number system, dates, times, and scheduling'. In addition, we may want to measure their knowledge of and ability to perform the basic mathematical operations of addition, subtraction, multiplication, and division. Moreover, if we did not know in advance whether the children had topical knowledge of these mathematical operations, we could develop two sets of test tasks that involve reading, each with separate scoring criteria.

The first set of tasks, focusing on language ability, could include written instructions about when to report for different activities. Test takers could be required to give short written answers, consisting essentially of numbers, to simple questions about times for activities. Scoring criteria would be whether or not the test takers provided the factually correct times. The second set of tasks, focusing on topical knowledge, could include solving simple pencil-and-paper arithmetic problems involving addition, subtraction, multiplication, and division. Scoring criteria would be based upon whether or not the children could calculate the correct answers to the problems.

Comments

In situations where the test developer knows very little about the test takers' areas or levels of topical knowledge this is probably the most justifiable approach in terms of validity of inferences. However, while this may be so, it makes the greatest demands on resources and may not always be feasible.

Dealing with the problem of topical knowledge in language tests

How to deal with the potential effects of differing levels of topical knowledge on language test scores is a problem fundamental to all language tests. There are no easy solutions, and there is certainly no universal solution for all testing situations. The particular solution that the test developer arrives at will be a function of the various factors discussed above. What is clear is that the test developer cannot simply assume, either explicitly or by default, that topical knowledge need not be addressed simply because the focus of the test is on language ability. It is equally clear that in all situations the language test developer needs to obtain as much information as possible about potential test takers' areas and levels of topical knowledge, and should consult with content specialists in determining the areas of topical content to include in the test and the accuracy of the information that is included. Furthermore, in situations where the test developer/user wants to make inferences about test takers' language ability and areas of topical knowledge, it is crucial for the test development team to include specialists in both language and the content area(s) to be assessed.

Role of language 'skills' in construct definitions

In Chapter 4 of this book we have taken the position that the familiar 'language skills' (listening, reading, speaking, and writing) should not be included in the construct definition. This is because, if we distinguish among the language skills only in terms of mode (productive or receptive) and channel (audio or visual), we end up with skill definitions that miss many of the other important distinctions between language used in particular tasks. For example, suppose we have two tasks. In one, test takers prepare a speech in which they compare and contrast the positions taken by two authors in two different stories. In the second task, test takers write a two-line note to the mail carrier. Nominally, the first task is a speaking task, while the second is a writing task. Yet these two tasks differ in many other ways as well. In the first task, the length of the response is long, the language of the input is long and complex, the language of the expected response is highly organized rhetorically and in a formal register, and the scope of relationship between input and response is broad. In the second task, the length of the response is short, there is no input in language form, the language of the response is not highly organized and is in informal register, and the scope of relationship between input and response is narrow. Thus, focusing only on the difference between the so-called 'skills' (speaking versus writing) misses much that goes into distinguishing between these two language use tasks. That is, it suggests that the names of skills alone are sufficient to define the critical characteristics of language use tasks.

Another reason for not including a specific skill in the construct definition is that, as Widdowson (1978) has pointed out, many language use tasks involve more than one 'skill'. What he calls the communicative ability of 'conversation' involves listening and speaking, while what he calls 'correspondence' involves reading and writing. Therefore, rather than defining a construct in terms of 'skills', we suggest that the construct definition include only the relevant components of language ability, and that the 'skill' elements be specified as characteristics of the tasks in which language ability is demonstrated.

Exercises for Section 4

1   Read Project 1 in Part Three. How might the construct definition be changed if we wanted to measure specific components of strategic competence? What additional scoring procedures might we need to implement?

2   Obtain a copy of a published language test and test manual. Read whatever material is available dealing with the construct definition. How is the construct defined? What kind of construct definition is supplied: syllabus-based or theory-based? Does the construct definition involve language ability only, or is topical knowledge included in the construct definition? Does the construct *definition* include the metacognitive strategies? How adequate do you find the construct definition to be? How might you revise it?

3   Recall the last language test you developed or used. How did you define the construct to be measured at the time? How might you define it now? If you did not define the construct to be measured, how did that affect the usefulness of the test?

4   Has the discussion of defining the construct to be measured helped you distinguish components of language ability from characteristics of test tasks used to measure language ability? How? Do you find this distinction useful? Why or why not? What would be the consequences of defining the construct to be measured in such a way as to include characteristics of the TLU setting (such as 'ability to take an order in a restaurant')?

5   Are there any testing situations in which you feel it would be justified not to define the construct to be measured? Why or why not? If we want to predict the ability of a test taker to perform a specific TLU task and we know exactly what that task is, is it still necessary to define the construct to be measured?

Suggested Readings for Section 4

See Bachman 1990 and Bachman and Palmer 1982.

Chapter summary

The process of test development begins with the preparation of a set of descriptions and definitions. We begin by describing the test purpose, which in the case of a language test is primarily to make inferences about language ability. Additional purposes may include using these inferences to help us make decisions affecting test takers, teachers or supervisors, or programs. In addition, tests may also be used for research purposes.

Next we describe the TLU situation and tasks so that we can design test tasks that correspond in demonstrable ways to specific target language use situations and tasks, enabling us to develop authentic test tasks. We start by identifying the TLU situation and tasks. We then describe these in terms of their distinctive characteristics. If we are designing a test for use in a language instructional setting, we need to look beyond the instructional tasks to identify the TLU situation and tasks.

Next we describe the characteristics of the language users/test takers, which allows us to develop test tasks that will be appropriate to the test takers. The characteristics of test takers that we believe are particularly relevant to test development can be divided into four categories:

1   personal characteristics,
2   topical knowledge,

3   general level and profile of language ability, and
4   predictions about test takers' potential affective responses to the test.

Preparing this description will be relatively straightforward as long as we have in mind a specific TLU situation and specific language users. Otherwise, it will be more difficult.

Finally, we need to define the construct to be measured so that we can know how to interpret test scores. During the design stage, we define the construct, language ability, abstractly, and we can base this definition on either the content of a language syllabus or a theory of language ability. Although strategic competence will be involved in test performance, the test developer may or may not want to make specific inferences about this component of language ability, and thus must decide whether or not to include it explicitly in the definition of the construct. Test takers' topical knowledge will also be involved in test performance, and thus the test developer must also decide on the nature of the inferences to be made, and define the construct accordingly. There are essentially three options for this:

1   do not include topical knowledge in the construct definition, and make inferences about language ability only,
2   include topical knowledge in the construct definition, and make inferences about the ability to interpret or express specific topical information through language, and
3   define language ability and topical knowledge as separate constructs, and make separate inferences about these two constructs.

Typical situations in which these three approaches might be appropriate are presented, along with potential problems and solutions.

To conclude, we reiterate and reinforce our contention, presented in Chapter 4, that language 'skills' are not part of language ability, but consist of specific activities or tasks in which language is used purposefully. We would therefore include only the relevant components of language ability in the construct definition, and specify the 'skill' elements as characteristics of the tasks in which language ability is demonstrated.

Notes

1   Note to the teacher: This chapter deals with a number of important, related issues in test design, which are relatively complex. For this reason, it is relatively long. One way of teaching the material might be to assign each section to be read and worked with individually. To this end, independent exercises and suggested readings are provided after each section.

2 The test developer and test user may perform different functions. However, they may be one and the same individual, as is typically the case for a classroom test developed by a teacher. Or they might be different individuals, as with a test developed by testing specialists for use by admissions officers in colleges and universities. Or the test user might be one member of a team of test developers, as with a test developed by a team of teachers with a testing specialist coordinating the effort.

3 McNamara (1996) states that these two types of inferences are based on different hypotheses. The first type of inference, about individuals' ability to perform TLU tasks successfully, is based on what McNamara calls the *strong performance hypothesis*, while he calls the second type, about the individuals' ability to use language, the *weak performance hypothesis*.

4 For stylistic reasons, from now on we will use the acronym 'TLU' only where it is essential for distinguishing TLU domains and tasks from test tasks. Thus, where the meaning is clear from the context, we will refer simply to 'domain' and 'task'.

5 We would note here that the broader the TLU domain for which we are designing a test, the more difficult it may be to design a useful test. This is because the problem of sampling from the domain of TLU tasks becomes more difficult as the domain of TLU tasks becomes larger and hence more diverse. Thus, with a very large, diverse domain, both authenticity and the validity of inferences about test takers' ability to perform in the TLU domain may be compromised by practical restrictions on the number of test tasks that can be included in the test.

6 In keeping with our stylistic decision, rather than using the complete terms 'real-life TLU domain', 'language instructional TLU domain', we will refer to these simply as 'real-life domain' and 'language instructional domain'.

7 We recognize that our view that specific components of language ability need to be delineated and clearly defined in the construct definition is not universally held among language testers. Indeed, a fairly large number of language testers view language ability as a holistic, unitary ability, and thus do not attempt to delineate different components in the way they assess this. The most prominent example of this is the view which has informed the ACTFL Oral Proficiency Interview, and its predecessor, the FSI oral proficiency interview (Lowe 1988). Suffice it to say that the authors do not agree with this view, for reasons that have been widely discussed in the research literature, and refer those readers who are interested in this debate to the relevant references at the end of this section.

8 At present the role of strategic competence in language use, and hence in language test performance, is a relatively new area of research, and

we cannot be more specific about it. However, we believe that this is a promising approach to researching the ways that strategies work.

9 We would point out that allowing test takers the choice of taking tasks with different topical content introduces another potential source of inconsistency across test tasks, and that the test developer must take appropriate steps to determine the extent to which these tasks are equivalent and of comparable levels of difficulty.

7 Developing a plan for the evaluation of usefulness

Introduction

Since the purpose of this book is to describe procedures for developing useful language tests, usefulness will be an essential consideration at all stages of test development. (See Chapter 5, Figure 5.1 and discussion.) In fact, considerations of usefulness will probably begin from the first idea of developing a test. We will probably have some initial notion of the constructs or areas of language ability to be measured, which pertains to construct validity, and also of some of the resources available for developing the test, which relates to practicality. During the design, operationalization, and administration stages, we will continue to evaluate the usefulness of our test. Sometimes we will do so informally, while sometimes we will use more formal procedures, such as going through checklists and collecting data on usefulness.

In this chapter we discuss the ways in which considerations of usefulness play a role in the design stage of test development, through the preparation of a plan for evaluating usefulness. First, we discuss considerations in determining the appropriate balance among the qualities of usefulness and setting minimum acceptable levels for each. Next, we provide a set of questions for use in the logical evaluation of these qualities of usefulness. Finally, we briefly discuss considerations in collecting evidence of usefulness.

General considerations in developing a plan for evaluating the qualities of usefulness

In addition to being aware of usefulness while developing specifications, we also need to develop a formal plan for assessing the qualities of usefulness. This plan will be in three parts:

1   an initial consideration of the appropriate balance among the six qualities of usefulness and the setting of minimum acceptable levels for each,
2   the logical evaluation of usefulness, which involves using the questions

and checklist below to evaluate the design statement, blueprint, and test tasks, and

3   procedures for collecting qualitative and quantitative evidence during the administration stage.

We would emphasize that although we discuss these as three separate sequential parts, they are, as they apply in the process of test development, interrelated and iterative.

This plan will specify the various points at which we will collect evidence regarding usefulness and the kinds of evidence to be collected at each point. It is important that we have a formal plan so that the assessment of qualities of usefulness is not left to chance and carried out haphazardly, which can result in either wasted energy or a test that is not as useful as it might be. Finally, we need to keep in mind that the plan for evaluating the qualities of usefulness should not be regarded as fixed, but rather as a flexible set of considerations and procedures that can and probably will be modified at various stages in the test development process. We may find out, for example, that our initial plan is more ambitious than there are resources for, or we may think of additional ways to evaluate usefulness as test development proceeds.

The appropriate balance among the qualities of usefulness: setting minimum acceptable levels

In considering the qualities of usefulness two extremes must be avoided:

1   the unrealistic expectation that the highest level possible for every quality must or can be achieved, and
2   the indefensible view that one or more of these qualities can be given priority to the virtual exclusion of others.

Our view is that these extremes can be avoided by seeking to achieve a *balance* among the qualities of usefulness. This is done by determining minimum acceptable levels for each and recognizing that what constitutes an appropriate balance and appropriate minimum acceptable levels will vary from one testing situation to another.[1] Thus, achieving an appropriate balance among the qualities of usefulness entails, in our view, the initial specification of minimum acceptable levels for each quality by the test developer during the design stage, and attention to and refinement of these minimum levels during the stages of operationalization and administration.

In specifying initial minimum acceptable levels for the qualities of usefulness during the design stage, the test developer will need to consider the intended purpose of the test, including the consequences of using the test results for this particular purpose, the way the construct has been defined, and the characteristics of the TLU task types that will be used as a basis for developing test tasks. The test developer will also need to recognize that these levels will most likely be stated in different terms for different qualities. Furthermore, as stated in Principle 3 in Chapter 2 (page 18), it is not possible to prescribe, or even suggest, minimum acceptable standards in general, since these must be determined for each specific testing situation. What we will try to do in this section, however, is provide some guidance as to how one might go about setting minimum acceptable standards for the various qualities. We would note that setting minimum acceptable standards for the various qualities will be facilitated by referring to the questions for guiding the logical evaluation of usefulness, discussed below.

Reliability

Probably the most important consideration in setting a minimum acceptable level of reliability is the purposes for which the test is intended. Thus, for a relatively high-stakes test, the test developer would want to set the minimum acceptable level very high, while for a relatively low-stakes test, a lower level of reliability might be acceptable. While the test developer will want to set the minimum acceptable level of reliability as high as possible, this level needs to be realistic, and thus two other considerations need to be kept in mind—the way the construct has been defined and the nature of the test tasks—as these will affect the level of reliability that one can expect to achieve. If the construct definition focuses on a relatively narrow range of components of language ability, the test developer can reasonably expect to achieve higher levels of reliability than if the construct is complex, including a wide range of components of language ability, as well as topical knowledge. Finally, if the test tasks are relatively uniform in their characteristics, higher levels of reliability can be expected than if the test includes a wide variety of types of test tasks. A minimum acceptable level of reliability will most likely be stated in terms of an appropriate statistical estimate of reliability.[2] (An example description of minimum levels of reliability is provided in Project 1 in Part Three.)

Construct validity

A minimum acceptable level of construct validity cannot be stated in terms of a single statistical estimate, but must rather be specified in terms of the amounts and kinds of evidence that need to be provided to support a given score interpretation in a particular testing situation. The amount of evidence needed will be a function of the purposes for which the test is intended, so that more evidence will need to be gathered for high-stakes than for low-stakes uses. In addition, the test developer will need to consider the construct definition and the domain of generalization, in terms of the correspondence between the characteristics of the TLU tasks and test tasks. (See Chapters 2 and 6.) In virtually all situations, the evidence for construct validity of interpretations will involve gathering several types of information, but this is particularly crucial when the construct is complex, including language knowledge, metacognitive strategies, and topical knowledge, and when the domain of generalization is relatively broad or heterogeneous. This evidence is likely to be both quantitative and qualitative, and can be collected using some of the approaches discussed in Chapter 12. (An example description of minimum levels of construct validity is provided in Project 1 in Part Three.)

Authenticity

An important consideration in setting levels for authenticity is the potential impact of the test on language instructional programs. Where the potential for such impact is high, then the test developer needs to make every effort to insure that the authenticity of the test tasks is also high. Another consideration is the TLU domain, or domain of generalization. If this domain is very broad, or is varied, then it may be realistic to expect only a moderate level of authenticity.

The minimum acceptable level of authenticity might be stated in two ways:

1   in terms of task characteristics and
2   in terms of expected perceptions on the part of test takers and test users.

In developing test tasks, the test developer lists the numbers and types of distinctive TLU task characteristics that the test tasks share (see Chapter 6). This comparison can provide an indicator of the degree of authenticity of a given test task, and minimum acceptable levels could be stated quantitatively, in terms of the percentage of distinctive characteristics shared, or qualitatively, in terms of descriptions of specific task characteristics. Information on test taker and test user perceptions of authenticity can be gathered during the pre-testing cycle of test administration, using the qualitative methods described in Chapter 12, and minimum acceptable levels could be stated in terms of these. (An example description of minimum levels of authenticity is provided in Project 1 in Part Three.)

Interactiveness

As was indicated in Chapter 2, the level of interactiveness will be a function of the characteristics of the test takers—personal characteristics, language ability, topical knowledge, and affective schemata—and of the characteristics of the test task. For the purpose of setting minimum acceptable levels of interactiveness, however, the test developer will focus on those characteristics of the test taker that are included in the construct definition, and will probably set the minimum acceptable levels very high for these components. At the same time, the test developer will want to design the test task so as to optimize the interactiveness of all relevant components, not just those that are included in the construct definition.

As with authenticity, information on interactiveness can be gathered during the pre-testing cycle of test administration, using the qualitative methods described in Chapter 12, and minimum acceptable levels could be stated in terms of these. (An example description of minimum levels of interactiveness is provided in Project 1 in Part Three.)

Impact

Important considerations in setting minimum acceptable levels for impact include the kinds of decisions to be made and the possible effects of using the test and of making these decisions. Minimum acceptable levels of impact might be stated in terms of a list of specific influences we would want the test to have on the various stakeholders, as well as on the educational system and on society. Minimum acceptable levels of impact on test takers could include descriptions of the amount and types of test preparation expected, of their experience of taking the test, and of their expected perceptions of the kinds of feedback provided. Impact could also be specified in terms of the minimum acceptable percentages of incorrect decisions made, and statements of the degree to which the decisions made are fair. If impact on instruction ('washback') is an intended outcome of the test, minimal acceptable levels could be stated in terms of descriptions of the specific components (for instance, teaching method, curriculum, materials) to be affected and the degrees to which they are affected. Minimal levels for impact on the educational system and society are likely to be stated in terms of specific types of negative impact that are to be minimized. (An example description of minimum levels of impact is provided in Project 1 in Part Three.)

Practicality

As indicated in Chapter 2, practicality is unlike the other qualities, in that it is not continuous, with some tests being relatively more or less practical. Rather, practicality is an either-or quality, with the minimum acceptable level being the threshold level at which the resources available equal or exceed the resources required. In setting this threshold level for practicality, we need to design procedures into our test development for monitoring the allocation of resources to insure that we do not start to exceed those that have been allocated. We also need to consider the consequences of exceeding the threshold level at any stage in the test development process. Thus, it may be possible to reallocate resources at one stage while not at another, so that the test developer might have to consider altering the development plan.

During the operationalization stage, considerations of usefulness will focus on designing test tasks and allocating available resources so as to maximize attainable levels for all the qualities, while not going below the minimum acceptable level for any. This will involve both the logical evaluation of usefulness described later in this chapter, and the allocation of available resources, described in Chapter 8. Finally, during the administration stage, through iterative cycles of try-out, analysis, feedback, and revision, the test developer may need to refine the specifications of minimum acceptable levels for the individual qualities, keeping a clear view to the overall usefulness of the test. (An example description of a threshold level of available resources is provided in Project 1 in Part Three.)

Insuring an appropriate balance among the qualities of usefulness by setting and refining minimum acceptable levels is an essential component in the evaluation of usefulness. At the same time, the test developer must recognize that there is a certain amount of indeterminacy in this. Perhaps the best way to think of achieving an appropriate balance is as a process of gradual approximation. This begins with some initial targets, in terms of minimum acceptable levels, and a plan for collecting evidence about these levels. In practice, we would encourage the test developer to start with what she feels are appropriate criteria for levels of usefulness, and to recognize that the specific details of these criteria will evolve as part of the test development process. Through try-out and revision, the developer will discover the levels for the individual qualities that can be reasonably attained, given the resources that are available. These attainable levels then need to be considered in terms of the overall usefulness of the test, to determine if this is acceptable. If it is not, then it must be determined whether adjustments in the minimum acceptable levels are justifiable, or what reallocation of resources is possible.

The logical evaluation of usefulness

In this part of the chapter, we provide a list of questions for use in the logical, or conceptual, evaluation of usefulness. You may not need to use all of these questions for a given project, and you may find that there are additional questions that need to be considered for a given project. Nevertheless, these questions may help you develop your plan for assessing usefulness. In particular, they can be used as a first step in setting minimum levels for the different qualities of usefulness.

Questions for the logical evaluation of reliability

The following are questions that can be asked in the logical evaluation of reliability. As noted in Chapter 2, the essence of reliability is consistency, so the questions below are designed to focus attention on aspects of test design that affect consistency of test scores. The basic premise behind the questions is that variations in test task characteristics should be related to, or *motivated* by, variations in the characteristics that are distinctive of tasks in the TLU domain. That is, we believe that variation in test task characteristics for its own sake may be counterproductive if this variation does not reflect critical variation in TLU tasks. Thus, what we will call *unmotivated* variation in test task characteristics may result in inconsistencies in test performance that are not related to differences in the ability we want to measure. The following example may help clarify this distinction between motivated and unmotivated variation.

In developing a writing test we might choose to vary the types of prompts, as a way of sampling the range of writing tasks that are required in a particular TLU domain. Thus, we might include a prompt that requires a chronological narration, one that requires an explanation of a procedure, and another that requires the test taker to write a persuasive letter to a potential customer. In this case, some of the differences in the characteristics of the rubric, input, and expected response across the three prompts are appropriate to the definition of the construct and the intended domain of generalization, and would not be considered sources of inconsistency. Variations in task characteristics that are not specified as part of the construct, however, such as different forms of input (for example, a diagram versus a verbal description) or different topical content across the three prompts could be considered potential sources of inconsistency and should be controlled as part of the test design.

The following questions move systematically through the major task characteristics: setting, rubric, input, response, and relationship between input and response. (You may wish to review Chapter 2, in which the logic behind the questions is discussed.)

1 *To what extent do characteristics of the test setting vary from one administration of the test to another?*
   For example, if the test setting is noisy one day and quiet the next, test takers' performance may vary for that reason alone.

2 *To what extent do characteristics of the test rubric vary in an unmotivated way from one part of the test to another, or on different forms of the test?*
   For example, if an extensive set of instructions is used on one form of a test and an abbreviated set on another, test takers' performance on the two forms may be unstable. Similarly, differences in time allotment

and scoring method can lead to differences in test performance and hence to instability in test scores.

3   *To what extent do characteristics of the test input vary in an unmotivated way from one part of the test to another, from one task to another, and on different forms of the test?*

For example, test takers' performance on two forms of a listening test may be different if a listening comprehension selection is presented live on one form of the test and recorded on the other.

4   *To what extent do characteristics of the expected response vary in an unmotivated way from one part of the test to another, or on different forms of the test?*

For example, if we vary the response format from selected to limited production for no reason other than a feeling that we should be innovative, test takers may lose track of what they are supposed to be doing.

5   *To what extent do characteristics of the relationship between input and response vary in an unmotivated way from one part of the test to another, or on different forms of the test?*

Suppose, for example, that we wanted to assess an individual's ability to participate in an informal conversation, and decided to use an oral interview for this purpose. If, in the middle of the interview, the test taker was presented with a role-play or simulation, simply for the sake of variety, their performance on this part might differ from that in the conversational part of the interview. This difference in performance, however, might not be relevant at all to the oral language use in the TLU domain.

Questions for the logical evaluation of construct validity

The following are questions that can be asked in the logical evaluation of construct validity. As was noted in Chapter 2, the essence of construct validity is the appropriateness of the inferences made about the test takers' language ability, so the questions below are designed to focus attention on aspects of test design that may affect our ability to make such inferences. The questions are divided into two types: questions that focus on the relationship between the construct definition and the test tasks, and questions that focus on possible sources of bias in the task characteristics.

Clarity and appropriateness of the construct definition, and the appropriateness of the task characteristics with respect to the construct definition

6   *Is the language ability construct for this test clearly and unambiguously defined?*

For example, the label 'oral communication' would not be clear enough in most situations to serve as a basis for making ability interpretations on the basis of test scores.

7 *Is the language ability construct for the test relevant to the purpose of the test?*
For example, for the purpose of placing students into a course in conversation, defining the construct to include only pronunciation would most likely be too narrow.

8 *To what extent does the test task reflect the construct definition?*
For example, asking the test taker to describe a picture orally would not adequately reflect a construct broadly defined as 'the ability to participate in conversations'.

9 *To what extent do the scoring procedures reflect the construct definition?*
For example, using a single rating scale for a writing test may not be appropriate if the construct definition of writing ability includes grammar, cohesion, and organization.

10 *Will the scores obtained from the test help us to make the desired interpretations about test takers' language ability?*
For example, scores obtained from tests of grammar and vocabulary may not permit us to make inferences about test takers' ability to read to follow the structure of an argument presented in written materials.

Possible sources of bias in the task characteristics

The premise behind these questions is that the ability to make valid inferences about the test takers' capacity for language use will be compromised if all test takers do not have an equal opportunity to perform at their best.

11 *What characteristics of the test SETTING are likely to cause different test takers to perform differently?*
If characteristics of the test setting favor some test takers over others, construct validity may be compromised. For example, testing equipment such as computers or word processing equipment may favor some test takers over others. Care should be taken to insure that the test setting is equally conducive to all test takers' performing at their best.

12 *What characteristics of the test RUBRIC are likely to cause different test takers to perform differently?*
If characteristics of the rubric, such as the instructions, favor some test takers over others, not all test takers will be able to perform at their best. For example, instructions too complicated for all test takers, or instructions given in the target language, may favor test takers with higher ability levels. The rubric should be designed with the least proficient test takers in mind.

13   *What characteristics of the test* INPUT *are likely to cause different test takers to perform differently?*
For example, if the purpose of a test is to assess test taker's ability to evaluate the argument presented in a written text, differences in the topical content of the reading passages may lead to differences in performance that are not directly related to test takers' ability to read.

14   *What characteristics of the* EXPECTED RESPONSE *are likely to cause different test takers to perform differently?*
For example, if not all test takers are capable of writing responses to a listening task in the target language, the test may be biased against them as a test of their ability to comprehend aural input.

15   *What characteristics of the* RELATIONSHIP BETWEEN INPUT AND RESPONSE *are likely to cause different test takers to perform differently?*
For example, if not all test takers have the same topical knowledge background, and if the test tasks involve an indirect relationship between input and response (require test takers to use topical information outside of the input itself), some of them may not be able to perform at their best.

Questions for the logical evaluation of authenticity

As noted in Chapter 2, the essence of authenticity is the degree of correspondence between the characteristics of TLU tasks and those of the test task. The questions below are designed to focus attention on aspects of test specification and operationalization that affect these correspondences.

16   *To what extent does the description of tasks in the TLU domain include information about the setting, input, expected response, and relationship between input and response?*
If the description of the TLU domain is not complete and detailed, this information cannot be used to evaluate the degree of correspondence between TLU tasks and test tasks.

17   *To what extent do the characteristics of the test task correspond to those of TLU tasks?*
Even if the characteristics of the TLU tasks and test tasks are carefully specified, they may not be comparable.

Questions for the logical evaluation of interactiveness

As noted in Chapter 2, the essence of interactiveness is the involvement of the major components in the model of language use: language knowledge, metacognitive strategies, topical knowledge, personal characteristics, and affective schemata (see Chapter 4, Figure 4.1 and Chapter 2, Figure 2.5) in the execution of test tasks. Thus, the questions below are designed to focus our attention on the extent to which these components are called into play in the performance of test tasks.

Involvement of the test takers' topical knowledge

In Chapter 4 we argued that language use involves topical content, and thus engages the topical knowledge of language users. The engagement of topical knowledge is therefore an important determinant of the relative interactiveness of test tasks.

18   *To what extent does the task presuppose the appropriate area or level of topical knowledge, and to what extent can we expect the test takers to have this area or level of topical knowledge?*
For example, if a test task requires the test takers to compare and contrast aspects of two different educational systems, to what extent are both equally engaged by the topic in this task?

Suitability of test tasks to the personal characteristics of the test takers

If we want to make inferences about language ability for a specific group of test takers, clearly the characteristics of the test tasks must be suitable for the personal characteristics of the test takers. (See Exercise 7 in Chapter 4.)

19   *To what extent are the personal characteristics of the test takers included in the design statement?*
For example, simply *naming* a group of test takers, such as 'immigrant elementary school children', will not provide sufficient information on the test takers' ages, nationalities, native languages, educational backgrounds, and type and amount of prior experience with test taking to allow one to design appropriate test tasks. (See the discussion in Chapter 6.)

20   *To what extent are the characteristics of the test tasks suitable for test takers with the specified personal characteristics?*
Even if one has carefully specified the personal characteristics of test takers, steps must still be taken to insure that the characteristics of the test tasks will allow these test takers to perform at their best, while also providing information on their language ability consistent with the purpose of the test.

Involvement of the test takers' language knowledge

Clearly, if we want to make inferences about language ability, the test task must engage the test takers' areas of language knowledge.

21   *Does the processing required in the test task involve a very narrow range or a wide range of areas of language knowledge?*
    For example, even if a construct is defined narrowly, such as 'knowledge of cohesive devices', a test task that requires the test taker to use other areas of language knowledge as well, such as grammatical, functional, and sociolinguistic knowledge, will be relatively highly interactive.

Involvement of language functions in the test tasks

A number of language testers have noted that every test task involves the function of requesting a demonstration of knowledge.[3] Consider the following example of some exchanges that might take place in an oral interview:

Are you wearing something red? (Yes)
Please point to it.
Are you wearing something blue? (No)
Is there something green on your desk? (Yes)
Please point to it.

The functions performed by the questions in this example appear to consist of requests for information and requests for actions. However, the 'questions' do not constitute genuine requests for information at all, since the examiner already knows the answers and the test taker is aware of this. Furthermore, when the test taker points to an object, the examiner does nothing with this, other than noting it and using it to score the test item. What is missing from these exchanges is any sort of involvement in a function other than getting the test taker to demonstrate knowledge of the language.

If our objective is to design language test tasks that correspond to non-test language use, then test tasks must incorporate the goal-directed, purposive nature of language as communication, which means that they must involve the test taker in functions other than simply demonstrating knowledge of the language. We would propose that interactive test tasks are those in which some language function is involved in addition to that of demonstrating the test takers' language knowledge. We can thus ask the following question, as we consider the involvement of language functions in designing a given test task:

22   *What language functions, other than the simple demonstration of language ability, are involved in processing the input and formulating a response?*

For example, a test task involving correcting subject-verb agreement errors in a series of unrelated sentences does not require the test taker to perform any language function other than demonstrating knowledge of this aspect of English grammar.

Involvement of the test takers' metacognitive strategies

The extent to which a test task requires the test taker to use a wide range of metacognitive strategies in completing it will affect the task's interactiveness.

Questions that can be asked as we consider the involvement of the metacognitive strategies in designing a given test task include the following:

23 *To what extent are the test tasks interdependent?*
    For example, a series of short writing tasks, all of which depend on each other, will require the test taker to do more goal setting, assessment, and planning than a series of short, independent tasks, because the test taker will have to work out how to integrate the tasks.
24 *How much opportunity for strategy involvement is provided?*
    For example, if we were testing ability to give a speech, providing the test takers with sufficient time to prepare and materials with which to plan will allow them more opportunity to assess their knowledge, set goals, and plan the speech.

Involvement of test takers' affective schemata in responding to the test tasks

The test takers' assessment of the characteristics of the test task will determine their affective response to that task and their flexibility in using his language ability to complete it. We would thus expect a positive affective response to the test task to make the test task relatively more interactive, and a negative affective response to have the opposite effect.

We can ask the following question, as we consider the test takers' affective response, when we design a given test task:

25 *Is this test task likely to evoke an affective response that would make it relatively easy or difficult for the test takers to perform at their best?*
    For example, does the input of the test task contain emotionally charged or controversial topical information that may evoke a negative affective response in the test taker?

Questions for the logical evaluation of impact

As noted in Chapter 2, impact involves the various ways in which test use affects society, an education system, and the individuals within these.

Impact on individuals

The following questions may help evaluate the positive and negative impact on stakeholders of using a test in a particular situation. Here we will focus attention on the impact on those individuals who are most directly affected by the test use.

Impact on test takers

The following questions focus on the impact on test takers of three aspects of the testing procedure:

- the experience of taking the test,
- the feedback test takers receive about their performance on the test, and
- the decisions that may be made about test takers on the basis of their test scores.

26   *To what extent might the experience of taking the test or the feedback received affect characteristics of test takers that relate to language use (such as topical knowledge, perception of the target language use situation, areas of language knowledge, and use of strategies)?*
For example, if international students coming to the US are asked to read and comment in writing on a story describing how foreign tourists to the US have been murdered, will this tend to mislead the students about the prevalence of violence in the US?

27   *What provisions are there for involving test takers directly, or for collecting and utilizing feedback from test takers in the design and development of the test?*
For example, have students in a language class been asked to suggest appropriate test tasks and scoring criteria for use in an achievement test?

28   *How relevant, complete, and meaningful is the feedback that is provided to test takers?*
Are the scores that are reported meaningful? Is qualitative feedback provided? Have students been provided simply with raw or percentage scores without an indication of what these scores mean in terms of mastery of subject matter? Have students been provided with a profile of their language ability if this information is available?

29   *Are decision procedures and criteria applied uniformly to all groups of test takers?*
For example, if students are promised that grades will be based solely on the basis of test scores, is the teacher then allowed to modify the decisions about some students, based on other factors such as attendance, participation, or attitude?

30   *How relevant and appropriate are the test scores to the decisions to be made?*

For example, are language test scores used as the sole basis for grading when other factors are also important?

31 *Are test takers fully informed about the procedures and criteria that will be used in making decisions?*
For example, have students been told how scores from different tests will be combined in assigning course grades?

32 *Are these procedures and criteria actually followed in making the decisions?*
If there is inconsistency in following stated procedures and criteria for making decisions, test takers are likely to feel as if they are treated unfairly.

Impact on teachers

The questions that might be asked in considering the potential impact on teachers (an aspect of 'washback', as discussed in Chapter 2), as we design language tests include the following:

33 *How consistent are the areas of language ability to be measured with those that are included in teaching materials?*
If tests used in a course of instruction measure abilities not taught, the teacher may feel uncomfortable about either the instruction or the tests.

34 *How consistent are the characteristics of the test and test tasks with the characteristics of teaching and learning activities?*
For example, if teachers have taught grammar using a series of written editing tasks, are students then asked, on the final exam, to write a composition in which they have no time to edit what they have written?

35 *How consistent is the purpose of the test with the values and goals of teachers and of the instructional program?*
For example, do teachers who are required to use a standardized test to assign grades feel that the test tasks are consistent with the goals of the course?

Impact on society and education systems

The following questions can help evaluate the potential impact on society and education, both positive and negative, of using a particular test.

36 *Are the interpretations we make of the test scores consistent with the values and goals of society and the education system?*
For example, if language program administrators use language test scores as the sole basis for making decisions to hire language teachers, and if the society values highly the ability of the teacher to relate to

students, the impact on the society and education system of using the test in this way may be negative.

37   *To what extent do the values and goals of the test developer coincide or conflict with those of society and the education system?*

If a person from another country is hired as a consultant to develop a language test, and does not have the same values and goals as individuals in the education system or society, the test may have a negative impact upon the education system and society.

38   *What are the potential consequences, both positive and negative, for society and the education system, of using the test in this particular way?*

For example, will using a placement test to put higher and lower ability students in different classes discriminate between students from different socio-economic backgrounds and thus reinforce distinctions that the society and education system may be trying to minimize?

39   *What is the most desirable positive consequence, or the best thing that could happen as a result of using the test in this particular way, and how likely is this to happen?*

For example, we may need to design a test for assessing achievement, and believe that the most important positive consequence of using this test would be positive impact on instructional practice.

40   *What is the least desirable negative consequence, or the worst thing that could happen as a result of using the test in this particular way, and how likely is this to happen?*

For example, in order to design a test with high authenticity and interactiveness, we may choose topical content from current affairs, not anticipating that the topic we have chosen is highly controversial, and that test users will refuse to allow students to take the test.

Questions for the logical evaluation of practicality

As discussed in Chapter 2, a test's practicality is a function of the amount of resources required and available during the different stages of the test development process. To evaluate practicality, we can ask the following questions:

41   *What type and relative amounts of resources are required for: (a) the design stage, (b) the operationalization stage , and (c) the administration stage?*

42   *What resources will be available for carrying out (a), (b), and (c) above?*

Collecting evidence of usefulness

The logical considerations discussed above are essential to the evaluation of usefulness, and must inform all stages of test development. These considerations need to be kept in mind not only in the design stage, but also during the operationalization and administration stages, during which we collect qualitative and quantitative information relevant to the empirical evaluation of usefulness. Thus, evidence of usefulness can and should be collected starting early on in the development process, for this can help keep test development on track and avoid wasted effort. Qualitative evidence of usefulness can be collected even in the initial stages of operationalization of test tasks. Quantitative evidence is likely to be collected later on, during the administration stage. The plan should indicate when the various kinds of evidence will be collected

Kinds of information

The kinds of evidence we collect in our evaluation of qualities of usefulness will be both qualitative and quantitative. *Qualitative evidence* that can be collected includes verbal descriptions of observations by test administrators, self-reports by test takers, interviews, and questionnaires. In our plan for collecting qualitative evidence, we can specify the kinds of questions we will ask about test tasks and test use. *Quantitative evidence* of usefulness is based upon the statistical analysis of numerical data, including test scores and scores on individual test tasks, that are obtained from administering the test. Our plan should include the specific kinds of quantitative evidence we plan to provide, as well as the statistics to be used to produce this evidence.

Procedures for collecting evidence of usefulness

A variety of specific procedures for collecting qualitative and quantitative evidence of usefulness are available. (See the references provided in Chapter 12.) The specific procedures to be used should be included in the plan.

A checklist for evaluating usefulness

In order to facilitate the use of the questions we have discussed for both the logical and empirical evaluation of usefulness, we suggest listing them in the form of a checklist, presented in Table 7.1 on pages 150–5. This checklist includes places to indicate the degree to which and how the quality has been satisfied in the particular test under consideration. (An example of a completed checklist is given in Table P1.3 in Project 1, Part Three, pages 280–4.)

Questions for logical evaluation of usefulness	Extent to which quality is satisfied	Explanation of how quality is satisfied
Reliability		
1 To what extent do characteristics of the test setting vary from one administration of the test to another?		
2 To what extent do characteristics of the test rubric vary in an unmotivated way from one part of the test to another, or on different forms of the test?		
3 To what extent do characteristics of the test input vary in an unmotivated way from one part of the test to another, from one task to another, and on different forms of the test?		
4 To what extent do characteristics of the expected response vary in an unmotivated way from one part of the test to another, or on different forms of the test?		
5 To what extent do characteristics of the relationship between input and response vary in an unmotivated way from one part of the test to another, or on different forms of the test?		
Construct validity		
Clarity and appropriateness of the construct definition, and the appropriateness of the task characteristics with respect to the construct definition		
6 Is the language ability construct for this test clearly and unambiguously defined?		
7 Is the language ability construct for the test relevant to the purpose of the test?		

8 To what extent does the test task reflect the construct definition?		
9 To what extent do the scoring procedures reflect the construct definition?		
10 Will the scores obtained from the test help us to make the desired interpretations about test takers' language ability?		
Possible sources of bias in the task characteristics		
11 What characteristics of the test *setting* are likely to cause different test takers to perform differently?		
12 What characteristics of the test *rubric* are likely to cause different test takers to perform differently?		
13 What characteristics of the test *input* are likely to cause different test takers to perform differently?		
14 What characteristics of the expected *response* are likely to cause different test takers to perform differently?		
15 What characteristics of the relationship between *input* and *response* are likely to cause different test takers to perform differently?		
Authenticity		
16 To what extent does the description of tasks in the TLU domain include information about the setting, input, expected response, and relationship between input and response?		

17 To what extent do the characteristics of the test task correspond to those of TLU tasks?		
Interactiveness		
Involvement of the test takers' topical knowledge		
18 To what extent does the task presuppose the appropriate area or level of topical knowledge, and to what extent can we expect the test takers to have this area or level of topical knowledge?		
Suitability of test tasks to the personal characteristics of the test takers		
19 To what extent are the personal characteristics of the test takers included in the design statement?		
20 To what extent are the characteristics of the test tasks suitable for test takers with the specified personal characteristics?		
Involvement of the test takers' language knowledge		
21 Does the processing required in the test task involve a very narrow range or a wide range of areas of language knowledge?		
Involvement of language functions in the test tasks		
22 What language functions, other than the simple demonstration of language ability, are involved in processing the input and formulating a response?		

Involvement of the test takers' metacognitive strategies		
23 To what extent are the test tasks interdependent?		
24 How much opportunity for strategy involvement is provided?		
Involvement of the test takers' affective schemata in responding to the test tasks		
25 Is this test task likely to evoke an affective response that would make it relatively easy or difficult for the test takers to perform at their best?		
Impact		
Impact on individuals		
Impact on test takers		
26 To what extent might the experience of taking the test or the feedback received affect characteristics of test takers that pertain to language use (such as topical knowledge, perception of the target language use situation, areas of language knowledge, and use of strategies)?		
27 What provisions are there for involving test takers directly, or for collecting and utilizing feedback from test takers, in the design and development of the test?		
28 How relevant, complete, and meaningful is the feedback that is provided to test takers?		
29 Are decision procedures and criteria applied uniformly to all groups of test takers?		

30 How relevant and appropriate are the test scores to the decisions to be made?		
31 Are test takers fully informed about the procedures and criteria that will be used in making decisions?		
32 Are these procedures and criteria actually followed in making the decisions?		
Impact on teachers		
33 How consistent are the areas of language ability to be measured with those that are included in teaching materials?		
34 How consistent are the characteristics of the test and test tasks with the characteristics of teaching and learning activities?		
35 How consistent is the purpose of the test with the values and goals of teachers and of the instructional program?		
Impact on society and education systems		
36 Are the interpretations we make of the test scores consistent with the values and goals of society and the education system?		
37 To what extent do the values and goals of the test developer coincide or conflict with those of society and the education system?		
38 What are the potential consequences, both positive and negative, for society and the education system, of using the test in this particular way?		

39 What is the most desirable positive consequence, or the best thing that could happen, as a result of using the test in this particular way, and how likely is this to happen?		
40 What is the least desirable negative consequence, or the worst thing that could happen, as a result of using the test in this particular way, and how likely is this to happen?		
Practicality		
41 What type and relative amounts of resources are required for: (a) the design stage, (b) the operationalization stage, and (c) the administration stage?		
42 What resources will be available for carrying out (a) (b), and (c) above?		

Photocopiable © Oxford University Press

Table 7.1:   A checklist for evaluating usefulness

Summary

Usefulness is an essential consideration in all stages of test development. It serves first of all as a general orientation for test development, which keeps us on track during the process. It also surfaces in a formal plan for assessing the qualities of usefulness. This plan contains three parts:

1 an initial decision about minimum acceptable levels for and balance among the six qualities of usefulness,
2 the logical evaluation of usefulness, and
3 procedures for collecting qualitative and quantitative evidence during the administration stage.

The appropriate minimum acceptable levels for the qualities of usefulness will be a function of how we have conceived of our balance of test qualities and the amount of resources we have to devote to them. The logical or conceptual evaluation of usefulness is facilitated by asking a series of questions about each quality, the answers to which may help the test developer develop a plan for evaluating usefulness.

Exercises

1 Think about the questions for the logical evaluation of authenticity. How helpful are these questions to you? Can you think of any other questions to help with this process?
2 Read the description of Project 2 in Part Three. Describe a possible set of minimum acceptable levels of usefulness for each quality.
3 Read Project 2 in Part Three. Go through the questions for the logical evaluation of usefulness and evaluate this test. Then follow the same procedure for Project 3 and compare the usefulness of the two tests for their intended purposes. To what extent is such a comparison possible? Might such a comparison be useful? If so, when?
4 Bring to class a language test you intend to use. In a small group, use the questions for the logical evaluation of usefulness to evaluate the test. Does each question seem helpful? Can you think of any additional questions you might ask to help you evaluate the usefulness of this test?
5 Interview someone not in this class who has developed a language test. Ask her how she would evaluate the usefulness of her test in terms of the six qualities of usefulness. See what her process is and whether she comes up with additional helpful questions or criteria.

Notes

1 The field of educational and psychological testing has developed an authoritative set of standards for evaluating the appropriateness and acceptability of educational and psychological tests and their uses. These standards are discussed in *Standards for Educational and Psychological Testing* (APA 1985). Our view that one should seek an appropriate balance and minimum acceptable levels for the various qualities of usefulness is consistent, we believe, with the position stated in the APA Standards: 'Evaluating the acceptability of a test or test application does not rest on the literal satisfaction of every primary standard in this document, and acceptability cannot be determined by using a checklist. Specific circumstances affect the importance of individual standards. Individual standards should not be considered in isolation' (APA page 12).
2 Approaches to and methods for estimating reliability are discussed in Bachman (1990) and in the references listed in Chapter 12.
3 Searle (1969) calls questions that only require the demonstration of knowledge 'exam questions', and does not consider them to be real questions, since they do not function as requests for information. Bachman (1990) points out that this function of requesting a demonstration of knowledge is a rather trivial criterion for considering a test task to involve functional language use.

8 Identifying, allocating, and managing resources

Introduction

One of the most important steps in any test development process is to take stock of the available resources and estimate the resources required. (As noted in Chapter 2, practicality is the relationship between available and required resources.) If steps are not taken to be realistic about resources, one may take on a project that will either be impossible to complete or will be exhausting. One way to get a better feel for the kinds of resources that may be needed is to list the major steps in test development and ask what kinds of resources will be involved in carrying out each step. One can then brainstorm a list of available resources. We now discuss some of the resources typically required for test development.

Identifying and allocating resources

Human resources

One critical component of test development is the individuals who carry it out. Human resources can best be thought of in terms of roles or functions. In some situations, individuals will have very clearly defined roles and functions, while in other cases they may take on different roles and functions as test development proceeds. In most projects several roles will be filled by the same person.

Test developer

One role or function that will be referred to frequently is that of test developer. There are a number of possible relationships between the test developer and others involved in test development. In some cases, the same person is both test developer and test writer. In others, the test developer may be working as a consultant or project director, in which case many of the decisions can be made interactively with the members of the test development team, since resource allocation and decisions made in the planning process will directly affect the test developers.

The test developer supervises the test development from beginning to end, from specification to administration, try-out, and use, and to archiving. For complicated projects one may want a director with extensive training and experience in test development. For other projects (such as developing a small classroom quiz) the teacher is the most likely person.

Test writers

The test writers are key personnel in the test development process. (We use the term 'test writers' in a general sense to refer not only to writing *per se* but also to other test development tasks such as collecting material already written, editing, recording, etc.) The qualifications of test writers and the amount of time they will need to put in on the project will vary. For example, suppose one person 'writes' a short test in which words are deleted at random from a reading passage and replaced by blanks. The test takers respond by trying to fill in the blanks with the original, deleted words. Preparing this kind of test may involve very little 'task writing' expertise and time. On the other hand, developing a script for a lengthy oral interview may be very demanding. We have noticed that when tests are developed with authenticity as a major design consideration, the writers often tend to be involved in writing the entire test, rather than just a part of it. This is because relatively more authentic tests tend to be unified and cohesive, so that all of the parts have to fit together. In any case, it is important to think in terms of the abilities of test writers to write different kinds of test tasks and consider assigning writers to tasks accordingly.

Scorers

Test raters and scorers also play an important role in test development. In tests such as face-to-face oral interviews, for example, the raters/scorers need either to be on hand during each test administration or to have access to tape recordings. They can also provide valuable input into the scoring procedures of the test. Depending on the particular scoring method used, raters may need to be highly proficient in the language being tested.

Test administrators

Test administrators carry out the process of giving the test. For some tests such as group administered paper-and-pencil tests, relatively little training may be required to administer the tests, although administrators will still need to be coached on how to interact with the test takers. For others, such as face-to-face oral interview tests, much more training may be necessary.

Clerical support

Many test development projects require extensive clerical support, including typing, photocopying, record keeping, etc., and this needs to be taken into consideration in advance. In one large overseas project, we did not know until we were well into the project that we would have to type all of the original test copy ourselves, not only for the pre-test but also for the final version. Since the complete pre-test was over 50 pages long, this turned out to be a huge job which took energy away from writing and editing.

Material resources

Space

Space can be particularly critical and requires careful planning and management in tests that involve a variety of task types requiring different types of space, such as an examination that includes paper-and-pencil parts, listening tasks that need to be administered to smaller groups, and a one-on-one oral interview. In one of our research projects, sixty students had to take eight subtests in a single day, and each subtest had to be administered in a different room. This required a number of the instructors' offices to be used, as well as the language laboratory.

Equipment

Equipment also plays an important role in test development and production. The list is long, and includes, for example, typewriters, word processors, overhead projectors, tape recorders, video recorders, computers, language laboratories, machine scoring devices, etc. While the need to plan for necessary equipment from the beginning may seem obvious, situations do arise where equipment that is generally assumed to be available is not. For example, in some of our assignments word processors and photocopiers were not available, which made revision much more time consuming.

Test materials

Test materials include whatever the test itself is made of and whatever may be used in the process of taking the test. This may include pencils, test booklets, answer sheets, computer disks, videotapes, audio tapes, etc.

Time

Time is a critical resource which needs to be considered with respect to each of the other resources. There are two aspects to this:

1 development time and
2 the time required to complete the parts of each stage of the test development process.

It is important to estimate the total amount of time available from personnel and equipment such as computers, language laboratories, etc.

Prioritizing and allocating resources

Different kinds of tests require different allocation of resources. For example, to develop a high quality, discrete-point multiple-choice test, a great deal of energy needs to be put into item writing and editing. Administration and scoring, on the other hand, are relatively simple and require little effort. In contrast, the time and effort required to prepare a prompt to which students will respond by writing a thirty-minute composition may be considerably less (although this should not be an excuse for using slip-shod, inadequate, inconsistent prompts). However, considerable resources may be required not only to actually score the test but also to train the raters in the scoring procedures. By prioritizing and allocating resources in advance, one can avoid unpleasant surprises, such as taking on a project and only later finding that available personnel are unwilling or unable to help, leaving no alternative but to do it oneself or to abandon part of the project.

Preparing a table of tasks and resources

To prioritize and allocate resources, prepare a table of tasks and resources as in Table 8.1. Within each cell, note the amount of resources needed. The information will be in terms of the most convenient units. For example, when allocating personnel, their time could be specified in terms of numbers of hours or days, and also perhaps salary figures. When allocating space, we might enter a value for the area required (for instance, square feet or meters or the number of usable seats).

Determining total cost of project and preparing a budget

In order to determine the total estimated cost of the project, we add up the estimated costs of the resources as follows:

1 The estimated monetary cost of physical resources, including equipment, space rental, printing, computer time, etc.

	ACTIVITIES				
Resources	**Design**	**Operational-ization**	**Adminis-tration**	**Scoring**	**Analysis of feedback**
Personnel					
Project director	50 hours				10 hours
Test writers		25 hours			
Editors		10 hours			10 hours
Raters				30 hours	
Administrators			10 hours		
Clerical support	5 hours	10 hours	5 hours	5 hours	5 hours
Space					
Test development	225 sq. ft.	225 sq. ft		225 sq. ft.	225 sq. ft.
Test admin	@ rate of $.0016 per sq. foot per day	@ rate of $.0016 per sq. foot per day	900 sq. ft. @ rate of $.0016 per sq. foot per day	@ rate of $.0016 per sq. foot per day	@ at rate of $.0016 per sq. foot per day
Equipment					
Computer	NC				NC
Recording studio		$500			
VCR and monitor			$50		

Table 8.1:   Allocation of resources

2 The estimated monetary cost of human resources, including salary of test designers, preparers, scorers, administrators, clerical staff, etc.
3 The estimated monetary cost for the test takers (if they are charged for taking the test).

In most teacher-directed projects, the total cost is much less of a concern than determining the practicality at each stage. If the project is not practical at one stage, the test developer may need to shift resources from another stage or delay starting the next phase. For example, if the developer discovers that the operationalization stage is requiring more human resources for writing than anticipated, she/he may need to ask for more released time for task development specialists or delay the start of the administration stage. In larger projects, it is almost always necessary to prepare a budget, including an estimate of the project's total cost.

An example budget based upon the information in Table 8.1 is provided in Table 8.2.

Preparing a time line

A time line is a document specifying the tasks involved in the test develop-

Personnel	
Project director: 60 hrs @ $50/hr	$3,000.00
Test writers: 25 hrs @ $15/hr	$375.00
Editors: 20 hrs @ $15/hr	$300.00
Raters: 30 hrs @ $10/hr	$300.00
Administrators: 10 hrs @ $10/hr	$100.00
Clerical support: 30 hrs @ $8/hr	$240.00
SUB TOTAL	$4,315.00
Space	
Design: 225 sq. ft. for 55 hrs @ $.0016/hr	$81.67
Operationalization: 225 sq. ft. for 45 hrs. @ $.0016/hr.	$66.82
Giving the test: 900 sq. ft. for 15 hrs. @ $.0016/hr.	$9.80
Scoring: 225 sq. ft. for 35 hrs. @ $.0016/hr.	$51.97
Analysis of feedback: 225 sq. ft. for 25 hrs. @ $.0016/hr	$37.12
SUB TOTAL	$247.48
Equipment	
Computer	NC
Recording studio	$500.00
VCR and monitor	$50.00
SUB TOTAL	$550.00
GRAND TOTAL	$5,112.48

Table 8.2:   Budget

ment process, the sequence in which they will be carried out, and the time by which each needs to be completed. Each task is put into a sequenced list which specifies its temporal relationship to the other tasks in the project. The following are the steps in developing a time line:

1   Write down your objectives. Specify what you want to accomplish and when you want to accomplish it.
2   Break your objectives down into major steps or activities.
3   Organize the activities in a logical order.
4   Estimate how long each major activity will take to complete, and assign a calendar date to each.
5   Break down each major activity into minor activities and add these to the time line.

The following is an example of a time line for a large test development project at a general stage of development.

Example time line

Objective: Develop a set of three fully scripted oral interview tests and videotaped tests of listening comprehension to be administered at the end of the first, second, and third year Spanish courses. To be completed by 5/30/96.

1 Start-up
   (6/1/95)

   Complete initial draft of table of specifications

2 Secure resources
   (7/1/95)

   Consult with departmental chairperson
   Consult with Dean
   Prepare preliminary budget proposal
   Secure final approval of budget

3 Appoint director from within department
   (7/15/95)

   Prepare list of possible candidates
   Determine availability of candidates
   Prioritize list of available candidates
   Contact candidates in order of priority

4 Assemble development team
   (7/30/95)

5 Revise table of specifications, as needed, with the development team
   (8/15/95)

6 Operationalization (including all scripts and videotapes)
   (12/1/95)

7 Trialing
   (2/1/96)

   Train test administrators
   Obtain space for trialing
   Obtain subjects for trialing
   Arrange payment for subjects for trialing

8 Analyze results
   (2/30/96)

   Obtain data processing facilities, code data, enter data, run statistical analyses

9 Interpret results
   (3/30/96)

10 Revise specifications, blueprints, and tests
    (5/30/96)

In simple projects, this process will be relatively uncomplicated and can be handled rather informally. In larger projects involving a number of inter-related tasks and a critical deadline, a more sophisticated time line may be needed. In either case, preparing a time line allows one to become conscious of what needs to be done and when.

Resource management: Test developers and test development

Amount of time and effort spent in test development

Classroom tests

We believe that the activities involved in design, operationalization, and administration need to be carried out for every test we develop. What differs from situation to situation is the amount of detail, resources, etc. involved. For some classroom tests, relatively few resources may be required. For example, suppose a course teacher wanted to prepare a short vocabulary quiz whose primary measurement use was for assigning course grades and whose instructional use was to encourage students to do their homework. It might be possible to plan the design statement rather quickly because at the outset there would be a fairly clear idea of the purpose, the TLU domain and tasks, the test takers, the construct to be measured, as well as how to evaluate the qualities of usefulness. Moreover, the teacher would probably do all of the actual writing, administration, analysis of results, and archiving her- or himself.

High-stakes tests

A high-stakes test will involve the same kind of planning but this will be much more detailed and require many more resources. For example, suppose you were responsible for developing a final exam for a multi-section course, something very common in many language teaching programs in several different countries. Since these tests are frequently given to hundreds of students, and since students' grades depend heavily upon the results, a lot of resources go into the planning, including time spent by the department chairperson, the director of the testing program, a testing committee, and the instructors teaching the courses for which the test is developed. In such situations, a team of teachers typically prepares the initial pool of test tasks. These are then revised by a smaller team of teachers with skills and experience in test development, before being submitted for final review to the project director. A secretarial pool prepares the final version of the test and reproduces the test booklets. Another team scores the test, prepares grade reports, and makes recommendations to the developer regarding score criteria for assigning grades.

Classroom teachers may find their planning needs lie somewhere between the two extremes described above. In writing a mid-term test covering several chapters in a textbook, a teacher might need to spend some time planning how to define the construct, to sample the content of the chapters, to allocate time for the different sections of the test, to score those parts of the test employing subjective scoring procedures, and so on.

Individual and team efforts

Over the past quarter of a century, the authors have been involved with a variety of test development efforts, and in doing so have become increasingly impressed by the effectiveness of team as opposed to individual test development efforts. One of the authors once worked for a small, private company overseas writing pseudo-TOEFL tests for students to take as practice for the TOEFL. In this project the developer worked entirely alone. He was given some examples of the test items and then had to write, revise, and edit the entire test. It became clear both that he could not do all things equally well and also that he did not enjoy the process, with no one to get feedback from and no opportunity for humor.

Immediately after this, the developer directed the development of a test for selection and placement of all entering students in English courses at a major university. From the start he worked closely with the department chairperson and her main assistant. They discussed the purposes of the test and reviewed past test development efforts. In the early planning stages, he had the opportunity to discuss ideas and proposals with these colleagues before investing any effort into putting them into action. Many unsatisfactory proposals were reviewed and rejected at this stage without creating any problems.

The general plan for the test was then taken to all of the teachers in the department, who gave immediate feedback so that appropriate revisions could be made. The developers thus knew that the procedures for test development and use had the approval of most of the teachers who would have to live with the results.

The teachers were also involved with most of the remaining steps in the test development process. Procedures were developed by which teachers would help produce the initial pool of items, then certain particularly skillful teachers assisted in the editing. All of the teachers were present at the try-out and helped with the tabulations needed for the analysis of results and revision. As a result, they knew just how much work went into developing the test, and they went to great pains to make sure that the test was properly administered and kept secure.

The developer's experience in this project was entirely different from what he had experienced just months before. The team effort was much more rewarding than the individual one in terms of both the process and the product, because of the interaction and cooperation. He felt supported instead of isolated, and acknowledged for his work, rather than merely paid for it. He felt confident that the test would make a difference because he knew the teachers (and students) and knew how much the test was needed. He knew the test had passed before many eyes and that they were not likely to suddenly discover glaring mistakes or gaps after the project was finished. The product of the team effort was certainly better, because of both the numbers of points of view incorporated in the planning process and the greater diversity of creative thought that went into the items themselves.

Interactive team efforts may offer many of the benefits of the concurrent development planning process that is now widely used as an alternative to the linear development of new products. Linear development operates in a series of discrete stages in which an inventor gives an idea to a designer, who gives it to an engineer, who gives it to a manufacturer, and so on. In terms of test development, a linear process might involve the department chairperson deciding a test is needed. A project director would prepare the design statement and blueprint. The blueprint might be passed to someone who supervises a group of item writers. The items might be returned to the designer and put into the test, which would then be given to the teachers for use. Finally, a statistical or measurement specialist might be contracted to provide some quantitative analyses of the results.

In concurrent development, all members of the team meet together on a regular basis to provide input. Thus, the design statement is created with input from the people who will be using the test, as well as those responsible for try-out, use, and analysis. If the task writers know that a certain kind of task is difficult to create, the whole team can make appropriate changes in the design statement before a commitment is made to a project. Similarly, if the person responsible for scoring and analysis indicates that a particular task type will require greater resources for the development of an appropriate scoring method, the entire team needs to consider this during the operationalization stage, before the test is tried out. Likewise, the teachers and students would have an opportunity to make suggestions about the design.

Finally, while we find team efforts particularly effective and enjoyable, we also acknowledge that there is a place for one-person efforts. In particular, experimental tests are often the result of one person's creative thinking. Moreover, for many classroom tests the individual teacher may want to do the whole thing alone. However, we believe that once a test starts to affect a number of people, the participation of all involved will tend to produce a more satisfactory test in the long run.

Steps in an interactive team effort

The following are some of the major steps in an interactive team effort.

Selecting a team

One of the first steps in interactive team test development is to decide who to involve in the planning. We might start by brainstorming a list of the various people who might be affected by the project as a whole. The list of steps in the test development process provides a number of categories to work with.

In addition, we might want to consider including people who might be affected by the test but who might not necessarily be involved in the writing itself. These might include fellow teachers, school administrators, (department head, principal), students, and even parents and other interested parties outside the school. An important test given to students is likely to affect their parents, and including them makes the final plan more acceptable to a wider range of people. Finally, good members of a team may be creative and need an outlet for their creativity, or may learn from the project and use this in other positive ways.

Eliciting input

Having determined whom to involve, the next step is to elicit input from all those affected by the test. With a project to develop a new placement test, one might begin by giving each member a statement of the purpose of the test and a list of the steps in the development process. Then the team could be invited to brainstorm any ideas that occur as they consider each step. They should be encouraged to write down *anything* that comes to mind, no matter how outrageous. Even if 90 per cent of the ideas are not used, the 10 per cent that are might never have come up without the freedom to explore.

Creating a first draft of a proposal

After eliciting input, a draft of the development proposal can be developed, including some beginning ideas about the remaining steps in the development process.

Eliciting reactions to the first draft

The first draft of the proposal could then be circulated among a representative sample of people from whom the initial input was elicited, for comment. Care needs to be taken to respond in a way that will not discourage comments from being offered. This involves not evaluating the comments, but simply hearing them and writing them down.

Revising the proposal based upon comments

A revised draft can now be prepared, incorporating appropriate suggestions.

Determining the amount of support

The next step in the process is to determine the amount of support for the proposal. This is extremely important, for test developers do not want to find themselves unpleasantly surprised to discover that they have little support. One reason that the university proficiency test development project described above worked so well was because of the large number of teachers involved in the planning.

In contrast, we later developed another proficiency test for use in placement at a different university in the same country. Here, the planning was not interactive and the teachers were not involved. As a result, considerable dissension arose as to the appropriateness of the test, which was soon dropped from use.

Dealing with lack of support

You may not always be fortunate enough to have total support for a development plan, and in such cases we suggest the following strategy. First, find out who you can count on to support and work with you, and how much energy you can expect others to provide. How much work will you have to do yourself in the worst case scenario?

Next, ask yourself whether you are willing to take on the project with little support. If you are, go ahead. If not, there are two options. One involves being flexible. Use the usefulness framework to think about various degrees of usefulness you can achieve with varying degrees of effort and support. In one case a colleague working with very little official support mobilized volunteers to get what she called 'quick fixes' to a really bad test. This drew attention from potential support givers, and put her in the position to argue for official support. Even though the 'quick fixes' were not the project that she wanted, that approach acted as a first step. Another option is to simply decline to take on the project. Taking on a project without an appropriate amount of support leads to extra work and resentment. In any case, a test development project taken on when it is not really feasible is not likely to produce a useful test, so it is always best to be aware in advance of what is expected and what resources will be made available.

Summary

Resource allocation and management is one of the most important steps in the test development process, for it allows us to determine whether or not a project is feasible. Resources include human resources (the project director, test writers, scorers, test administrators, and clerical support) and material resources (space, equipment, test materials, and time). Resources are prioritized and allocated by means of a table of tasks and resources. Tasks are then sequenced by means of a time line, which specifies for each their temporal relationship to other tasks in the process. How complex these processes are depends upon the size of the project. For high-stakes tests, the resource allocation and management may require a great deal of effort.

Test development can be carried out either individually or by a team. While individual efforts may be appropriate for the development of low-stakes classroom tests or for individuals who really prefer working alone, interactive team efforts offer many benefits. The process is frequently more enjoyable and the product is often better thought out. Finally, whenever taking on the development of a test with wide-ranging impact, it is important to determine at the outset how much support exists for the project and to decide whether one is willing to work with that level of support, or perhaps modify the project.

Exercises

1   Recall a test you developed or helped develop. Prepare a table of tasks and resources for your project. Compare your table with those of other classmates.
2   Think of a test you are planning to develop. Prepare a table of tasks and resources for your future project. Discuss possible areas in which anticipated resources may exceed available resources.
3   Prepare a time line for specifying the test development tasks in Exercise 2.
4   Recall a time when you developed a test in cooperation with other individuals. What was your experience of working in a team? What were the rewards? What were the problems? How might you avoid such problems in future team efforts?
5   Invite someone who has prepared a high-stakes test to tell the class about the process and how resources were allocated to each step in the process. Ask how resources might be allocated differently given another chance to develop the same test.
6   Form a group of classmates all of whom are interested in developing a test for a single purpose. Give out a list of steps in the test development process. Brainstorm input from all members on each step of the process. During this session, have one person write down each idea. (No negative comments or evaluation of other people's ideas should be allowed.)

9   Operationalization: Developing test tasks and blueprints

Introduction

Operationalization is the process of using the components of the design statement that is produced in the design stage to guide us in developing test tasks, a blueprint for the test as a whole, and actual tests. In order to maximize the qualities of usefulness, these will have been considered in the selecting and describing of TLU task types for possible development as test tasks. In operationalizing TLU task types as test tasks, we again need to take into account the qualities of usefulness. In order to do this, we will consider ways in which we can either modify TLU task types for use as test tasks, or create original test tasks whose characteristics correspond to those of TLU task types. In this chapter we describe two interrelated activities in operationalization:

1   developing test tasks and test task specifications, and
2   developing a blueprint for the test as a whole.

Developing test tasks

The test task is the elemental unit of a language test, and so the central activity in operationalization should be the development of test tasks, focusing on the qualities of usefulness. We believe that the best way to insure these qualities is to begin with the descriptions of TLU task types, as discussed in Section 2 of Chapter 6, as templates for designing test tasks. This should help insure that our test tasks will have a high degree of authenticity and interactiveness. In addition to considering these qualities in developing test tasks, we also need to consider the other qualities of usefulness that are associated with testing: reliability, construct validity, impact, and practicality. Thus, in determining exactly what characteristics the test tasks and the test as a whole will have, we need to consider the distinctive characteristics of the TLU task types, the purpose for which the test is intended, the definition of the construct we intend to measure, and the resources that are available for test development and use. This can be illustrated as in Figure 9.1.

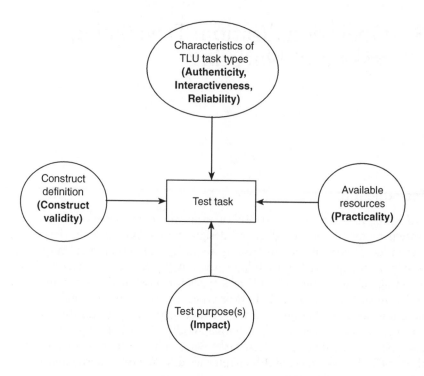

*Figure 9.1:   Considerations of design components and qualities of use-
fulness in developing test tasks*

Developing test task specifications

In the process of operationalization we begin with the TLU task types and
modify their task characteristics as necessary to satisfy the qualities of usefulness. In addition, we will include the specific purpose and construct
definition for each type of test task. The resulting sets of task characteristics
constitute, in effect, the *test task specifications* that will be used as a template for developing actual test tasks. For any given type of test task, the
specifications will include the following:

1   The purpose of the test task

This will be the same as one of the purposes which have been specified in
the design statement for the entire test. The reason for including the purpose here is so that test writers, who will use the test task specifications
for guidance in writing test tasks, will not lose sight of the specific purpose
for which the particular test task is intended.

2 The definition of the construct to be measured

This is needed because different constructs are frequently included in the design statement for the entire test, and the test developer and task writers must be as clear as possible as to what a given test task is supposed to be measuring. This is also helpful for test users in interpreting the results of tests. (See Chapter 6 for a discussion of how to define constructs.)

3 The characteristics of the setting of the test task

These may vary from task to task and need to be specified here. (See Chapter 3 for a discussion.)

4 Time allotment

Since different types of test tasks may require more or less time to complete, and since test developers often want to maintain some control over the amount of time test takers have to complete the test, the estimated time allotment needs to be specified.

5 Instructions for responding to the task

Different types of test tasks will require different types of responses, and so it may be necessary to specify separate instructions for each type of test task. (See Chapter 10 for a discussion of preparing instructions.)

6 Characteristics of input, response, and relationship between input and response

These can be conveniently provided in a table, as illustrated in Projects 1 and 8 in Part Three.

7 Scoring method

Different types of test tasks may be scored differently, so the scoring method needs to be specified for each. (See Chapter 11 for a discussion of scoring method.)

While we believe that the test task specifications need to include all of these characteristics, we would repeat the point made in Chapter 5, that the *order* in which the parts of the test task specifications are included is likely to vary from one test development situation to another, depending on what order proves to be the most effective for the test developer and task writers. An example of a complete set of test tasks specifications is given in Project 1, Part Three.

General strategies for developing test tasks

There are two general strategies that we can use in developing test tasks,

1   modify TLU task types, or
2   create original test tasks based on a set of test task specifications. With
either strategy, we must consider both the qualities of usefulness and
the distinctive characteristics of the TLU task type upon which the test
tasks are to be based. These two strategies are illustrated in Figure 9.2.

In some situations we may find that either one strategy or the other
provides the greatest potential for yielding a maximally useful test, while
in others the usefulness of the whole test is maximized by using both strategies. It is not possible to recommend one strategy over the other, since
both have the potential for yielding useful tests. Furthermore, whether the
test developer decides to use one or the other or both will depend on the
situation, as this has been specified in the components of the design
statement.

Modifying TLU task types to meet our criteria for usefulness

In some circumstances, the TLU task types may meet many of our criteria
for usefulness and can be used as the starting point for test task development. Consider, for example, Project 2, in which we have designed a test
to measure the ability of potential employees in a company to perform a
routine writing task, such as writing letters in response to written letters
of complaint. In this situation we could probably produce most of the distinctive characteristics of the TLU task type in our test tasks. We could
also supply the test takers with comparable input, perhaps in the form of
actual letters of complaint the company has received. In addition, we have
required the test takers to produce responses with characteristics comparable to those of responses in the TLU task. In this project, the characteristics of the input and response, as well as the major characteristics of the
relationship between input and response for the test tasks, correspond very
closely to those of the TLU task type.

In most cases, however, considerations of usefulness will mean that we
need to modify the TLU task types in developing test tasks. To make such
decisions, we evaluate each TLU task type against our requirements for
usefulness. For example, suppose our purpose for testing required a short
writing task for international students applying to a university, and that
one of the TLU task types for these test takers involved writing a research
paper. We would most likely not be able to use this entire task type as a
test task because of its length. We might, however, be able to include in
the test certain sub-tasks, such as preparing an outline for the term paper
or developing an introductory paragraph.

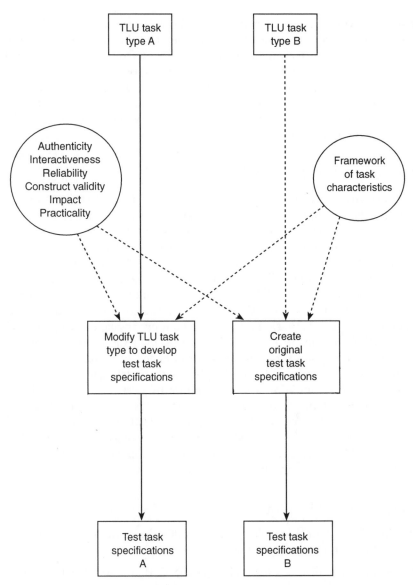

Figure 9.2: Operationalizing TLU task types as test task types

When, as we advocate here, TLU task types are used as a basis for developing language test tasks, the specific characteristics of the test tasks will differ somewhat from the specific characteristics of TLU tasks. This is because certain characteristics of TLU tasks will be selectively modified to accommodate the demands of testing. Because of the importance we attach to authenticity, we would point out that the highest priority in developing test tasks will be given to maintaining those characteristics of TLU task types that are considered to be distinctive. Thus we believe that, rather than leading to relatively inauthentic language tests, our approach will yield test tasks whose distinctive characteristics correspond very closely to those of TLU tasks, and which also provide a basis for obtaining reliable measures upon which we can base valid inferences and make decisions that are fair and defensible, given the values of the society and educational system in which the test is used.

Creating original test task types

In other circumstances, specific TLU task types in a given TLU domain may not be an appropriate place to *begin* to develop test tasks. We may then want to create original test task types whose characteristics nevertheless correspond in demonstrable ways to the distinctive characteristics of TLU tasks. This situation is illustrated in Project 4. Because we were not dealing with a restricted TLU domain in this project, we could not locate a single, specific, limited TLU task type that would serve as an appropriate starting point. We therefore developed a series of original test tasks based upon an analysis of question types carried out by language testing researchers in US Government agencies (Lowe 1982). In these tasks we elicited speech by means of a series of questions designed to require the test taker to use a progressively wider and wider range of language knowledge in responding. Each question and its response by itself was quite authentic, in that many of the characteristics of input, response, and relationship between input and response are consistent with questions one might encounter in a real-life extended conversation of areas of expertise. However it is unlikely that tasks of this sort would be linked in real-life language use discourse as they are in the test itself.

Developing a blueprint

A *blueprint* is a detailed plan that provides the basis for developing an entire test. The blueprint includes two parts:

1   the task specifications for each type of task that is to be included in the test, and
2   the characteristics that pertain to the structure of the test: the number of parts/tasks, the salience of parts/tasks, the sequence of parts/tasks, the relative importance of parts/tasks, and the number of tasks per part.[1]

In developing a blueprint, we begin with the specifications for the various test task types to be included, and determine how best to combine these in a test, taking into consideration the qualities of usefulness.

Uses of the task specifications and blueprint

A blueprint, which includes the specifications for each type of task that is included in the test, can be used for a number of purposes.

To permit the development of other tests or parallel forms of the test with the same characteristics. By knowing what characteristics the test developers have specified, we can know what characteristics to include in developing other forms of the test. One way to develop parallel forms of a test is to use the test task specifications to generate a *test task bank*, which is a set of test tasks developed from the same test task specifications. Tasks from this test bank can then be used, following the blueprint, to construct whole tests. For example, for a test that involves speaking tasks, we might want to prepare a variety of prompts in different areas of topical knowledge for use with test takers from a variety of backgrounds. (See Project 4 in Part Three.)

To evaluate the intentions of the test developers. A blueprint provides an independent means of knowing what the test developers were trying to accomplish. This is not always evident from the test itself.

To evaluate the correspondence between the test as developed and the blueprint from which it was developed. This is useful in determining the extent to which the test writers were able to implement the specifications of the blueprint in a given test.

To evaluate the authenticity of the test. Authenticity is defined as the correspondence between the characteristics of the TLU tasks and those of the test tasks. Since the blueprint provides a detailed description of the test and test tasks, it can be useful in evaluating the correspondence between the test and test tasks and the TLU domain and tasks.

Tests

Once the blueprint, including the test task specifications, has been developed, this provides the basis for generating actual test tasks and compiling them into either a single test or several comparable forms of the test. In many cases the purpose of a test development project is to produce a single test, for example, a classroom quiz to determine whether a group of students is ready to go on to the next lesson. Or we might need a single test to place students transferring from another college or university into upper division university language courses.

In other cases it may be necessary or desirable to produce several comparable tests, for example, a series of tests to measure progress at various stages in a course of instruction. Or we might need a set of equivalent forms of the same test when repeated use of a single form of the test might result in a loss of test security. We cannot be sure that multiple forms of a test will provide equivalent measures of test takers' abilities until we have tried them out and analyzed their results.[2] However, if they are developed from the same blueprint, following the procedures described, we can be reasonably certain that they will be comparable in terms of their content and tasks. Furthermore, the blueprint provides a basis for investigating and demonstrating the comparability of the different forms, and it is our view that without comparability of constructs and task characteristics, any demonstration of statistical equivalence will be meaningless.

While we include a complete set of characteristics in the specifications for each different test task type, it may be the case for a given test that there will be some overlap between characteristics of different test task specifications, so that these may need to be included only once in the actual test. For example, even though a given test includes several different test task types, these may be similar enough in their formats to permit them to be grouped together with one set of instructions.

In Part Three we have provided a number of examples of test development projects that illustrate the process of using components of the design statement to develop test blueprints and actual test tasks. We refer to these projects in the exercises at the end of this chapter and provide specific suggestions as to how to read the projects. We also suggest ways to read and evaluate other examples of blueprints for tests.

Summary

The second stage in test development is operationalization: the process of using fairly abstract components in the design statement to produce specifications for test tasks, a blueprint, test tasks, and an actual test. There are two interrelated parts in the operationalization process:

1   developing test tasks and test task specifications, and
2   developing a blueprint for the test as a whole.

To develop actual test tasks, the test developer may either modify TLU tasks or create original test tasks whose characteristics correspond to TLU tasks. To develop test tasks from TLU tasks, the developer starts by using needs analysis to identify and select those TLU tasks that test users or subject matter specialists consider most important. These tasks should meet the minimum requirements for authenticity and interactiveness specified in the plan for evaluating usefulness in the Table of Specifications. The test developer makes the second cut by evaluating this pool of TLU tasks against the minimum levels of usefulness for the remaining qualities of usefulness: reliability, validity, impact, and practicality. Some of the TLU tasks in the pool may need very little modification to satisfy these minimum requirements, and these tasks would be retained. Other TLU tasks may need so much modification that the initial qualities of authenticity and interactiveness may suffer, and these tasks would be rejected. The final step in the operationalization is to modify the characteristics of the retained TLU tasks for use as test tasks, so as to satisfy minimal levels that have been set for the qualities of usefulness, or to develop original test tasks whose characteristics correspond to those of TLU tasks and also satisfy minimal levels on the qualities of usefulness.

A blueprint is a detailed plan that provides a basis for developing an entire test. In addition, the blueprint is used to evaluate the intentions of the test developers, to permit the development of other tests or parallel forms of the test with the same characteristics, to evaluate the correspondence between the test as developed and the blueprint from which it was developed, and to evaluate the authenticity of the test.

Exercises

1 Read through the test task specifications for Project 1 and Project 7. How do these specifications help the test developer to operationalize the purpose and definition of construct(s) in the design statements?

2 Find a test and the blueprint from which it was written. To what extent does the blueprint provide a complete description of the test structure and test task specifications? In what areas do you find the blueprint lacking? What problems would you have developing test tasks based upon the existing blueprint?

3 Consider the following situation. You have been asked to develop a classroom test for a beginning language course that is based on a structural syllabus. The grammatical testing points have been specified, so you have a specific construct definition to work with. The instructional tasks are highly inauthentic: decontextualized structural pattern drills, yet you want to develop a useful test of the students' control of the grammar points. Your supervisors decide that they want the test you develop to have an impact on instruction by nudging it toward a more communicative approach.

First, imagine a set of tasks in a TLU domain that would be compatible with the TLU needs of at least some of the students. Describe the characteristics of these tasks. From this set of tasks, select specific tasks that would not be intimidating to the students.

Use the TLU tasks you have selected as the basis for developing test tasks and describe how the characteristics of the test tasks will contribute to the test's usefulness.

4 Recall a testing situation with which you are familiar. Prepare a table of specifications for a test for use in that situation. Then incorporate these into a blueprint for a test which will meet those specifications.

5 Locate a language test. Analyze the test tasks in terms of the qualities of usefulness, with respect to the specific testing situation for which the

test is intended. Then see if you can prepare a blueprint from the test. Does this present any difficulties? Of what sort? If you had to develop a parallel form of the test without the blueprint, how would you proceed? What problems might you encounter? How would the blueprint help you in developing a parallel form of the test?

6   Obtain a manual for a commercially produced test. Try to determine from the manual what the blueprint for the test might look like. How might the usefulness of the manual be improved with the inclusion of some of the information found in a blueprint?

7   Read Project 7. Then suppose that live examiners were no longer available to administer the test. How might you change the characteristics of the test tasks in response to this change of resources?

Suggested readings

Lowe (1982) provides useful guidance on oral interview testing.

Notes

1   Our conception of a blueprint is quite different from that which is found in traditional language test development, which typically treats test tasks holistically rather than as sets features. In the traditional orientation, a test blueprint is conceived as a table that specifies the numbers and types of items. For example, a blueprint of this type might specify 20 'multiple-choice vocabulary' items, 20 'grammar completion' items, and 10 'reading comprehension' items, as well as the desired statistical properties of the items. Our approach is different in that it (1) focuses on the sets of characteristics that define types of test tasks, and (2) relates each task type to the whole test through the design statement and blueprint.

2   There are certain statistical characteristics that the scores from different forms of a test must satisfy in order for these scores to be considered equivalent, or 'parallel'. These are discussed at length in Bachman 1990 Chapter 6, as well as in the statistical and measurement references provided in the Suggested Readings for Chapters 3 and 11.

10 Preparing effective instructions

Introduction

As discussed in Chapter 3, the way test takers perform on language tests is affected to some extent by the characteristics of the tests themselves. In keeping with the maxim that we want to make it possible for test takers to do their best, it is essential that they clearly understand how they are to proceed in taking the test, the types of tasks they are going to encounter, the ways in which they are expected to respond to these tasks, and how their responses are going to be evaluated. The test instructions are particularly important because it is through them that we inform test takers how they are expected to approach and attempt the test tasks.

The instructions will reflect the considerations that we have included in the design of the test (discussed in Chapters 5–8) and will thus communicate to the test takers our intentions as test developers. These include matters such as the purpose for which the test is being used, the language abilities to be tested, and the relative importance of different parts of the test. We convey these intentions explicitly by what we include in and the way we present the instructions. In this chapter we will discuss ways in which instructions can be most effectively specified to promote the best test performance in a given group of test takers. We will discuss general principles and what we believe are the essential components of instructions, along with suggestions on how these can be effectively written and presented to test takers.

Purpose of instructions

The instructions are typically the first part of the test that test takers encounter. It is the instructions, therefore, that bear much of the responsibility for setting the test takers' expectations and appropriately motivating them to do their best on the test. The primary purpose of the test instructions is thus to insure that the test takers understand the exact nature of the testing procedure and of the test tasks, how they are to respond to these tasks, and how their responses will be evaluated. The essential components of the test instructions, therefore, are:

1   statement of the purpose(s) for which the test is intended,
2   statement of the language abilities that the test is intended to measure,
3   specification of the procedures and tasks, and
4   specification of the scoring method, including criteria for correctness.

Test instructions also serve as an important affective goal: motivating students to do their best. Effectively presented test instructions can go a long way toward assuring test takers that the test is relevant, appropriate, and fair, and does not make unreasonable expectations.

The different components of instructions can be presented at different times and at different levels in the test. With published tests, general instructions are often available to test takers well before the test is taken, and are usually repeated in greater detail at the time of the test administration. In most situations, however, general instructions covering all parts of a test are presented either orally by the person who administers the test, or in writing in the first part of the test itself. In addition, specific instructions may be given for different parts of the test. Irrespective of when or at what level instructions are provided, their overall purpose is to facilitate the test taking process and to encourage students to perform at their highest level.

Making instructions understandable

If instructions are to accomplish their purposes, then we must do whatever is necessary to assure that they can be understood by the test takers. They should *not* be considered part of the test itself, since they are not part of the input to which test takers are expected to respond directly. In deciding how best to make the instructions understandable, we need to consider:

1   the language and
2   the channel through which the instructions are presented,
3   the need for providing examples, and
4   the need to pre-test the instructions with test takers.

Language of presentation

Instructions may be presented in either the test takers' native language or, depending on their level of ability, in the target language (the language being tested). Where test takers share a common native language, if there is any doubt about misunderstanding it is best to present the instructions in the native language. Often, however, test takers come from many different first language backgrounds, so that the instructions must be presented in the target language. In such situations, care should be taken that the level of difficulty of the language of the instructions is not greater than that of the test questions themselves.

Channel of presentation

Understandability can also be facilitated by presenting the instructions in a channel that is most appropriate to the purpose and abilities being tested, and that test takers are most likely to find easy. In tests whose input is presented in the visual channel (written), instructions are also typically presented in this way. Instructions for completing a test with tasks that require reading, for example, would typically be presented in writing, as would instructions for composition tests. However, in tests with listening or speaking activities, which typically involve input in the aural channel, instructions would also be presented in this channel. Thus, if the test were presented 'live' by the person administering the test, the instructions would be read aloud to the test takers, and if the test were presented via an audio or video tape player, the instructions would be presented on the tape. Some test takers may be able to perform one type of language use activity better than another, in which case it may be helpful if instructions are presented both orally and in writing. If students are relatively good at reading activities and weak at listening activities, for example, test takers could be given a set of written instructions for the tasks that involve listening and asked to follow these as they are presented orally, either by the test administrator or on a tape player. If, on the other hand, they are more able at listening tasks than at reading tasks, the test administrator might read the written instructions aloud while test takers read them silently. The purpose of presenting the instructions both orally and in writing is to insure that students understand. However it is possible that some students will find this distracting, and that it interferes with comprehension of the instructions. Since different test takers vary as to whether both oral and written instructions will facilitate or interfere with understanding, the test developer must base the decision on a thorough understanding of the personal characteristics of the particular test takers, and, if possible, on the feedback obtained from pre-testing.

Providing example tasks

Providing example tasks can also facilitate test taking, particularly when test takers may not be familiar with the specific task type, or with complex question types. Consider the following test task, for example:

> Instructions: Make the necessary changes and additions to the following sets of words and phrases to produce a complete sentence for each. Write the sentence in the space provided.

> I just finish/six-week data processing course/local college.

Even with fairly detailed instructions, it may not be entirely clear to all test takers just what their response is supposed to be. An example task such as the following could help:

Example: I be quite happy/receive/letter/you yesterday.
Answer: I was quite happy to receive a letter from you yesterday.

While we generally recommend providing examples as a means for insuring that test takers understand test tasks, there are two types of costs involved. First, providing good examples can be as difficult as writing good test tasks. Second, reading through examples requires additional time on the part of the test takers. However, if the test developer feels that a new type of test task is particularly useful, or if the ability cannot be easily tested in another more familiar way, example tasks need to be provided. The burden of writing example tasks can be alleviated to some degree by using test tasks that have been discarded after pre-testing as too easy for the test. This has the added benefit that the example tasks will be easier and hence more understandable than the tasks in the test.

Components of instructions

Many language tests are aimed at measuring more than one aspect of language ability, or employ more than one method of testing, and thus include more than one part. With such tests, it is useful to provide, at the beginning of the test, a set of *general instructions* that apply to all parts of the test. In addition, if the different parts include different task types, require different procedures, or use different criteria for correctness, then these need to be made explicit in *specific instructions* for each part. Thus, tests with multiple parts may include both general and specific instructions. In tests with only one part, on the other hand, there need be only one set of instructions. In either case, instructions need to include descriptions of the following:

Test purpose
Language abilities to be tested
Parts of the test and their relative importance
Procedures to be followed for all parts of the test
Scoring method

Test purpose

The purpose of the test is its intended use, and we have discussed a variety of uses in Chapter 6. How will the information obtained from the test be used? What inferences or decisions are to be made on the basis of the test scores? These will all be specified during the test development process, as part of the test specifications. If the test is designed to serve several purposes, then the instructions should be specific to each given purpose. Furthermore, if the test is used for some purpose other than that stated in the specifications, then this may constitute a misuse of the test. The reason we want test takers to know what the test will be used for is twofold. First, it provides a justification for giving a test. If there is no legitimate use for the test results, then test takers may well question why they should take the test at all. Second, as a matter of fundamental fairness, we believe that test takers are entitled to know how their test scores will be used. We believe that if test takers understand that there is a fair and legitimate use for a given test, they will be more likely to take the test seriously and to attempt to do their best. Furthermore, an explicit statement of intended test use helps insure that both the test developer and potential test users are accountable to test takers for how the results of the test are used.

In most classroom testing, the purpose of a given test will be obvious to students, particularly if certain uses of tests, such as diagnosis, progress, and grading, are an integral part of the instructional program. Even so, decisions of varying importance may be made on the basis of students' test performance, so that it is essential that students clearly understand the particular use of each test. Thus, while we want our students to attempt to do their best on all tests, high motivation and effort are probably more important for a test that will be used to assign course grades than for a daily quiz that may be used primarily for diagnostic feedback. In classroom testing, the purpose can be provided as part of the orientation to the instructional program. In a writing class, for example, the teacher may inform the students at the beginning of the course that short daily writing tasks will be used to diagnose their writing problems and to provide feedback for correction, a weekly in-class essay will be given to assess their progress and provide feedback, and two longer essay exams, to be given at specified times, will be used to assign course grades. If testing is not a routine part of the instructional program, then the classroom teacher will need to inform students of the purpose of the test, either before the test itself, or as part of the test administration.

In large-scale achievement and proficiency testing programs, the purpose of the test is usually known to test takers by virtue of their having chosen or been required to take it. Students who have taken a foreign language in secondary school, for example, may either choose or be required to take a language test to determine which level of college or university foreign language course is appropriate for them, or to determine if credit can be given for having achieved a specified level of ability in the foreign language. Another example is that of non-native English-speaking students who take a standardized test of English proficiency as part of the requirements for admission to institutions of higher learning in countries where English is the medium of instruction.

Language abilities to be tested

The rationale for informing students of the language abilities we intend to measure is essentially the same as that for informing them of the test's purpose. In addition, providing a statement of the abilities to be measured gives test takers the means for assessing the relevance of these abilities

1 to the test's intended purpose,
2 to a particular course of instruction, either already completed or about to be entered,
3 to their TLU tasks, and
4 to the types of test tasks used.

As with stating the purpose of the test, we believe that an explicit statement of the abilities to be measured will help motivate students to do their best and will also help insure accountability of test use. In multi-part tests that measure different aspects of language ability, statements of the abilities to be tested should be given in the specific instructions to the different parts.

Since very few individuals who take language tests are either language teachers or trained linguists, it is important that our descriptions of the language abilities to be tested should be stated in non-technical language. In classroom testing, a 'label'—a word or phrase—may be sufficiently clear for tests that are directly related to learning objectives and activities. In large-scale testing, however, where test takers may come from a wide variety of learning backgrounds, labels are seldom sufficient, in that even an apparently obvious label, such as 'reading comprehension', for example, may have different connotations for different test takers and test users. For such situations we would recommend that the instructions include more than a label, and that a brief description of the areas of language ability being measured should be provided. Since terms such as 'proficiency', 'competence', 'comprehension', and 'communicate' are ambiguous even to language teachers, it is not likely that they will be clear to test takers. We would therefore recommend that the abilities to be measured should be described in terms of specific language use activities, since it is these that are more likely to be understood by test takers. Thus, rather than a statement such as 'This test is a measure of your listening comprehension', for example, we would prefer a statement such as 'This is a test of how well you can understand spoken English in lectures and classroom discussions.'

Parts of the test and their relative importance

With tests that consist of several different parts, it is important for test takers to understand

1 how many parts there are,
2 how many tasks there are in each part,
3 the relative importance of each part, and task, often stated in terms of a maximum score per part or task, and
4 how much time will be allocated to each.

The general instructions should thus include descriptions of the different parts of the test, including the types and numbers of tasks in each, and how much time test takers will be given to complete each part. Depending on the number of different parts and how distinct they are, it may also be helpful to provide a summary table, as in Table 10.1.

Part	Task type	Number of tasks	Time allowed
I Listening tasks	Short answer questions	20	10 mins
II Reading tasks	Reading passage followed by short answer questions	Two passages; 15 questions	20 mins
III Writing tasks	Prompt requiring an extended written answer	Two prompts	30 mins
Total			60 mins

Table 10.1: Example description of test parts

Different types of test tasks may be appropriate for different areas of language ability for a given test purpose or group of test takers, and these tasks may vary in their efficiency in terms of adequately measuring the specific area in a given amount of time. For this reason there is not necessarily a one-to-one relationship between the relative importance of the parts of a given test, the number of tasks in the different parts, or the amounts of time allowed for the different parts. Test takers thus may not be able to determine accurately the relative importance of the different parts from either the number of tasks or the times allowed, and we therefore believe it is important to provide an explicit statement of the relative importance of each part. In the example above, although the listening and reading parts are equally important (30 per cent each), there are more tasks in the former. This may reflect the test developer's perception that reading tasks are relatively more difficult for the intended test takers. Furthermore, although there are more listening than reading tasks, more time is allowed for the latter. This difference may also reflect the test developer's perception of the difference in difficulty. The test developer may also know that the test takers for whom this test is intended typically require more time for reading tasks than for listening tasks.

Procedures to be followed

For many tests that consist of several parts, there will be general procedures for test takers to follow with regard to how to proceed from one part to the next, and how and where to indicate their responses. It is often desirable, for standardization in large-scale testing, to make sure that test takers complete the parts in the order presented, and that they adhere to the time allocations for the different parts. In such situations, the instructions need to state explicitly that test takers must stop at the end of each part and wait to begin the next part until they are told to do so.

On the other hand, in less formal testing situations, such as in a class progress test, it may not matter whether test takers complete the parts in the order presented, or that they rigorously adhere to the times allowed for each part. In this case, the instructions should indicate those parts of the test that may be completed in any order, that the times indicated in the instructions are suggested times, and that test takers may, if they choose, spend more or less time on the various parts than indicated by these suggested times. In the example above, it is likely that the listening part would be presented aurally first, and would be timed by the test administrator, so that there would be no flexibility with either the order or timing. However, the test developer might want to give test takers the flexibility of completing either the reading or the writing part next, as long as they complete both parts within the total time allowed. In this way, the test developer provides the opportunity for test takers to set their own goals and plans for how to respond to the different parts of the test.

Test takers also need to understand exactly how and where they are to indicate their responses to the test questions. If all the parts of the test follow the same question format, directions can be given in the general instructions. Otherwise, separate directions need to be provided in the specific instructions for each part of the test. In paper-and-pencil tests, responses can be written either on the test itself or on a separate answer sheet. In either case, the instructions should explicitly state how test takers are to indicate their responses. For selected responses, the instructions should state how and where test takers are to indicate their response (for example, circle or check the letter of their choice), while for limited and extended production responses they should be told where to write their response (for example, in the space provided). If machine-scannable answer sheets are used, the general instructions must explain how students are to mark their choices so that they will be clearly legible to the machine. If a separate answer sheet is used, test takers need to be told in the general instructions to mark their answers on the answer sheet and not in their test booklets (particularly if the test booklets are to be reused). For tests administered by means of a computer, specialized instructions on how to use the computer may be necessary, depending upon the personal characteristics of the test takers.

In other types of tests, in which either the input or the response or both are in the audio channel, the order in which test takers answer questions and indicate their responses may be controlled as part of the administration. In a test with tape-mediated speaking tasks, for example, in which test takers listen to aural input from a tape player and record their spoken responses on a tape recorder, the order in which they answer the different parts or tasks is controlled by the tape that presents the input. Similarly, the type and length of each spoken response will be controlled by the type of tasks posed and amount of time allowed on the tape.

Scoring method

In order for test takers to understand what they are expected to do, and hence to perform at their best, they need to know how their responses are going to be evaluated. If the test includes several parts that will be scored in the same way, the criteria for correctness can be stated in the general instructions. If different parts will be scored differently, then these criteria should be given in the specific instructions for each part.

For selected responses, there are generally two considerations that need to be made explicit. First, the test taker needs to understand whether the item is a 'correct answer' type (there is only one correct answer and this is provided among the choices) or a 'best answer' type (there may be many possible answers, and the test taker must choose the best one from among those provided in the choices). Second, will the test taker's score be corrected for guessing? Although corrections for guessing are not widely used in language tests, some test takers may come from countries or educational systems in which this is routine for multiple-choice tests. Such individuals may be reluctant to guess on the basis of partial knowledge (i.e. they can rule out one or two incorrect choices), and thus may perform differently from other test takers who are willing to do so. (These considerations are discussed more extensively in Chapter 11.)

For tasks that require a limited or extended production response, the test takers' understanding of the criteria for correctness may affect the way they approach the given test task and hence the way they perform. For example, test takers are likely to approach a writing task differently if they believe that the primary criterion for correctness is grammatical accuracy than if they know that it will be scored primarily on its content. Since test takers are likely to have preconceptions about what criteria of correctness will be applied to their answers, and since these are likely to influence the way in which they construct their responses, we believe that it is crucial for the instructions to state explicitly what criteria will be used in evaluation.

How extensive should instructions be?

From the discussion so far, it may appear that instructions need to be long, complex, and extremely detailed. This need not be the case. Efficient, effective test instructions have three qualities:

1 they are simple enough for test takers to understand,
2 they are short enough not to take up too much of the test administration time, and
3 they are sufficiently detailed for test takers to know exactly what they are expected to do.

The best basis for writing understandable instructions and for knowing how much of the test administration time they will take is a thorough knowledge of the personal characteristics of the test takers for whom the test is intended, combined with actual try-outs of the instructions with test takers. For classroom tests, in addition to trialing the instructions, a very effective way to insure that test instructions are appropriate for the students is to ask them to write the test instructions as a learning activity.

The amount of detail required in the instructions will depend on two factors:

1 how familiar test takers are with the test tasks, and
2 the number and variety of task types used in the test.

Tests that consist of multiple parts and employ a variety of relatively unfamiliar test tasks are likely to require complex instructions. Thus, while there may be legitimate reasons for using a variety of task types in a given test, such as promoting authenticity and positive impact on instruction, there is no particular virtue in proliferating different task types simply for the sake of variety or novelty.

Summary

In order for test takers to have the opportunity to perform at their best, it is essential that they be provided with clear instructions. The purpose of these is to insure that the test takers understand the exact nature of the testing procedure and of the test tasks, how they are to respond to these tasks, and how their responses will be evaluated. Effective instructions help assure test takers that the test is relevant, appropriate, and fair. The essential components of the test instructions are:

1 a statement of the purpose(s) for which the test is intended,
2 a statement of the language abilities that the test is intended to measure,
3 a specification of the procedures and tasks, and
4 a specification of the criteria for correctness.

With tests that consist of several different parts, it is important for test takers to understand

1   how many parts there are,
2   the relative importance of each,
3   what each part is like, and
4   how much time will be allocated to each.

Instructions can be made understandable by taking into consideration and controlling the language of presentation and the channel through which the instructions are presented. In addition, providing example tasks can help to clarify to test takers just what their response to a task is supposed to be. In any case, the instructions should not be considered part of the test itself and should not increase the difficulty of responding to the test tasks. Trialing provides an opportunity to revise instructions based upon feedback from test takers. Finally, instructions need to inform test takers of the relative importance of the parts of the test. This will provide them with the opportunity to manage their test-taking time so as to maximize their performance.

Exercises

1   Read the instructions for Project 1 in Part Three. Evaluate them according to the criteria in this chapter.
2   Obtain a language test. Do the instructions provide a statement of the purpose(s) for which the test is intended, a statement of the language abilities that the test is intended to measure, a specification of the procedures and tasks, and a specification of the criteria for correctness? How might you revise the instructions to provide any missing information?
3   Recall a language test you have taken. What kind of instructions were provided? How did you react to them? What changes do you wish had been made in the instructions?
4   Obtain a published test. Compare the information provided in the general instructions with the information provided in the specific instructions for each part. Does the division of information seem appropriate for this test? Why or why not?
5   Obtain a language test that consists of several parts. Do the instructions indicate how many parts there are, the relative importance of each, what each part is like, and how much time will be allocated to each? If not, how might the instructions be improved to provide this information?
6   Prepare a set of instructions for a test that you are developing. Explain how your decisions with respect to the instructions helped you maximize the usefulness of the test.

11 Scoring method

Introduction

The results of language tests are most often reported as numbers or scores, and it is these scores, ultimately, that test users will make use of. Because test scores are commonly used to assist in making decisions about individuals, the methods used to arrive at these scores are a crucial part of the measurement process. This process, which plays a key role in insuring that the test scores are reliable and that the uses made of them are valid, consists of three steps. The first step, defining the construct theoretically, is discussed in Chapter 6. The second step, defining the construct operationally, is discussed in Chapter 9. The last step of the measurement process, establishing a method for quantifying responses to test tasks, has to do with how scores are derived from test takers' responses to test tasks, and constitutes an essential component of the operational definition of the construct. In specifying the scoring method—the criteria by which test takers' responses are evaluated and the procedures followed to arrive at a score—we are essentially determining how to quantify test takers' responses. Scoring is thus the essential step to arrive at a measure, in addition to any qualitative, descriptive information obtained from the test takers' responses.

Deciding what type of scoring method to use is an integral part of the process of operationalization, discussed in Chapter 9, and can only be done interactively with decisions about other aspects of the blueprint. In some cases, considerations of scoring may influence the specific tasks or intended responses included in the test. If, for example, we had limited resources for writing test tasks but still needed a test that could be scored fairly quickly, then we might decide to avoid multiple-choice items, which typically require considerable resources to write, and include limited production tasks, such as completion or short answer items, which can be written with fewer resources and can still be scored quickly and efficiently, using a scoring key. Or if we wanted to measure individuals' ability to use formal and informal registers appropriately in speaking tasks, we might build into an oral interview some role-plays intended to elicit both formal and informal registers. In other situations, we may decide to include a particular test task because of its relationship to the tasks in the TLU domain, and determine our scoring method later, once we have written the specific task. For example, we may decide to use a dictation test to measure a job applicant's ability to take dictation, but may not decide on exact criteria and procedures for scoring until we have selected the specific text to be used as the dictation.

In determining what scoring method to use, we need to consider two aspects of test development discussed in the previous chapters: the theoretical definition of the construct to be measured, which is part of the design statement, and the test task specifications, which are part of the blueprint. The way we define the construct for a particular testing situation will determine which areas of language ability we need to score and the role, if any, of topical knowledge in the scoring method. The construct definition will also determine the type of score to be reported, whether this is a profile of scores for different areas of language ability, a single composite score, or both. The way we specify the test task will determine the type of intended response, and this has clear implications for scoring. Thus, tasks intended to elicit a selected response can generally be scored objectively, whereas if the intended response is a limited or extended production response, it is necessary to consider the nature of the language of the intended response (for example, length, organizational characteristics, pragmatic characteristics) in determining the specific scoring method to be used.

As with most decisions in designing and developing language tests, the initial decisions about scoring must be checked by actually giving the test and evaluating the testing procedures and results in terms of their usefulness. That is, until we have given the test, observed test takers, scored their responses, and analyzed and interpreted these results, the initial decisions about the scoring method must be considered tentative. Thus, a critical step in the development of a scoring method is to try out the test tasks with one or more groups of individuals who are representative of the intended test takers, score their responses, and analyze the results. (A detailed discussion of pre-testing procedures is provided in Chapter 12.)

Because of the wide variety of uses made of language test scores, as well as the large number of different tasks used in language tests, many different specific scoring methods have been developed. However, all of these methods fall into two broad approaches. In one approach, the score is defined as the number of test tasks successfully completed, so that the number of correct responses are added up. This approach is typically used with items that require selected or limited production responses. Specifying a scoring method in this approach involves

1 defining the criteria for what constitutes 'successful completion', and
2 determining whether responses will be scored as right or wrong, or with varying degrees of correctness.

The other general approach is to define several levels on one or more rating scales of language ability, and then to rate responses to test tasks in terms of these scales. This approach is typically used with prompt-type tasks that require test takers to produce an extended response. Specifying a scoring method in this approach involves

1 defining rating scales in terms of the areas of language ability to be assessed, and
2 determining the number of levels of ability on the different scales.

Thus, in both approaches, the specification of a scoring method involves two steps:

– specifying the criteria for correctness, or the criteria by which the quality of the response is to be judged, and
– determining the procedures that will be used to arrive at a score.

In this chapter we will discuss these two general approaches to scoring, and various criteria for correctness and procedures for scoring within each. We first discuss scoring methods for items that elicit either selected or limited production responses. We then discuss the scoring of extended responses, focusing on an approach to developing rating scales that is based on two principles:

– scales are defined according to the way we have defined the specific construct to be measured, and
– scale levels are criterion-referenced from zero (no evidence of knowledge) to mastery (evidence of complete knowledge).

We argue that this approach offers the greatest potential for maximizing test usefulness, and provide specific examples of rating scales developed within it. We then discuss some potential problems with the development and use of rating scales, along with procedures for minimizing them. Finally, we discuss ways of deriving scores from both approaches, and considerations in interpreting scores.

Scoring as the number of tasks successfully completed

General considerations

Tasks that consist of items (see Chapter 3) can be used to measure specific areas of language knowledge, as well as the ability to use language in receptive language use tasks—listening and reading comprehension. In tests that consist of items, test takers are typically required either to select an answer from among several options (selected response) or to produce a limited sample of language in response to the task (limited production response). For both of these response types, the most commonly used approach to scoring is to add up the number of tasks successfully completed—the number of correct responses. Assuming that the task is sufficiently well defined by the way the item is designed and written, the main considerations for scoring are

1   specifying the criteria for what constitutes a correct response to the task, and
2   determining procedures for scoring the responses, that is, deciding whether responses will be scored as right or wrong or in terms of degrees of correctness (partial credit scoring).

Specifying the criteria for correctness

Areas of language knowledge

A variety of criteria for correctness can be used with both selected and limited production responses, depending upon the areas of language knowledge to be assessed. In one tradition that still informs many language tests today, it is considered essential to use a single criterion for correctness, in the attempt to achieve a 'pure' measure of a specific area of language knowledge. Thus, for an item intended to measure only grammatical knowledge, for example, one might reasonably use grammatical accuracy as the sole criterion for correctness. This can be done quite easily with selected response items, by providing only one alternative that is grammatically correct, the 'key', while all the other choices, or 'distractors', are grammatically incorrect, even though they may be appropriate in terms of lexical choice, as in example (1).

1   My neighbor asked me ⎯⎯⎯⎯⎯⎯ away the tall weeds in my yard.
   a   clear
 *b   to clear
   c   cleared
   d   clearing
   (* indicates the key, or correct response)

While the use of a single criterion may work reasonably well with selected responses, this may create problems with limited production responses. For example, using grammatical accuracy as the sole criterion for correctness may result in counting as correct some answers that are lexically inappropriate as in example (2).

2   She turned the wheel quickly to *preserve* a tractor and her car went off the road.

In items designed to measure lexical knowledge, on the other hand, the test developer might not consider grammatical accuracy at all, but use meaningfulness as the sole criterion, as in the following example, which would be counted as a correct answer if grammatical accuracy were not considered.

3   We mailed out several hundred *copy* of the advertisement to our customers this morning.

Examples (2) and (3) illustrate how the criteria for correctness need to be determined by the way we define the construct we want to measure. They also illustrate the kind of problem that can arise when we attempt to design test tasks involving limited production responses to measure a single area of language knowledge in isolation: we may end up giving credit for an answer that would be perceived as somehow incorrect or inappropriate in non-test language use situations.

Given our view of language use as an interactive process involving multiple areas of language knowledge, and our belief in the importance of authenticity and interactiveness of test tasks, we would argue that, in order to make inferences about test takers' language ability on the basis of their responses to test tasks, multiple criteria for correctness will necessarily be involved in the scoring of these responses. In developing a scoring procedure, we would therefore employ multiple criteria for correctness, including (but not limited to) grammatical accuracy, meaning, and appropriateness, as would be the case in non-test language use situations. If this combination of criteria were used, neither of the answers given in examples (2) and (3) would be counted as correct, while 'avoid' and 'dodge' might both be considered correct responses for example (2) and 'copies', 'offprints', and 'duplicates' might all be acceptable responses to example (3).

Topical content and topical knowledge

In tests intended to measure language use in receptive tasks, such as listening or reading comprehension, the criteria for correctness may be based on topical content in the input for interpretation. The following item, for example, focuses primarily on the comprehension of content in a reading passage, rather than on a particular area of language knowledge.

4   According to the passage, the most effective way to avoid procrastination is to _____ .

In scoring items such as this, we face a problem that has been discussed throughout this book: whether to try to distinguish language ability from topical knowledge, and if so, how. We have argued that our primary interest in language testing is to make inferences about test takers' language ability and not about their knowledge of a particular discipline or topic. Thus, if we wanted to try to make 'pure' inferences about test takers' ability to perform reading tasks, the criteria for correctness for items such as the one above could be limited to the specific information that is included in the input for interpretation. However, test takers' topical knowledge will almost always affect their performance on such tasks to some degree, just as their topical knowledge plays a vital role in their non-test language use. If test takers already happen to know specific information that is supplied in the input for interpretation and correctly answer questions on the basis of this knowledge, rather than from reading the passage, how are we to know? It may therefore not be possible to completely isolate language ability from topical knowledge in some test tasks, no matter how we score test takers' responses. Furthermore, not to consider test takers' use of topical knowledge in scoring such items would appear to reduce their potential for authenticity and interactiveness. If we only accept as correct the information that is contained in the reading passage, we are, in effect, denying test takers the possibility of answering the questions on the basis of whatever relevant real-world knowledge they may already have.

Thus, there would appear to be somewhat of a trade-off in the scoring of tasks aimed primarily at testing comprehension. We can include in our criteria for correctness only information that is provided in the item input by adding a phrase such as 'according to the reading passage' in each item, in the hope that this will enable us to make clearer inferences about language ability, but we do so at the risk of somewhat reducing the authenticity and interactiveness of the task. Or, we can accept as correct any accurate information the test takers may provide from their own topical knowledge, in the hope that this will increase the authenticity and interactiveness of the task, but do so at the risk of making it more difficult to make clear inferences about language ability. Which way to go in this trade-off should be decided with respect to the Table of Specifications: the purpose of the test, the nature of the TLU setting, and the definition of the construct. In making this decision, however, the test developer must recognize that the focus chosen will be relative, and that the inferences that can be made are most likely to vary somewhat from one test taker to another. That is, the reality of language testing is that a given test task will involve varying degrees of language ability and topical knowledge for different test takers. Similarly, a test task is likely to be perceived as relatively authentic and interactive by some test takers and as relatively inauthentic and non-interactive by others.

There remains the problem of quantifying the content. That is, how do we count the information in the test takers' responses? It might appear quite obvious simply to count up the bits of accurate information included in the response. But what counts as a 'bit'? How many bits of information, for example, are in the following possible response to example item (4): 'break your project up into smaller tasks and then work on these one at a time'? Assuming that we can determine what to count as a bit of information, will we count all bits as equally important? In attempting to address these issues in developing criteria for scoring, the test developer may be able to refer to specific materials and guidelines in a teaching syllabus, or to research in reading and listening that pertains to identifying information units.[1]

It is not our intention, in this discussion of topical content and topical knowledge, to discourage language testers from attempting to measure test takers' ability to comprehend the information in the input. The ability to interpret discourse is at the heart of language use, and is one that we must, in many situations, try to measure. Nevertheless, we hope this discussion will lead to a greater appreciation of the complexities and uncertainties involved in scoring responses to test tasks which are aimed at enabling us to make inferences about cognitive processes and representations of meaning that are essentially internal and therefore not directly observable.

Determining procedures for scoring the responses

Both selected and limited production responses can be scored in one of two ways: right/wrong or partial credit. With right/wrong scoring, a response receives a score of '0' if it is wrong and '1' if it is correct. With partial credit scoring, responses can be scored on several levels, ranging from no credit ('0') to full credit, with several levels of partial credit in between.[2] Many language testers have tended to favor right/wrong scoring for selected and limited production responses, largely because the techniques available for statistically analyzing the characteristics of test items—difficulty and discrimination—were designed to work best if responses were scored according to a single criterion for correctness (such as grammatical accuracy or meaning), and if scores on test items were dichotomous, that is, having only two possible values ('0' for wrong and '1' for right).

This method of scoring works reasonably well if we only want to measure a single area of language knowledge, and thus decide to score responses in terms of a single criterion for correctness. However, if we are interested in assessing responses as instances of language use, several areas of language knowledge are likely to be involved, so that responses may be scored according to several criteria for correctness, either implicitly or explicitly. In example (2), test takers might give a number of different answers, some of which are grammatically accurate, some of which are semantically appropriate, and some of which meet both of these criteria for correctness. When we have multiple criteria for correctness and use right/wrong scoring, the score of a wrong response fails to reflect the specific area(s) of language knowledge in which the test taker is deficient. Thus, with right/wrong scoring, the following answers to example (2) above would all receive a score of '0': 'hitted', 'avoided', and 'preserve', even though they are wrong for different reasons. 'Hitted' is wrong according to both grammatical and semantic criteria; 'avoided' is grammatically inaccurate but semantically appropriate, and 'preserve' is grammatically accurate but semantically inappropriate.

In order to capture information about which criteria for correctness the response failed to satisfy, there are essentially two options: give *multiple* right/wrong scores for each item, or use partial credit scoring. Using the former approach for example (2), each of the example answers would receive two scores, as follows:

Response/Criterion	Grammar	Meaning
'hitted'	0	0
'avoided'	0	1
'preserve'	1	0
'avoid'	1	1

Multiple right/wrong scores for responses to a single item

With partial credit scoring we apply multiple criteria for correctness to arrive at a *single* score for each item: we give full credit for a response that satisfies all criteria for correctness, partial credit for responses that satisfy some of the criteria, and no credit for answers that satisfy none of the criteria. The way we assign the scores will depend on how, if at all, we prioritize the areas of language ability to be measured. Assuming that grammar and meaning are to be given equal priority in scoring, using partial credit scoring for example (2), the answers would receive the following scores:

Response/Primary criterion	Grammar	Meaning	Both
'hitted'	0	0	0
'avoided'	0	1	1
'preserve'	1	0	1
'avoid'	1	1	2

Single partial credit scores for responses to a single item

There are two advantages with either of these approaches—multiple scores or partial credit scoring. First, they offer the test user the potential for capturing more information about responses, and hence more information about test takers' areas of strength and weakness, than does giving a single right/wrong score. With the multiple-score approach it is possible to report separate scores for different areas of language ability that are tested. In the above example, the grammar scores for all the items could be added up to yield a total score for grammar, and similarly for meaning. Reporting separate scores like this may be particularly useful where tests are to be used for diagnostic purposes, that is, for providing feedback to students on their areas of strength and weakness and to teachers on which areas of the syllabus appear to be working effectively to promote learning and which areas need improvement.

In order to realize this potential advantage, both the assignment of multiple scores and partial credit scoring need to be based on a clear specification of the components of language ability required for correct responses, and the criteria for correctness, which must themselves derive from the definition of the construct to be measured. This requirement, in our view, is a second advantage of these scoring approaches, since it strengthens the link between the scores we derive and the constructs they are intended to measure. Thus, neither multiple marks nor partial credit scoring should be used simply to resolve uncertainties about the relative correctness of specific responses, but should be implemented in a principled way, deriving from the design specifications of the test itself.

The disadvantage of these approaches is that they are more complicated than giving single right/wrong scores, in terms of both the actual scoring and the analysis of scores. One aspect of this complexity is determining how many different levels to assign for responses to a given item. That is, should one give points of 0, 1, 2, 3, and 4, or just up to 3? In reaching a decision, we can consider the qualities of usefulness as they relate to this particular issue. With respect to validity, probably the best guide is to look at the specific nature of the intended response and the criteria for correctness and consider the degree to which different responses reflect the construct to be measured. With respect to reliability, information about the number of levels that are actually functioning can be obtained through the analysis of test results. (See references in Chapters 2 and 12 for a discussion of some procedures for doing this.) We can also collect feedback from people who score the test to see what problems, if any, they encounter with a given number of points. It may be, for example, that assigning a wide range of points makes scoring more difficult or inconsistent. Feedback such as this can also provide information about practicality.

In general we recommend using either multiple scores or partial credit scoring with items in which multiple criteria for correctness are used, and where the primary use of the test is to make inferences about profiles of language ability, such as in diagnostic or achievement testing. In such situations, considerations of consistency with construct definitions that involve several areas of language ability would dictate partial credit scoring. We suggest that single right/wrong scores should be used only where there is a single, clearly defined construct, and where a single criterion for correctness can be justified.

Selected responses

Specifying the criteria for correctness

Test tasks that require a selected response are of two types, in terms of the criteria of correctness of the options from which the test taker must select a response. One type is the 'best answer' type, in which the test taker is expected to choose the best answer from among the choices given. In multiple-choice tests of vocabulary, for example, it is common for test takers to choose, from among several alternatives, the word that is closest in meaning to an underlined word or phrase in the stem of the item. This is a best answer type, since it is possible that there is another word, not given in the choices, that is as close a synonym as any of the choices given. This is because the meaning of any lexical item involves more than a single aspect, so that different words may be synonymous with the underlined word or phrase in different ways. Thus, before selecting one word from among those given, the test taker must first determine the basis of the synonymy. For an item such as the following, this may be quite simple:

5   All professors at the university <u>ceased</u> their teaching because of the large pay raises given to top administrators while faculty salaries were frozen.

    a   began
    b   changed
  *c   stopped
    d   increased

This item would be considerably more difficult with the following options, which are much closer in meaning, so that the basis for identifying the synonymy is much more subtle:

    a   terminated
    b   finished
  *c   discontinued
    d   completed

Another example of a best answer task is when we ask test takers to choose the best title for a reading passage, meaning 'best' from among the choices given, even though the test taker may be able to think of a better title than any of the choices provided.

The other type of selected response task is the 'correct answer' type, which implies that there is only one correct answer in the world, and that this answer is among the choices provided. Multiple-choice tests of grammar, for example, are typically correct answer types, since there is (presumably) only one answer that is grammatically acceptable in the particular variety and register of the target language.

One variation of the selected response task that is sometimes used is an editing task, in which the test taker is asked to identify something in the input that is actually incorrect or inappropriate according to some specified criterion. Consider the following example, in which test takers are asked to indicate which of the underlined words is stylistically inappropriate:

6   One way to <u>determine</u> the <u>appropriateness</u> of the <u>method</u>
                    a   b   c
    is by <u>shooting the breeze</u> with <u>individual practitioners</u>.
              d   e

Editing tasks can also require the processing of larger texts, either with specific words and phrases underlined to focus the task for test takers, or a more open-ended task, with no indication of which words or phrases are potentially incorrect. In any of these tasks, either the best (worst) or correct (incorrect) answer criterion can be used.

Whether the test developer designs a question to be a best answer type or a correct answer type will be determined primarily by the area of language ability that is being tested, and by the domain of possible options within that area. If the construct to be measured requires fine discriminations and involves multiple components of language ability, then the best answer type will be the most appropriate. Suppose, for example, we were interested in assessing students' ability to make inferences from a reading passage. Such a task is likely to involve many, if not all, the components of language ability. In this case, for a selected response task type the best answer type would be the most appropriate. If, on the other hand, the construct is defined in terms of a single area of language knowledge, then the correct answer type may suffice. However, we would again express our view that language use, including the responses that we are interested in eliciting with test tasks, involves the interaction of multiple components of language ability, so that there are very few cases in which the correct answer type will be appropriate for language tests. In language use there is virtually no situation in which there is only one appropriate response. That is, the domains from which we make choices in language use are all very large and, in most cases, open sets. Even in the area of grammatical knowledge we are seldom limited to a single form when we want to accomplish a particular communicative goal. Thus, even though it is certainly possible to provide a set of options that constrains the test taker to choosing what the test developer believes to be the only correct answer, in our view this results in test tasks that are relatively inauthentic.

We believe that the best answer type for tasks that require a selected response is more appropriate for most language testing situations. However, it is important to bear in mind the view among measurement specialists that this type generally tends to be more difficult than the correct answer type. This is because of the more precise discriminations that may be required and because the best answer type tends to be used to measure more complex and integrated aspects of language ability, such as the ability to comprehend discourse through reading or listening. Because of this, it is essential that the test taker be clearly informed of what type the item is, since if he thinks he is expected to choose the 'correct' synonym, for example, and knows of a close synonym that he believes is better than any of the choices given, he may find the task difficult or confusing.

Determining procedures for scoring the responses

Tasks that require a selected response have traditionally been scored according to a single criterion, so that right/wrong scoring is generally used with this task type. This is not to say, however, that partial credit scoring cannot be used with selected task types. Indeed, it is our view that best answer tasks, as discussed above, lend themselves particularly well to partial credit scoring. Consider a typical type of reading comprehension question, the 'main idea' question. The test developer typically presents test takers with several choices, each of which might have some elements of the main idea, but only one of which adequately captures the entire main idea. Differing amounts of partial credit could be given for the choices that contain only some elements of the main idea.

Correcting for guessing

For most selected response type items, there is some possibility that test takers will be able to select the correct response by guessing.[3] With this type of item the test taker is presented with a small finite set of options from which to choose, so that the probability of chance success can be calculated, and procedures for 'correcting' for chance guessing are available. Because of this, test users sometimes want to employ correction for guessing when selected response type items are used.

In deciding whether or not to do so, several issues must be considered. First, we need to realize that the tendency to guess is affected by a number of different personality characteristics and varies greatly from one individual test taker to the next. The 'cautious' type of test taker will typically omit most, if not all, responses to items of which they are unsure, while the 'risk taker' may not omit any responses at all. The intention of correction procedures is to remove any advantage the risk taker may gain, by guessing at random, over the cautious test taker. However, we only know which items test takers omit, and not why they omit them, so corrections for guessing actually correct for differential omissions and not for guessing itself. Furthermore many other factors, including the test taker's level of ability and the nature of the test task itself, affect guessing. Finally, there is a difference between random guessing and informed guessing, in which test takers are able to narrow down the number of possible correct responses on the basis of partial knowledge. Corrections for guessing fail to take this into account, since they are based on the probability of random guessing. If a test taker is able to respond correctly through partial knowledge, we feel that this should be rewarded, preferably through partial credit scoring, and that correction for guessing would be inappropriate.

In summary, it is our view that correction for guessing with selected responses is virtually never useful in language tests. Our recommendation is to include, in the test design, provisions for eliminating or reducing the potential causes of random guessing, rather than correcting for it after the fact. First, we need to provide ample time for the majority of test takers to complete all the tasks in the test. Second, we need to match the difficulty of items with ability levels of test takers. Both of these provisions can be checked empirically by trialing the tests, observing test takers' patterns of response, analyzing their responses, and collecting self-reports from test takers on their reasons for choosing specific options. Finally, we recommend encouraging test takers to make informed guesses on the basis of partial knowledge. One way to accomplish this is to instruct them to answer every item, and, for items where they are not completely sure of the correct answer, to eliminate as many incorrect choices as they can, and then guess from among those remaining.

While we make these recommendations in the context of equalizing the effects of differential guessing or omissions, we believe that they are all consistent with the principles outlined in this book. With respect to adequate time and appropriate difficulty of test tasks, we believe that this reflects non-test language use, in which participants in a speech event have numerous means at their disposal for controlling or accommodating the speed and complexity of the discourse they must process. And even where we get lost because of either the speed or the complexity of the discourse, we virtually never make a totally random guess at meaning; rather, we use the means at our disposal—language knowledge, topical knowledge, and metacognitive strategies—to arrive at a possible understanding of the meaning. Finally, these recommendations are in accord with our emphasis on the importance of planning and test design as the crucial step in producing useful language tests.

Limited production responses

Unlike tasks aimed at eliciting a selected response, in which the range of possible responses is generally quite small and fixed, in limited production tasks the range of possible responses is very large, if not infinite. Even in tasks that require only a single word to complete a sentence, the domain of options from which the test taker can choose may be quite large, depending on her level of ability in the area being measured and the size of her domain in that area. Consider again example (5), which could be revised and presented as a limited production task, as follows:

7   All professors at the university ＿＿＿＿＿ their teaching because of the large pay raises given to top administrators while faculty salaries were frozen.

For test takers toward the low end of the ability range, the domain of possibly correct responses might be limited to those verbs having the general meaning of modifying an activity (teaching, in this case), so that verbs such as 'stopped', 'halted', 'delayed', 'started', 'began', 'changed', 'altered', 'modified', 'increased', and 'decreased' might appear equally correct. For test takers at the high end of this ability range, on the other hand, the domain of possible lexical choices might be further constrained to include only verbs that have to do with the interruption or termination of an activity. Nevertheless, the choice may still be from among a fairly large set of options, such as 'ceased', 'stopped', 'terminated', 'finished', 'discontinued', 'completed', 'concluded', and 'quit', depending on the test takers' lexical knowledge. Not only is the range of possible responses very large, but in many limited production tasks there are likely to be several acceptable answers. Thus, in the example above, 'ceased', 'stopped', and 'quit' might all be considered correct responses. The size and range of both possible and acceptable responses is even greater for limited production tasks that require the test taker to produce more than a single word or phrase. Consider, for example, the range of acceptable responses to the following item:

8   All professors at the university ceased their teaching because of the ＿＿＿＿＿ given to top administrators while faculty salaries were ＿＿＿＿＿＿＿.

The potentially large range of acceptable responses that limited production tasks are likely to elicit has two implications for scoring. First, insuring that the criteria for correctness correspond to the construct definition is more complicated, since responses that are identified as being acceptable may not all fit the specified criteria for correctness. That is, even though in the test design the test developer may specify criteria for correctness that reflect the way the construct to be measured is defined, some of the actual responses that are identified as acceptable, through trying out the test items with various groups of individuals, may not satisfy the specified criteria for correctness. Consider, for example, the following item from a cloze test:

9   The teaching staff wants to use the ＿＿＿＿＿ to improve presentations and teaching methods of the course.

The words 'results', 'study', and 'evaluation' occur elsewhere in the passage, and if the test designer intends for this blank to measure test takers' sensitivity to lexical cohesion, all may be considered acceptable. However, a number of other possibly acceptable responses, such as 'outcomes', 'research', and 'materials', might be produced by test takers. In this case, the test developer could consider expanding the original list of acceptable answers, and would thus need to respecify the criteria for correctness. This in turn would require a reconsideration of the definition of the construct measured by this item, recognizing that the different responses reflect different areas of language knowledge. If, on the other hand, the test developer wants to include items in the test that focus only on lexical cohesion, she would most likely decide that this item is not suitable, since there are acceptable responses to it that do not depend on knowledge of lexical cohesion. Thus, with limited production tasks, determining if the criteria for correctness correspond to the way in which the construct is defined will depend on the different types of acceptable responses that are identified in the trialing of the items. But rather than considering this complication a disadvantage, we would argue that it is an advantage, since it leads the test developer to constantly consider the relationship between construct definitions and criteria for correctness. Furthermore, it strengthens the tryout and revision cycle that is part of the evaluation of usefulness in the test development process.

A second scoring implication of limited production tasks is that the test developer will need to develop a scoring key which lists those responses that will be considered acceptable, and, if partial credit scoring is used, how much credit each of these responses will be given. This is necessary in order to avoid introducing inconsistencies in the way scorers apply criteria of correctness. If a scoring key is not provided, the individuals who score the responses will need to exercise their own judgment in assigning scores. While there is nothing inherently wrong with such subjective scoring, it does introduce another potential source of inconsistency, which we will need to investigate empirically, in order to estimate how great it is and its effects on test scores. (See Bachman 1990 Chapter 6, and the Suggested Readings for Chapter 12 for a discussion of procedures for estimating inter- and intra-scorer reliability.)

Specifying the criteria for correctness

As with selected response tasks, test tasks intended to elicit limited production responses can be used to measure specific areas of language knowledge, as well as comprehension in receptive language use tasks. Essentially the same considerations in specifying criteria for correctness that have been discussed under General considerations, pages 195–6, apply. Unlike selected response tasks, however, where the range of options is limited to a small finite set of choices, with limited production tasks test takers actually construct their own responses, so that the range of response options is virtually unlimited. For this reason, limited production tasks are by definition the best answer type.

Determining procedures for scoring the responses

Given the greater complexity and variety of responses that are possible with limited production tasks, we believe that our arguments in favor of partial credit scoring are even stronger with this type of test task. Since the probability of guessing the correct answer by chance is essentially nil for limited production tasks, correction for guessing is not generally a consideration.

Scoring as levels of language ability

There are many situations, most commonly when we want to test the use of language in tasks that involve speaking or writing, in which test takers are presented with tasks aimed at eliciting extended production responses. In contrast to selected and limited production responses, extended production responses deal with instances of discourse or situated language use and we cannot easily identify individual tasks or responses to score. Rather, we judge the quality of the response in terms of levels of ability demonstrated in completing the test task, using rating scales defined and developed for this purpose. In this section we present an approach to developing rating scales that incorporates the notion that language ability consists of multiple components, and that involves separate *analytic* ratings for each of the specific components in the construct definition. Before describing this approach, however, we feel it is important to point out some of the problems associated with a more traditional approach.

Global scales of language ability

One traditional approach to developing rating scales of language proficiency is based on the view that language ability is a single unitary ability, and yields a single score, called a 'global' rating. Many such scales, however, contain multiple 'hidden' components of language ability. Here are two examples of global scales of language ability. The first is an example of a portion of another global scale, developed by the United States Foreign Service Institute (FSI).

   10   Global Scale 1

        Limited working proficiency
        S-2   *Able to satisfy routine social demands and limited work*

requirements. Can handle with confidence but not with facility most social situations including introductions and casual conversation about current events, as well as work, family, and autobiographical information; can handle limited work requirements, needing help in handling any complications or difficulties; can get the gist of most conversations on non-technical subjects (i.e. topics which require no specialized knowledge) and has a speaking vocabulary sufficient to express himself simply with some circumlocutions; accent, though often quite faulty, is intelligible; can usually handle elementary constructions quite accurately but does not have thorough or confident control of the grammar. (Clark 1978: 10)

Here is a portion of another global scale:

11 Global Scale 2

80–90 These people can write English fairly well, but they are not good enough to carry a full-time academic load. They make frequent errors, more basic errors, and they use less complex grammatical structures. These compositions should be understandable, but the authors clearly need special attention and consideration in their written work.

Some problems with global scales

There are three major types of problems with global scales:

1 problems of inference,
2 difficulties in assigning levels, and
3 differential weighting of components.

The problem of inference

The use of global scales makes it difficult to know what a score reflects: multiple areas of language knowledge, topical knowledge, or multiple language use situations. An S-2 rating on Global Scale 1, for example, refers to multiple areas of language knowledge (vocabulary, accent, (grammatical) constructions), multiple areas of topical knowledge (current events, family, autobiographical information), and multiple TLU situations (casual conversation, limited work requirements). Global Scale 2 also refers to multiple components: the TLU situation (carry a full-time academic load), language ability (basic errors, less complex grammatical sentence structure), the composition reader (understandable), and instructional treatment (authors clearly need special attention and consideration in their written work). Thus it is difficult to know exactly what kinds of inferences can be made from a rating of 80–90 on this scale. That is, does the score reflect the test takers' capacity to function in the TLU situation, their accuracy of language use, how effectively they communicate, or the amount of further instruction in writing that they need? What it appears to reflect is a profile of a particular type of test taker, including a description of some aspects of language ability (errors), prediction of future performance (not good enough to carry a full-time academic load), and a prescription for treatment.

Difficulty in assigning levels

A second problem with global scales, related to the problem of inference, is that raters using them frequently have difficulty in assigning levels. Consider, for example, Global Scale 2, which includes reference to language, task, and reader. If all of these criteria are not satisfied at the same time (and this is often the case), the rater will have to determine which takes precedence. What if the composition uses highly complex grammatical structures with frequent errors? What if the composition does not contain frequent, basic errors (in grammar) but for other reasons (such as organizational problems), the composition is difficult to understand? What if other factors, such as the writer's intelligence, control of topical knowledge, or study habits, would tend to qualify her for full-time academic work? Furthermore, how are raters to assign specific scores within this band of 80–90?

Differential weighting of components

With global scales, there is always the possibility that different raters (or the same rater on different occasions) may either consciously or unconsciously weigh the hidden components differently in arriving at their single rating. This is also a potential problem with analytic scales. However, with these scales the components to be included and how each is to be rated are made explicit, so that we are in a position to control the weighting of the different components, either through rater training, or through statistical procedures.

In summary, many rating scales that are called 'global' include multiple components, with little or no indication as to how these different components are to be considered either in arriving at a single rating or in interpreting it. We recognize that much of the information included in global scales should be considered in the ultimate decision about the individual test taker. At the same time, we would point out that the test developer must carefully consider how much of this can be derived from the test score. That is, test developers need to be able to distinguish between everything that might be of interest in making a particular decision and the information that the test score can and should provide.

Analytic scales of language ability

Our approach to developing rating scales adheres to two principles. First, the operational definitions in the scales are based on theoretical definitions of the construct. These may be either theory-based or syllabus-based componential definitions of language ability, as discussed in Chapter 6. Second, the scale levels are referenced to specified levels in different areas of language ability, with the lowest level on our rating scales defined as 'no evidence of' the ability and the highest level as 'evidence of mastery of' the ability.

Ability-based scales

We have consistently argued that the design and development of language tests must be based upon a clear definition of language ability, which can be derived from either a theory of language ability or a set of specific learning objectives in a language teaching syllabus, and our approach to defining rating scales also follows this principle. In designing rating scales, we start with componential construct definitions and create *analytic* scales, which require the rater to provide separate ratings for the different components of language ability in the construct definition. In developing analytic rating scales we will have the same number of separate scales as there are distinct components in the construct definition.

In situations where it might be useful to provide a single score, we recommend deriving this by combining componential scores which are arrived at by the use of analytic rating scales, rather than developing a single global rating scale. This is because of the problems involved with the use of global scales.

Advantages

The use of analytic scales has two practical advantages. First, it allows us to provide a 'profile' of the areas of language ability that are rated. In most language teaching and testing situations, we will want to differentiate among areas of relative strength and weakness. For example, we might want to provide interpretations such as, 'Organizes writing very well, but doesn't have much control of register in formal writing; writes a formal business letter as if it were a conversation with a friend' or 'Has a large vocabulary but continually makes grammar mistakes when speaking about chemistry.'

A second advantage is that analytic scales tend to reflect what raters actually do when rating samples of language use. For example, even when expert raters are asked to sort writing samples into levels on the basis of *overall* quality, they report that they take into consideration specific areas of language ability (such as grammar, vocabulary, content) when they do so.[4]

Criterion-referenced scales of language ability

Our second principle is to define scales operationally in terms of criterion levels of ability, rather than as performance relative to other test takers or to native speakers of the language. The primary advantage of criterion-referenced scales is that they allow us to make inferences about how much language ability a test taker has, and not merely how well she performs relative to other individuals, including native speakers. We define the lowest level of our scales in terms of no evidence of knowledge or ability and the highest level in terms of mastery, or complete knowledge or ability. We will thus always have zero and mastery levels in our scales, irrespective of whether there are any test takers at these levels.

The main question that remains is how many levels to have between zero and mastery. This depends primarily upon considerations of usefulness. We need to consider the number of distinctions raters can reasonably be expected to make reliably and validly. It would be easy to create rating scales with, say, fifteen ability levels, but it is unlikely that raters could make so many distinctions with any kind of consistency. In terms of impact, the number of decision levels required on the basis of the intended use of the test must be taken into account. For example, in order to place a wide range of students into four levels of a writing program, a minimum of four scale levels is needed.[5] If the number of decision levels required exceeds the number of levels that raters can reliably distinguish, then it is possible to use a composite score by combining the ratings of the separate analytic scales to obtain a score with a larger number of levels. (Composite scores are discussed on pages 223–5.) A final consideration is practicality, as the number of levels decided upon will have implications for the selection and training of raters.

Scale definitions

The theoretical construct definitions from which rating scales can be developed may be based on either a theoretical model of language ability, such as that presented in Chapter 4, or the content of a language learning syllabus. Both these theoretical construct definitions refer only to areas of language ability, independent of any considerations of the characteristics of the specific testing situation and prompt with which they might be used. For example, we define grammatical knowledge to include rules of syntax and phonology/graphology without reference to language use situations such as 'conversation with an employer in an office environment'.

The *scale definition* includes two parts:

1 the specific features of the language sample to be rated with the scale, and
2 the definition of scale levels in terms of the degree of mastery of these features.

It is these specific features of language use that should be kept in mind when carrying out ratings, and the amount of detail provided in the scale definition will depend upon a number of factors.

1   *How are the ratings to be used?*

Are inferences about language knowledge to be made to a broadly defined or highly specific TLU situation? For example, in order to generalize to mastery of a specific body of course material, as in achievement testing, it is necessary to provide enough detail to relate the construct definition to instructional content. When rating writing samples in a composition course, for example, we might want to add to the construct 'knowledge of rhetorical organization' details such as 'knowledge of introduction, thesis statement, topic sentences, and topic headings'.

2   *How much detail do the raters need be given in order to provide reliable, valid ratings?*

This will be influenced by the characteristics of the raters. For example, if trained English composition teachers were rating punctuation, a construct definition that included a list of all of the punctuation marks in English might be unnecessary. On the other hand, if untrained native speakers of English were rating sociolinguistic knowledge, a fairly detailed definition of the construct would probably be required in order to familiarize them with what to look for.

Examples of criterion-referenced ability-based analytic scales

The following example scales illustrate ratings of construct definitions, with two different numbers of ability levels. These example scales could be used for placing students into a multi-level writing course. These examples are, however, intended to be illustrative, and although they may be appropriate for use in actual testing situations, this would need to be determined by the test developer, after taking into account the considerations of use-fulness. (For additional examples of criterion-referenced ability-based analytic scales, see Project 1 in Part Three.)

12   Knowledge of syntax

Theoretical construct definition:	knowledge of syntax
Operational construct definition:	evidence of accurate use of a variety of syntactic structures as demonstrated in the context of the specific tasks (as specified in the task specifications) that have been presented, and as rated on the following scale:

Levels of ability/mastery	*Description*
0 None	*No evidence of knowledge* of syntax

	Range:	zero
	Accuracy:	not relevant

1   Limited

Evidence of *limited knowledge* of syntax

Range:	small
Accuracy:	poor, moderate, or good accuracy. If test taker only attempts a very few structures, accuracy may be good.

2   Moderate

Evidence of *moderate knowledge* of syntax

Range:	medium
Accuracy:	moderate to good accuracy within range. If test taker attempts structures outside of the controlled range, accuracy may be poor.

3   Extensive

Evidence of *extensive knowledge* of syntax

Range:	large, few limitations
Accuracy:	good accuracy, few errors

4   Complete

Evidence of *complete knowledge* of syntax

Range:	no evidence of restrictions in range
Accuracy:	evidence of complete control except for slips of the tongue

13 Knowledge of register

| *Theoretical construct definition*: | knowledge of appropriate register |

Operational construct definition: evidence of the appropriate use of a range of markers of register in formulaic expressions and substantive discourse, as demonstrated in the context of the specific tasks that have been presented, and as rated on the following scale:

Levels of ability/mastery	*Description*

0 Zero

No evidence of knowledge of register

| Range: | zero |
| Appropriateness: | not relevant |

1 Limited

Evidence of *limited knowledge* of only one register

| Range: | evidence of only one register in formulaic expressions and substantive discourse |
| Appropriateness: | poor |

2 Moderate

Evidence of *moderate knowledge* of two registers

| Range: | evidence of two registers in formulaic expressions and substantive discourse |
| Appropriateness: | good for one register, poor for another |

3 Extensive

Evidence of *extensive knowledge* of two registers

| Range: | evidence of two registers in formulaic expressions and substantive discourse |
| Appropriateness: | good for two registers, few errors |

13 Knowledge of register—continued

Levels of ability/mastery	Description	
4 Complete	Evidence of *complete knowledge* of two registers	
	Range:	evidence of two registers in formulaic expressions and substantive discourse
	Appropriateness:	completely appropriate use of two registers, no errors

14 Knowledge of rhetorical organization: Thesis statement

Theoretical construct definition:	knowledge of the thesis statement as an organizing device which limits the topic and sets up procedures or divisions
Operational construct definition:	evidence of an explicit thesis statement which limits the topic and sets up procedures or divisions, as demonstrated in the context of the specific tasks that have been presented, and as rated on the following scale:

Levels of ability/mastery	Description
0 Zero	*No evidence of knowledge* of thesis statement
	No thesis statement, explicit or implicit, or thesis statement is irrelevant to topic
1 Limited	Evidence of *limited knowledge* of thesis statement
	Thesis is explicit but not limiting: does not set up procedures or divisions, or thesis is implicit but not expressed, or thesis depends upon title or assigned topic, or thesis is not completely relevant to topic
2 Complete	Evidence of *complete knowledge* of thesis statement
	Thesis is relevant to topic, explicit, limiting, and sets up procedure or divisions

Topical knowledge

In some situations we may want to make generalizations from test scores about the test takers' topical knowledge to be included in the construct definition. (See the discussion in Chapter 6, Section 4.) The way topical knowledge is handled in our approach is that the area of specific topical knowledge is defined operationally as an additional component of the construct and a separate rating scale is developed for this, so as to obtain distinct ratings for topical knowledge. This is quite different from the global approach, in which topical knowledge is generally hidden in the scale definitions, and thus cannot be distinguished from language ability. For example, suppose the control of grammar, vocabulary, and language functions of students completing a sheltered subject matter course in botany is to be rated. They might be asked to write a short essay comparing the processes of respiration and photosynthesis in plants. Following the construct definition, their essays would be rated on control of grammar, vocabulary, and functions. But suppose that while they used grammar, vocabulary, and functions correctly, they incorrectly described the process of photosynthesis. They might know what the words 'oxygen' and 'carbon dioxide' mean and use these words functionally to describe a process, in which case we could rate them high on vocabulary and functional knowledge. However, their topical knowledge would be incorrect.

The following is an example of a scale for rating topical knowledge.

15 Knowledge of topical information

Theoretical construct definition:	knowledge of relevant topical information
Operational construct definition:	evidence of knowledge of topical information relevant to the performance of the task, as demonstrated in the context of the specific tasks that have been presented, and as rated on the following scale:

Level of ability/mastery		*Description*
0	Zero	*No evidence of knowledge* of relevant topical information
		Range: zero, test taker demonstrates no knowledge of assigned topic
		Accuracy: not relevant
1	Limited	Evidence of *limited knowledge* of relevant topical information

15   Knowledge of topical information—continued

Level	Size	Description
		Range: small, test taker deals only with a small portion of assigned topic
		Accuracy: poor, moderate, or good accuracy within range
2	Moderate	Evidence of *moderate knowledge* of relevant topical information
		Range: medium
		Accuracy: moderate to good accuracy of knowledge within range
3	Extensive	Evidence of *extensive knowledge* of relevant topical information
		Range: wide, few limitations
		Accuracy: good accuracy throughout range
4	Complete	Evidence of *complete knowledge* of relevant topical information
		Range: evidence of unlimited range of relevant topical information
		Accuracy: evidence of complete accuracy throughout range

All of these scales include the distinction between range or variety in the use of realizations of the particular component (for example, syntactic structures, markers of register) and accuracy or appropriateness of use of those components. These are explicit in the grammar and register scales above. In the thesis statement scale, range is implicit in the number of criteria for thesis statement that are included (explicit, limits topic, sets up procedures or divisions), and accuracy is implicit in the degree to which they are controlled. It has been our experience over the years that this distinction is very useful for developing rating scales for a wide variety of components of language ability.

Ratable samples

In order for extended production responses to be rated reliably and validly, the language produced has to constitute what is called a 'ratable sample' of language. One characteristic of a ratable sample of language is that there is opportunity for the full range of components that are to be rated to occur. A second characteristic is that a ratable sample provides evidence of the test taker's highest level of ability on these components. What constitutes a ratable sample, therefore, depends directly upon the components of language ability to be rated, while the extent to which ratable samples can be obtained in a given language test depends on the characteristics of the test tasks. Consider, for example, the kinds of tasks that might be used to elicit a sample of spoken language that could be rated for 'knowledge of register'. Several highly authentic and interactive test tasks corresponding to the distinctive characteristics of TLU tasks would be set up, in the expectation that they will provide opportunities for the full range of appropriate markers of register to occur, and will enable test takers to perform at their highest levels of ability. In an oral interview, for example, several role-plays might be set up. In some the interviewer could play a role where it would be appropriate for the test taker to use an informal or intimate register, such as a close friend or sibling, while in others the interviewer could take a role where a more formal register would be appropriate, such as an older relative, a teacher, or a prospective employer. Tasks to elicit different registers in formulaic language, such as introductions, greetings, and leave-takings, would be included, as well as tasks to elicit appropriate register in extended discourse, such as a job interview or short presentation.

By providing a highly authentic and interactive test task, we try to insure that there is an adequate sample of language to rate. If this approach is not followed, the result is a discrete-point approach in which it is necessary to prepare a list of the specific elements of language to be measured and then specify test tasks that will elicit these elements. As can be readily seen, this can lead to the use of relatively inauthentic tasks, such as multiple-choice or short completion items. While there may be components of language ability which can be assessed efficiently with discrete items, we believe that any gain in efficiency would need to be balanced against the potential loss in authenticity and interactiveness.

Using rating scales

Rating scales have often been seen as inefficient, unreliable ways of scoring language tests, and it is partly for this reason that the use of 'objective' procedures—items with selected responses that can be scored efficiently by either untrained personnel or machines—has become so widespread in language testing. While inefficiency and unreliability are potential problems, they are by no means insurmountable. With sufficient planning and development, rating procedures can be highly reliable and relatively efficient.

Anticipating problems

Demand on resources

Ratings might appear to be the least efficient way of scoring language tests. After all, ratings involve subjective judgments in the scoring process, which is not the case for objectively scored tests. It is true that, relative to machine scoring, ratings are more demanding in terms of human resources. However, ratings can provide information very difficult to obtain from objective scoring, such as profiles of areas of language knowledge in tests that require test takers to produce samples of language. Ratings can also put human beings in contact with the test method in ways that objective scoring procedures may not. Raters are constantly in contact with responses and often, as in the case of oral interview procedures, in contact with input as well. Thus, ratings provide greater opportunity for assessing the effectiveness of the test task, as well as its impact on test takers. For such reasons, we believe that ratings are well worth their relatively high cost in human resources.

The use of rating scales places two kinds of demands on human resources:

1   the amount of time involved, and
2   the number of people involved.

Rating samples of language production always requires time to listen to or read them, and the longer the samples, the more time is required. Moreover, the total amount of rating time increases as we increase the number of times a sample is rated, but using multiple ratings and averaging them is one way to increase their reliability. Therefore, this demand on human resources must be recognized as an unavoidable cost of obtaining the kinds of information that ratings can provide. In terms of overall usefulness, we believe that the potential gains in validity, authenticity, and interactiveness more than offset any potential loss in practicality.

Inconsistency

Another potential problem with ratings is inconsistency, which can be attributed to three causes.

Different interpretations of scales

Different interpretations of a given rating scale, both by different raters and by the same rater on different occasions, can lead to inconsistent scoring. One reason raters may interpret scales differently is that the scales may be inadequately specified. For example, if we ask raters not sophisticated in linguistics to rate an oral interview on 'knowledge of register' without first carefully defining what we mean by 'register', some raters might interpret the use of a different regional variety as register. This can be a particular problem with so-called global ratings of language production, in which raters may tend to develop their own internal componential rating criteria, which differ from rater to rater and within a single rater on different occasions.

Different standards of severity

Another problem of inconsistency stems from lack of agreement on the meanings of the levels of ability within a scale. For example, two raters may agree on the definition of sociolinguistic knowledge for the purposes of rating, but they may disagree on how well test takers must perform in order to reach the different levels on the scale. Thus, one rater may rate a test taker a '2' in sociolinguistic knowledge while another may rate the same test taker a '3.' Or one rater may feel more severe during one rating session than another.

Reaction to elements not relevant to scales

Since ratings are subjective, and since the language sample is likely to include content or features not directly relevant to particular scale definitions, ratings may be influenced by this irrelevant material. For example, raters may be instructed to rate compositions only on textual and functional knowledge but may nonetheless be influenced by features such as the test takers' handwriting and knowledge of the topic, as well as by the positions they take on the issues. In addition, if raters know the test takers, they may find themselves influenced by prior knowledge of the test takers' performance.

Dealing with problems

While the use of rating scales brings with it a number of potential problems, there are ways of dealing with these and reducing their impact.

Preparing raters

One of the most effective ways of dealing with inconsistency is through the proper selection and training of raters. One primary consideration in the selection of raters is the required level of language ability. For some rating tasks, we might want to select only raters whose language ability is at the level of complete mastery in the types of production tasks being rated. This would certainly be the case if they were required to rate a full range of language ability. However, for rating subjects with only limited to moderate ability, raters with less than complete mastery might be selected.

Regardless of the backgrounds of the raters selected, it is important to provide them with adequate training. Here are six steps in a general procedure for training raters:

1   Read and discuss scales together.
2   Review language samples which have been previously rated by expert raters and discuss the ratings given.
3   Practice rating a different set of language samples. Then compare the ratings with those of experienced raters. Discuss the ratings and how the criteria were applied.
4   Rate additional language samples and discuss.
5   Each trainee rates the same set of samples. Check for the amount of time taken to rate and for consistency.
6   Select raters who are able to provide reliable and efficient ratings.

Obtaining a sufficient number of ratings

A second way to deal with inconsistency is to obtain a sufficient number of ratings. All other things being equal, the more ratings we obtain, the more stable their average becomes. So while any single rater can have a 'bad day', it is unlikely that two or three raters will do so at the same time or in the same ways. Thus, it is good practice always to obtain at least two ratings per sample. A typical procedure is to have all samples rated by two raters and to have a third rater rate those samples on which the first two raters differ by more than one scale level. Then the score can be derived by averaging the three ratings.

Estimating the reliability of the ratings

An important step in developing a test is the statistical analysis of quantitative information obtained in trialing, and this includes estimating the reliability, or the degree of consistency, of the ratings. This information will allow decisions to be made about how effectively inconsistency has been controlled, and if the results are unsatisfactory, additional steps can be taken to increase consistency. For ratings, we are typically interested in estimating the consistency between different raters (inter-rater consistency) and within the same rater, across occasions of rating (intra-rater consistency), although procedures for estimating the extent to which different raters rate different kinds of language samples differently are also available. (See Bachman 1990, Chapter 6, as well as the references listed in Chapter 12 of this book for discussions of appropriate procedures for estimating inconsistencies in ratings.)

Deriving test scores

Scores derived directly from the scoring procedures

Profile scores for parts of the test

In many cases we want to report a profile of scores corresponding to the different areas of language ability measured. With items that elicit either selected or limited production responses, the scores, derived through either right/wrong or partial credit scoring for the individual items in each part, can be added up and the total score for that part reported. The use of componential or analytic rating scales also allows profiles of language ability to be reported. In fact, if the rating procedures advocated in this book are followed and only analytic scales used, all scoring will, at some point, be in terms of profiles. (The reporting of profiles is discussed in greater detail in the references listed in Chapter 12.)

Composite scores

There are sometimes situations in which it will be useful to report a single score, in which case we recommend using a *composite score*. A composite score is one that is arrived at by aggregating the scores from different parts of a test, or from different analytic rating scales. A composite score can consist of either the sum or an average of the component scores. This sum or average can be arrived at by using the raw scores or ratings, or, if some components are considered to be more important than others, the test developer can weight these more heavily by multiplying them by a number greater than one. Suppose, for example, that it were necessary to select the top few candidates from among a large number of applicants for a language teaching position, and that language ability were one of the qualifications for the job. Assuming that this particular teaching position will require the teacher to use language in tasks that involve writing, reading, speaking, and listening, one could design a test that includes tasks requiring all of these language use activities, and design separate scoring methods for these different types of tasks. From this a profile of applicants' language ability across different types of language use tasks could be derived. In addition, in order to more easily rank applicants in terms of their language ability, a single assessment of their ability to use language in all of these types of tasks could be obtained by aggregating their scores on the different parts of the test. Another example is where the number of distinctions to be made, given the purpose of the test, exceeds the number of scale levels that raters can reliably and validly distinguish. In such situations a composite score based on scores from the separate scales can provide finer distinctions than can be made with any single scale. Two approaches to arriving at a composite score can be followed: compensatory and non-compensatory.

Compensatory composite scores

It is often assumed that individuals with high levels in some of the areas of language ability to be tested can use these high levels of ability to compensate for low levels of ability in other components. In such situations a *compensatory composite score* can be derived by summing or averaging the separate scores. This is because when the scores from the different parts of the test or different analytic rating scales are added up or averaged, the composite score arrived at balances out high scores and low scores. In the example above a compensatory composite score could be derived by adding up the scores on the different parts of the test. This might be reported in addition to the profile of scores on the various parts of the test. Or suppose it was necessary to derive a single rating for performance on speaking tasks from separate analytic ratings of organizational, textual, and sociolinguistic knowledge. The three ratings might be added up and averaged, in which case the relative importance of each individual rating in the overall score will simply be a function of its statistical characteristics. If there are reasons for wanting the individual scales to be weighted in a particular way, or if the individual scales should all be equally weighted, then a weighting system might be developed to insure that the relative importance of the individual scales in the composite score reflects this. (Procedures for doing this are discussed in the references in Chapter 12.)

Non-compensatory composite scores

In some situations the test user may feel that individuals must demonstrate a minimum level of ability in every component tested, and that high levels of ability in some areas cannot compensate for low levels in others. For example, teachers in a given language course may feel that students must demonstrate a minimum level of mastery on each component of the course in order to be placed or advanced into a given level. Or an employer may require that new employees have a minimum level of mastery in several areas of language ability. In such situations it might be appropriate to calculate and report a *non-compensatory composite score*, which is the lowest score achieved in any of the scoring areas. In the example above, if a certain minimum level of language ability were considered essential for language teachers, candidates' composite scores would be based on the lowest score received on any of the four parts. Or suppose a test taker's ratings, based on a writing sample, were '2' for knowledge of vocabulary, '3' for knowledge of rhetorical organization, and '3' for knowledge of register. This test taker would receive a non-compensatory composite score of '2'. (The fact that the test taker received '3's' on two of the scales does not compensate for the '2' that he received on the other.) (Procedures for calculating and reporting composite scores are discussed in the references in Chapter 12.)

Trialing

As with most aspects of test development, the development of a scoring method is iterative and cyclical, involving

1 initial specification,
2 try-out,
3 analysis, and
4 revision.

In developing a scoring method for items for eliciting selected responses, for example, we typically include in each item several choices from which test takers are to select, one of which is intended to be the 'correct' or 'best' answer. The items are then tried out with groups of test takers, and feedback on their performance collected, both qualitatively and quantitatively. Finally, based on these analyses, the items may be revised, including the choice intended to be the correct one. Items for eliciting limited production responses are often tried out with test takers in order to identify the expected range of responses, and to make an initial scoring key. If partial credit scoring is to be used, an initial specification will be provided of the number of points to be given for each response. Then the items are tried out and, on the basis of the analyses of the responses, the items may be revised and the scoring method refined. A very similar procedure is followed with rating scales. We begin with initial scale definitions, including the number of levels, for each of the areas of language ability to be rated. Then, based on feedback collected as part of the trialing of the rating scales, the definitions may need to be refined, and the number of scale levels either expanded or reduced. Thus, the development of a scoring method is not simply a matter of deciding on criteria for correctness and determining procedures for scoring responses during test specification. This is because although we can take into consideration the qualities of usefulness in the specification of a scoring method, it is only through trying out the method empirically and analyzing the results that evidence of its usefulness can be provided. (A detailed discussion of procedures for trying out test tasks and scoring methods is provided in Chapter 12, while procedures for analyzing results are discussed in the references in Chapter 12.)

Interpreting test scores

As indicated in the discussion of construct validity in Chapter 2, score interpretations have two components:

1   inferences about the components of language ability that have been rated, and
2   inferences about the TLU domain to which these inferences generalize.

Both of these components are included in the operational definitions of the constructs to be measured. Inferences about language ability are based on the construct definition, while inferences about the TLU domain will be based on the characteristics of the specific tasks included in the test. For these reasons, we believe that the score report that is provided to test users should include, *in addition to* the construct definition, a description of the types of tasks, including example tasks, and the scoring methods that were used to arrive at the test scores. (A more detailed discussion of reporting test results is provided in the references in Chapter 12.)

Summary

Developing scoring procedures involves establishing a method for quantifying responses to test tasks, and the scoring procedures constitute an essential component of the operational definition of the construct. Scoring methods fall into two broad approaches. In one approach, the score is defined as the number of test tasks successfully completed, so that we count and add up the number of correct responses. Specifying a scoring method in this approach involves

1   defining the criteria for what constitutes 'successful completion', and
2   determining whether responses will be scored as right or wrong, or with varying degrees of correctness.

The other general approach to scoring tests is to define several levels on one or more rating scales of language ability, and then to rate responses to test tasks in terms of these scales. The approach to developing rating scales that we advocate is based on two principles. First, scales incorporate the principle that language ability consists of multiple components, and this involves separate, *analytic*, ratings for each of the specific components included in the construct definition. Second, we argue that the scale levels should be criterion referenced, with the lowest level on our rating scales defined as 'no evidence of' the ability and the highest level as 'evidence of mastery of' the ability. Specifying a scoring method with this approach involves

1   defining rating scales in terms of the areas of language ability to be assessed, and
2   determining the number of levels of ability on the different scales.

Componential or analytic rating scales allow profiles of language ability to be reported. However, in situations in which it will be useful to report a single score, composite scores can be arrived at through the use of either compensatory or non-compensatory procedures.

With sufficient planning and development, rating procedures can be highly reliable and relatively efficient. Planning involves anticipating problems, including demand on resources and causes of inconsistency. Problems with inconsistency can be dealt with by preparing raters and obtaining a sufficient number of ratings, and by estimating the degree of consistency of ratings, based on trialing.

As with most aspects of test development, the development of a scoring method is iterative and cyclical, involving

1   initial specification,
2   try-out,
3   analysis, and
4   revision.

It is only through trying out the scoring method empirically and analyzing the results that evidence of its usefulness can be provided.

Irrespective of the specific scoring method used, test scores are interpreted in terms of the operational definitions of the constructs to be measured. Inferences are made about language ability from the construct definition part of the operational definition, and about the domain of generalization from the task and scoring parts of the operational definition. Therefore, in reporting scores from tests information must be provided about both the construct and the tasks. This is the case both for scores on rating scales and for scores based on number of tasks completed.

Exercises

1   Obtain a copy of a test involving either selected or limited production responses. Determine how the responses are supposed to be scored. Is provision already made for partial credit scoring? If not, can you tell from the test specifications why not? If so, can you tell how partial credit scoring strengthens the link between the scores and the constructs they are intended to measure?

2   Obtain a copy of a test involving either selected or limited production responses with single right/wrong scores. Examine the test specifications, and determine whether partial credit scoring might be used to strengthen the link between the construct to be measured and the test scores. Then develop a partial credit scoring procedure to establish this link.

3   Obtain a test involving selected response tasks. Determine whether the test takers are told to choose the 'best' response or the 'correct' answer. Are the instructions consistent with the actual criteria that the test takers use to select the responses? Why or why not?

4 Obtain a foreign language textbook. Develop a set of test tasks involving limited production responses to test several grammar points from the text. Determine how the construct to be measured might be defined. Then have a number of test takers complete the test tasks. From the responses, develop a partial credit answer key for scoring the responses.

5 Obtain a language test involving the use of 'global' rating scales. How do the scales address or deal with the problem of inference, difficulty in assigning levels, and differential weighting of components? How might the scales be revised to deal with difficulties that you foresee?

6 Obtain a language test involving the use of analytic scales. Are these scales based upon a clear definition of language ability or not? What components of language ability are measured by means of these scales? Are the scales criterion referenced, or are they referenced to the abilities of a particular kind of language user? How many levels are defined? Can you figure out the rationale for the number of levels included in the scales?

7 Are you faced with a testing situation for which it would be appropriate to use test tasks scored by means of analytic, criterion-referenced scales? If so, develop a set of specifications for a test, a preliminary description of one or more test tasks, and scales for scoring the responses.

8 Obtain a language test with tasks involving written responses scored by means of rating scales. Either administer the test or obtain copies of responses to the test tasks. Have several people score the responses using the rating scales. Then compare the scoring. If raters disagreed, have them explain the basis for their ratings in order to determine why they disagreed. Would it be possible to design a training program for raters which would reduce the amount of disagreement? What might such a training program look like?

9 Obtain a language test involving either written or spoken responses scored by means of rating scales. Examine the rating scales and the characteristics of the expected responses. Do the expected responses provide a ratable sample, one in which there is opportunity for a full range of components that are to be rated to occur? If not, how might the characteristics of the test task(s) be modified to provide a ratable sample?

10 Obtain a language test in which a single, composite score is derived from a profile of scores. Are the composite scores obtained through compensatory or non-compensatory procedures? Can you determine the rationale for the particular procedures? How do the procedures either enhance or limit the usefulness of the test?

Notes

1 See Davidson (1986) and the papers in Zakaluk and Samuels (1988) for discussions of these issues.

2 Partial credit scoring generally takes one of two forms: partial points or marks (for example, 0, 1/4, 1/2, 3/4, 1) or multiple points or marks (for example, 0, 1, 2, 3, 4). Since these two forms yield identical results with respect to statistical characteristics, choosing between them is largely a matter of whether one wants to deal with fractions or decimals, as in the case of partial points, or whole numbers, as in the case of multiple points.

3 When test takers are presented with a selected response task, the probability of getting the correct answer by chance alone depends on the number of options from which they have to choose. Thus, with a true/false question, the probability of getting the correct answer by chance is one out of two, or 50 per cent, while with a four-choice multiple-choice item the probability is one out of four, or 25 per cent. Thus the probability of getting a selected response question correct by chance is $1/n$, where 'n' is the number of options. From this it can be seen that by increasing the number of options, we decrease the probability of test takers getting the correct answer by chance. Procedures for correcting for guessing are discussed in most standard measurement texts.

4 See, for example, Vaughn (1991).

5 This minimum number of levels assumes, of course, that ratings are absolutely reliable and correspond perfectly to levels in the course. This is virtually never the case, however, so that we will generally need more scale levels than there are decision levels.

12 Language test administration: Procedures for administering tests and collecting feedback

Introduction

In the preceding chapters, we have described the first two stages in test development—design and operationalization—in which we develop a design statement, a blueprint, and a preliminary version of the test. In the final chapter of this book we focus on the third stage in test development: test administration. This involves a variety of procedures for actually giving a test and also for collecting empirical information in order to evaluate the qualities of usefulness and make inferences about test takers' abilities. For the first purpose, we will collect feedback from a variety of sources that will enable us to confirm or revise our original design statement, revise our test blueprint and test task specifications as needed, and carry out our assessment of usefulness.[1] For the second purpose, we will rely primarily on the scores we obtain from the test itself.

In this chapter we first describe some procedures for administering language tests. We then discuss two aspects of test administration: pre-testing and operational testing. Finally, we discuss the collection of feedback from test administration for purposes of evaluating the qualities of usefulness and making revisions that may be needed to improve these qualities.

Procedures for administering a test

In order to accomplish either of the two purposes of test administration—collecting feedback to assess usefulness and making inferences about test takers' language ability—it is necessary to have some control over the procedures for administering tests. These involve guiding test takers through the process of taking a test. This is done in accordance with the procedures specified in the test blueprint, which have been created in order to maximize the qualities of usefulness for specific kinds of test takers and specific TLU situations.

Preparing the testing environment

The first step in test administration is preparing the testing environment to be consistent with the specifications in the test blueprint. This involves arranging the place of testing, materials and equipment, personnel, time of testing, and physical conditions under which the test is administered.

For example, in one test developed by the authors that required speaking, the design specifications required a place large enough to allow us to create two separate testing areas with different characteristics, one suitable for a formal role-play and one suitable for an informal role-play. Materials and equipment included, among other things, two different kinds of desks designed to create both highly formal and highly informal atmospheres, recording equipment, two telephone headsets, test booklets with different colored covers, and a set of prompt materials for the interviewers (Bachman and Palmer 1983).

Personnel characteristics were closely controlled prior to and during the test administration. For the initial administration we acted as examiners because we felt that we were in the best position to maximize the qualities of usefulness during that stage of test design and development. We took the roles that best suited our personalities. Before administering the test, we went through a one-week training program supervised by experienced oral interviewers in a US government agency. We also practiced administering our test a number of times and made some design changes on the basis of our experience.

The time chosen for testing was influenced primarily by considerations of reliability and practicality. We administered the test during the day since we then had the best access to test takers, the majority of whom were students who were near the campus testing site during class hours. We scheduled the test at 40-minute intervals to allow sufficient time for debriefing following each test. We also scheduled longer breaks at regular intervals to avoid fatigue and loss of concentration, which could have adversely affected reliability.

The physical conditions under which we administered the test included a quiet, well-lit, uncluttered room where we would not be disturbed and with sufficient space to allow us to set up the scenes for the informal and formal role-plays.

A contrasting situation is that of large-scale group administrations of written tests, in which test takers need to have adequate writing equipment, which might include sharpened pencils, erasers, paper for writing notes, or computers and word processors, in other words, whatever they need to do their best work. In addition, test takers will obviously need an environment in which they will not be distracted by other test takers.

If one is concerned that test takers might exchange information, steps can be taken to provide adequate space between them. Or if misinterpreting the identity of test takers might be a problem, they could be asked to bring identification documents. The intention behind these procedures is not to focus attention on 'preventing cheating' (which would tend to cast the test-taking experience in a negative light) but rather on maximizing the usefulness of the test, which includes the validity of interpretation of test scores.

Communicating the instructions

The second step in administering a test is to give the instructions in such a way that they will be understood by all test takers. The preparation of effective instructions as well as the components of instructions have been discussed in Chapter 10. When administering the test it is essential that the test takers receive the full benefit of the instructions. This includes the obvious steps of providing suitable conditions (time, lighting, lack of distraction) for reading written instructions, as well as for listening to oral instructions. In addition, some selection and/or training of personnel in administering instructions orally may be needed.

Maintaining a supportive testing environment

The next step is maintaining a supportive testing environment throughout the test. This includes avoiding distractions due to temperature, noise, excessive movement, etc. For example, in large-scale group testing, test takers are frequently required to remain in their seats until the end of the test to avoid movement and noise. It also includes assisting test administrators and proctors in developing attitudes conducive to maximizing the overall usefulness of the test.

Before administering a test, test developers need to think through what kind of assistance they want the proctors to provide during the test itself. Traditionally, much of the focus of attention on the test-taking environment has been on controlling variability in order to increase reliability. While reliability is obviously an important quality of usefulness, we feel that equal consideration should be given to others. For example, to what extent might an attempt to create a highly stable test-taking environment lead to a reduction in the authenticity of the surroundings? Or to what extent might authoritarian attempts to control the test-taking environment result in a negative impact on test takers? For example, we once witnessed a large-scale administration of a standardized test in which the test administrator obviously felt hostile to the test takers. We could actually hear a rumble of discontent among the test takers prior to the start of the test, which was probably not conducive to their performing at their best.

Setting up a supportive test taking environment needs to be carried out with *all* qualities of usefulness in mind. Decisions need to be based on a consideration of the appropriate balance among the qualities of usefulness for the particular testing situation.

Collecting the tests

The final step in test administration is collecting the tests. While proctors might be tempted to focus only on making sure that the materials collected are those actually produced by the test takers during the test session, this might leave the test takers with a negative reaction. Therefore collecting the tests could be seen as one final opportunity to make personal contact with the test takers. Instead of hurrying to collect the tests, proctors might give the test takers a chance to write down a few comments on their experience. While the test takers are providing this feedback, the proctors can quietly collect the test booklets. Test takers may then leave at their own pace and, if they wish, talk with the proctors about their experience. If the proctors take notes on the test takers' suggestions, the feeling of being taken seriously could make a final, positive contribution to the overall usefulness of the test.

Pre-testing and operational testing

Test developers traditionally distinguish between pre-testing and operational testing. Pre-testing precedes operational testing in time, and its sole purpose is to collect information about test usefulness in order to make revisions in the test itself and in the procedures for administering it, rather than to make inferences about individuals.[2] When developing a test, much of the early pre-testing is done more or less informally with individuals and small groups, and involves collecting mostly qualitative feedback. After working out potential problems with specific tasks, instructions, and administrative procedures at this level, we generally move to larger groups, with which more quantitative feedback can also be collected. The last step in the pre-testing cycle is usually a field trial, in which the test is administered under operational conditions, that is, following the exact administrative procedures that will be used when the test is given for its intended purpose. The purpose of a field trial, however, is still to collect data for assessing usefulness, and not to make inferences about individuals.

The amount and kind of pre-testing data collection will vary, depending on the purpose and scope of the test. If, for example, a teacher were planning to base tasks for a classroom test on learning tasks with which students are already familiar, much of the feedback for developing the test tasks and the administrative procedures will have been collected as part of the instructional activity. For a large-scale test that will be used to make inferences and decisions about large numbers of individuals, on the other hand, pre-testing is likely to be much more extensive and rigorous.

During operational testing the test is administered for its primary purpose: to make inferences about test takers' language ability. However, it is also important to continue to collect information on the testing procedure itself, which gives information as to what modifications might be required in order to improve the usefulness of the test.

The third stage of test development—test administration—is cyclically related to the design and operationalization stages. In these first two stages, the initial planning is carried out and a preliminary version of the test is developed for trialing. In the third stage, we determine how well the test is working in order to evaluate the qualities of usefulness and to make appropriate changes. After pre-testing it might be necessary to make changes in the design statement. Or if the specifications are satisfactory revision might be focused on modifications to the test tasks and procedures which will yield results more in keeping with the original specifications. The amounts and types of revisions will vary, depending on the nature of the feedback obtained during pre-testing, from minor editing of single test tasks, to global revision, perhaps involving returning to the design phase and rethinking some of the components of the design statement. In major testing efforts, tests or test tasks are usually tried out before use. In classroom testing this is often omitted, although giving the test to selected students or fellow teachers in advance is always a good idea, since this can provide useful information for improving the test and test tasks.

Collecting feedback for assessing usefulness

As indicated above, the primary purpose of collecting feedback is to provide information relevant to evaluating the qualities of usefulness and to making revisions in the test. In this section we discuss specific purposes for which feedback can be collected, the kinds of feedback that can be collected, different sources of this feedback, the resources involved in obtaining feedback, and some methods for obtaining feedback.

Specific uses of information collected for assessing test usefulness

During the design and operationalization stages of test development, the primary sources of information for considering test usefulness are the qualitative judgments of the test developer and other members of the test development team, as well as potential test takers and test users. Collecting information during the test administration stage allows the test developer to obtain feedback from additional sources, permitting an initial evaluation of the usefulness of the test, based on empirical data and observations, and allowing modifications in the test or the testing procedures to improve its usefulness. There are a number of specific uses of information from test administration.

Determining the adequacy/appropriateness/efficiency of administrative procedures

Try as we may to anticipate potential problems in the testing environment and with the procedures for administering the test, and to design administrative procedures that avoid these, it is impossible to know how problem free the administrative procedures are without trying them out.

Problems with the testing environment

Problems with the testing environment have the effect of reducing one or more of the qualities of usefulness (such as reliability, validity, and impact). Such problems may be due to unexpected conditions with the physical setting, the participants, the time of the test, or to a combination of these. One type of problem stems from distracting noise at the test site, for example, noise from activities in adjacent rooms, noisy heating or air conditioning systems, test takers letting a door bang when leaving a test early, and so on. In one instance, when developing a listening test involving the use of recorded material and a test booklet we did not anticipate the possibility that the noise of turning pages might interfere with test takers hearing the recorded material. Early pre-testing of the materials with a few test takers did not reveal the problem—in fact, only a field trial with a large number of test takers at the actual testing site did so. Our solution was to allocate more time between those questions that occurred across page breaks in the test booklet.

Problems with the procedures for giving the test

Another type of potential problem comes from the test supervisors themselves. They may have insufficient training in answering procedural questions, may not be sufficiently supportive of test takers, may be unable to speak the test takers' native language, and so on. Some obvious solutions to these problems would include providing supervisors with more background information, providing simulated training sessions in which supervisors are given feedback on their non-verbal communication, providing debriefing sessions following operational test use, and so on.

Determining appropriate time allocations

A second purpose of pre-testing is to determine whether time allocations are appropriate and allow test takers to perform at their best. For example, suppose we were pre-testing a test with two separately timed sections. During pre-testing, the test developer might discover that the amount of time test takers needed to complete tasks in the first section varied widely, whereas they required essentially the same amount of time to complete tasks in the second section. One solution would be to change the order of the tasks so that the faster test takers did not need to wait for the slower ones during the first part of the test.

Another common problem is failure to anticipate how much time is required for test takers to read and understand instructions or examples, so that the actual amount of usable time for carrying out the test task varies from test taker to test taker. This may result in the test being less valid for some test takers than for others, and thus less useful overall. One solution would be to provide a separately timed period for test takers to read the instructions and ask questions. Other possible solutions would be to make the language of the instructions easier, to reduce the length of the instructions, to rely more on simple examples, or to provide instructions in the test takers' native language.

Identifying problems in task specification and clarity of instructions

A third purpose of pre-testing is to identify problems in task specification and instructions. For example, for a writing test that included a prompt for an essay, we would want to be sure that the prompt adequately specified the nature of the required writing sample, so that the characteristics of the expected response might match, to as great an extent as possible, the critical characteristics of the TLU tasks. In the operationalization stage of test development, we could go through all of the characteristics of the test task and try to determine what needed to be said about each set of characteristics (topical content, organizational characteristics, functional characteristics, sociolinguistic characteristics) in order to adequately describe the task to the test takers. In the administration stage, pre-testing might help identify any remaining problems and allow the procedures and instructions to be modified.

Discovering how test takers respond to the test tasks

A fourth purpose of pre-testing is to obtain preliminary information on how test takers respond to the test tasks in three areas: test-taking processes, their perceptions of test tasks, and test performance. To obtain information on the first two, we will typically rely upon qualitative assessment procedures. Feedback on test-taking processes typically includes observations of test takers as they take the test and various kinds of self-reports. Feedback on how test takers perceive a test and react to it typically comes from self-reports of perceptions of the relevance of the test, its difficulty, the appropriateness of the time allocation and administration procedures, and so forth.

To obtain feedback on test performance test takers' scores are collected for individual tasks, for individual parts, and for the test as a whole. These scores can be analyzed statistically to discover how difficult the individual tasks, the parts, and the whole test are, the degree to which individual tasks are functioning like other tasks, the reliability of the test as a whole, and so forth. These scores can also be used to help judge whether the test is providing the information it was designed to provide. For example, suppose a test is designed to provide information about the degree to which test takers have mastered two registers. And suppose it is pre-tested on a sample of test takers known to include individuals with differing levels of control of the two registers, but all the test takers obtain perfect scores on the test. It might then be necessary to re-examine the characteristics of the test tasks to determine what modifications to make so as to obtain the desired information. (See Suggested Readings at the end of this chapter for references on measurement and statistical analysis.)

To take another example, suppose that it was necessary to increase the interactiveness of the tasks on a writing test and therefore a writing task type was designed that required the test takers to assess a large amount of personal experience in order to respond. In the course of pre-testing the task, test takers might be asked whether they responded factually or with made-up information. Analyzing their responses to this question would provide an opportunity to compare the process the test takers actually used with the one they were intended to use. Or those who relied upon made-up information might be asked why they did so rather than using their real experience. It might then be discovered that the test takers did not all have the expected background knowledge and experience, in which case the test task might not be either appropriate or equally interactive for all test takers.

Kinds of feedback

Feedback about test takers' language ability

Feedback about test takers' language ability includes information on the extent to which the test tasks require the test takers to use components of language ability (organizational and pragmatic knowledge and the meta-cognitive strategies) and topical knowledge. This kind of information is useful in making a preliminary assessment of the construct validity, authenticity, and interactiveness of the test tasks. For example, suppose a writing task were designed to measure knowledge of textual organization of test takers with a wide range of language ability, from beginner to advanced. Quantitative analysis of the scores might indicate a problem if very little variability were found when more was expected. Subsequent qualitative feedback (from observation of procedures the test takers followed in organizing their compositions, from analysis of the test takers' compositions, or from self-reports of test takers) might provide additional information—perhaps indicating that the test task itself did not actually require high levels of organizational knowledge to complete satisfactorily.

Feedback about the testing procedure itself

Feedback about the testing procedure itself includes information on circumstances and events taking place during the test administration. This may pertain either to activities of the test takers or to circumstances or activities surrounding the test takers. This kind of information is useful in evaluating the degree to which the testing environment supports the test takers in doing their best work. For example, suppose during the pre-testing of a test involving a composition writing task, a number of test takers asked questions about the length of the composition, the relative importance of various grading criteria, and so forth. This information might be used to revise the instructions, perhaps by providing more information as well as some specific examples. Or during pre-testing of a test involving the use of an audio tape, it might be noted that it was not equally audible in all parts of the room. As a result more loudspeakers might be supplied for the final version of the test.

Where to get the feedback

During test administration, feedback can be obtained from test takers, test administrators, and test users. Test takers can provide feedback on their perceptions of and attitudes toward the test and test tasks, and on their performance. Test administrators/proctors can provide feedback on the degree to which the administration procedures are conducive to the test takers' performing at their best. Test users can provide feedback on the usefulness of the scores with respect to their particular needs.

The decision as to where to get feedback depends upon the use to be made of it. If the focus is on tailoring a test to the abilities of a specific group of test takers, they would be the primary source of feedback. For example, to determine if the test was appropriate for a given group of test takers, the test could be administered and it could be determined what proportion of the test takers performed well (or poorly) on the test. Or the test takers could be asked for their reactions to the instructions, clarity of the task, appropriateness of the task, and so forth.

If the purpose of collecting feedback were to determine whether or not the test was practical for the people administering and scoring it, it would be obtained from these individuals. For example, feedback from oral interview test administrators might be obtained using a questionnaire about their perception of the clarity of the test tasks, the amount of time they had to complete the tasks, the understandability of the rating scales, and so forth.

If feedback on the use of test scores was required, it would be natural to go directly to the users for this information. For example, a placement test might be given to a sample of students with whom the teachers affected by placement decisions are familiar, the students placed using the preliminary version of the test, and the teachers provided with placement levels, and then asked whether they thought the levels were appropriate.

Amounts of resources involved in obtaining feedback

In language testing practice, it is fairly common to end the process of collecting feedback to improve the usefulness of a test after the test has been used the first time, as is often the case with a classroom test used as an end-of-course examination. This can also happen, although probably not as frequently, in the development of high-stakes tests, if no more improvements are made to the test after the initial pre-testing and it is only used to obtain scores. It is our belief, however, that this practice of collecting feedback only the first time a test is used is generally counterproductive. We take the view that the more care taken to develop a test and the more feedback obtained on usefulness, the more useful it will be. Furthermore, we would argue that the process of obtaining feedback to improve test usefulness should continue as long as the test continues to be used. For example, if we were developing a comprehensive oral interview for use in evaluating the success of an entire undergraduate foreign language program, feedback might continue to be obtained on the usefulness of the test over its entire life span, perhaps by periodically debriefing examiners and test takers and making appropriate modifications to the test itself. In such a situation, the process of collecting feedback for assessing usefulness and improving the test might be considered to be an ongoing activity that is a part of every test administration.

This also applies to the development of teacher-made tests for classroom use. We feel that such tests will be much more useful if extra resources are allocated to designing them, collecting feedback on their usefulness, and revising them, rather than 'reinventing the wheel' each time a similar test is required. In this regard, it should be kept in mind that although collecting feedback on usefulness is essential, it need not necessarily be elaborate or cumbersome. Adopting our approach to test development thus implies that the test developer will be much less likely to develop a test and use it only once.

Of course, in order to decide how much and what kind of feedback to obtain in test administration, the usefulness of the feedback must be balanced against the cost (in terms of resources) of obtaining it. For example, if we were funded to develop a battery of placement tests for use in a large intensive English program, we might feel justified in using a portion of the funds to pay individuals to take the test and go through a lengthy debriefing process prior to the first operational use of the test. On the other hand, if we were developing a midterm examination for use in a current course, we might feel less justified in taking time from instruction to put students through an involved pretesting process. Instead, we might collect more feedback before, during, and following each operational use of the test. We might also use economical procedures such as short questionnaires attached to the end of the test or selective debriefing of a few of the test takers to obtain feedback. Ultimately, what is important is to balance the intended use of the test with the resources available.

Methods for obtaining feedback

Questionnaires

Questionnaires ask the test takers to respond to specific queries about various aspects of their test taking experience. Three commonly used formats for questionnaires are multiple-choice questions, rating scales, and open-ended questions.

Multiple-choice questionnaires

Multiple-choice questionnaires can be used to obtain quantitative feedback when test developers have in mind a number of specific test-taking strategies about which they want feedback from test takers. For example, Nevo (1989) describes a procedure in which test takers are provided with a list of test-taking strategies, each appearing with a brief description designed to prompt rapid processing of the checklist. The test takers are asked to indicate which of the strategies they used in responding to each item. In effect, in this procedure the test takers answered a 16-alternative multiple-choice question following each test item.

Example (1) illustrates how such strategies might be used:

1   After you answer each item, check which of the following strategies you used to answer the item:

   Item 1
   Strategies

   Background knowledge: general knowledge outside the text called up by the reader in order to cope with written material.
   Guessing: blind guessing not based on any particular rationale.

> *Returning to the passage:* returning to the text to look for the correct answer, after reading the questions and the multiple-choice alternatives.
> Etc.

The multiple-choice format can be modified in several ways. One modification would be to define the entire strategy only once at the beginning of the feedback form and list only the name of the strategy after each item. Another modification would be to name and define the strategies once at the beginning of the item and have the respondent simply list the numbers of the strategies used after each item. A strength of the multiple-choice format is that it allows the feedback collector to focus and limit responses to particular kinds of feedback. A weakness is that stakeholders may use strategies outside of the range of alternatives provided in the checklist, and these strategies may thus be missed by the person collecting the feedback.

Rating scales

Rating scales can also be used to obtain feedback from stakeholders on the strength and direction of their feelings about specific test-related issues. Several questions using rating scales (Sternfeld 1989, 1992) are illustrated in (2)–(7)

2 How well does this test measure the ability to write extemporaneously in German on a familiar topic?

very poorly				very well
1	2	3	4	5

3 How well prepared did you feel for this kind of test?

not at all				very well
1	2	3	4	5

4 How clear were the instructions?

not at all				very clear
1	2	3	4	5

5 How well do you think you did in absolute terms?

0%				100%
1	2	3	4	5

6 How well did you do relative to your hypothetical 'peak performance'?

worst performance				best performance
1	2	3	4	5

7 How useful was this test *to you* for learning about your German-language skills?

  not at all useful   very useful
  1   2   3   4   5

A strength of rating scales is that they elicit responses to specific questions in the form of scaled, quantifiable data which can then be subjected to powerful statistical analyses. A weakness is that they restrict the range and content of stakeholders' responses.

Open-ended questions

Open-ended questions provide a third format for a questionnaire. In this format, the test taker is simply asked to provide feedback by means of a free response to a question. Nevo (1989: 215) combines this method with multiple-choice questions by including the option 'other strategy' along with a space to describe it.

A strength of the open-ended questionnaire format is that it elicits responses that might not be anticipated. A weakness is that it does not insure that the respondent has considered specific responses which are of interest.

Think-aloud protocols

A second general method for obtaining feedback is by means of think-aloud protocols. Think-aloud protocols are accounts given by the test takers of the processes they go through while actually taking the test. They provide an opportunity for test takers to describe their test-taking processes while actually using them. Such protocols can be provided orally and in writing, as illustrated in (8) and (9).

8 In the following test of reading comprehension, as you take the test, describe whatever you are doing as you are doing it. Record your description by speaking into the microphone provided.

9 In the following test of writing ability, as you write your composition, briefly write down the process you are using.

A strength of the think-aloud protocol is that it is the most immediate of those described. Feedback is obtained on the test-taking process as it is being carried out (at least in the oral format). In the written format, responses may be slightly delayed. A weakness is the relative lack of control of the content of the feedback and the practical difficulty of obtaining immediate feedback for tests of listening and speaking in which the test taker is highly involved. For such tests even delayed feedback can be useful. (10) is an example of slightly delayed feedback that a test taker provided on her experience of taking an experimental videotaped lecture listening comprehension test.

10   Describe here your thoughts and feelings as you took the test [video-taped lecture listening comprehension test]

The Instructions were too fast for me. I couldn't get my sheets out in time, and gave up. Speech style for lecture was not ordinary spoken language. I got lost in the questions and couldn't figure out which question I was supposed to be on. I spent time searching the questions [written in German] for what I was supposed to be listening for and got upset, which interfered with my listening. I tuned out the last three quarters of the test.

Observation and description

A third general method of obtaining feedback from test administration is to have an outside observer monitor the test-taking process and describe what was observed. This can be done either in an open-ended format in which the observer simply notes whatever she happens to notice, or it can be done by providing the observer with directives or checklists which define specific categories of behaviors to be observed.

Interviews

A fourth method of obtaining feedback is by providing 'debriefing' inter-views for test takers after the test-taking process. Test takers can be invited to meet with test developers and talk about their test-taking experience. This can be used either as an opportunity for test takers to talk about whatever they want or for the interviewer to ask questions focusing on specific kinds of information.

The following is an example of notes from a relatively unstructured inter-view designed primarily to allow the test takers to express their feelings about a set of experimental tests.

11   Student 'A': Felt quite negative toward exams, no personal benefit. Thought she had done well in 5th quarter German, but felt like a failure on tests, which weren't representative of what she can do. Main gripes: too little time, no human content, tests not predictive of success in country with human contact. Thought other students felt the same, that tests were a total waste of time. Resented extra learning assignments in class along with testing. Varied reactions to the different tests. Felt tests were an imposition: 'I was forced to do it.' She tried to do her best, but felt discouraged because it was her

worst performance. She only relaxed because she knew she'd get credit for the course.

12 Student 'B': Didn't resent the tests, liked that they were different, but wondered how useful they were—what was in it for him? Disliked missing three and a half days of class time. Liked some tests, not others. Said some tests (such as writing) were mostly irrelevant for him. Liked to be able to be debriefed. Said tests were well organized and liked the researcher's comments on the difficulty of various listening tests. Generally positive comments.

As these two summaries indicate, one strength of a debriefing interview is that it provides test takers with an opportunity to interact personally with test developers. This lets them know that they have been heard and may contribute to positive impact. A weakness is that the format is costly in terms of time and may be less efficient if a large amount of feedback on specific issues is required.

Summary

The third stage in test development involves the collection of empirical data during the administration of tests to test takers, for the purpose of evaluating the qualities of usefulness. The collection of data typically takes place at two points in time: pre-testing, which takes place before the test is actually used for its intended purpose, and operational testing, which takes place when the test is used for the purposes for which it was designed. During pre-testing, two kinds of feedback are gathered: about the test takers' language ability and about the testing procedure and the test itself. During actual test use this kind of information continues to be gathered so that modifications can be made to improve the test's usefulness.

Procedures for giving a test involve guiding test takers through the process of taking the test in accordance with the procedures specified in the test blueprint. These are designed to maximize *all* of the qualities of usefulness of the test and include preparing the testing environment, communicating the instructions, maintaining a supportive testing environment, and collecting the tests.

Feedback obtained during test administration includes information about the administrative procedures, including time allocation, problems in task specifications, and test takers' responses to the test tasks. During pre-testing, feedback can be collected in a variety of ways, including qualitative case studies of individual reactions as well as qualitative and quantitative data from larger groups of stakeholders. During operational testing, the form of the test is relatively fixed and the test is already in use, so feedback collected at this point is generally used for the purpose of describing the characteristics of the test in order to inform test users of its qualities of usefulness.

The amount of time and energy involved in obtaining feedback will depend upon the importance of the test. In low-stakes tests, relatively fewer resources might be devoted to obtaining feedback, whereas in high-stakes tests, gathering feedback might be a large-scale operation. However, even low-stakes tests can be improved by planning to use them over an extended period of time and collecting feedback on usefulness during each operational administration. Feedback can be gathered via a variety of methods, including questionnaires, think-aloud protocols, observation and description, and interviews, and these methods can be selected, modified, and used according to the resources at hand.

Exercises

1   Consider the problems with the testing setting discussed on pages 232–4. How might different types of problems with the testing setting affect the qualities of reliability, construct validity, authenticity, interactiveness, impact, and practicality? Do different types of problems affect the different qualities in the same way?

2   Consider the problems with the procedures for giving the test discussed on pages 236–7. How might different types of problems with the testing setting affect the qualities of reliability, construct validity, authenticity, interactiveness, impact, and practicality? Do different types of problems affect the different qualities in the same way?

3   Recall a test you have developed in the past. Describe the process you used to pre-test and administer the test. Which of the procedures described in this chapter did you follow? Why? How might you change the procedures if you developed the test again?

4   Think of a test that you might develop. Prepare a list of pre-testing and administration procedures for this test.

5   Recall a test you took. To what extent did the administration procedures help you do your best work? To what extent did they get in the way? What changes would you suggest?

6   Recall a test you have used. What kinds of feedback on usefulness from stakeholders did you obtain? What kinds of feedback might you now want to obtain if you used the test again? What procedures might you use to obtain this feedback?

7   Recall a time when you developed a test for classroom use and then used it only once. What kinds of resources went into developing this test? What other opportunities may have existed for using this test again? How might you have allocated available resources toward developing a more useful test to be administered on multiple occasions?

8   If you are a teacher who regularly needs to develop classroom tests,

think of ways in which you might reorganize your current testing program in order to channel available resources into improving your tests,
rather than reinventing them.

9   How have you traditionally given tests? What kinds of impressions do
you think your procedures have made on the test takers? Do you think
these impressions have contributed positively to the usefulness of your
tests? If not, what changes might you make in your test giving
procedures?

10   Do some library research on recent controversies in educational measurement (not necessarily language testing). Try to find instances where
tests 'made the news' due to administrative issues, such as a cheating
scandal that was later solved by an administrative change, or a lawsuit
brought by an examinee who detected some questionable practice.
These are examples of operational feedback of a very critical nature.
What does it mean to a test developer or test user when his/her test
gets in the news? What kind of feedback is that, and how can it affect
later test practice?

Suggested readings

Educational Measurement and Statistical Analysis

Cronbach, L. J. 1989. *Essentials of Psychological Testing.* 4th Edn. New
York: Harper and Row.

Glass, G. V. and K. D. Hopkins. 1984. *Statistical Methods in Education
and Psychology.* 2nd Edn. New York: Prentice-Hall.

Guilford, J. P. and B. Fruchter. 1978. *Fundamental Statistics in Psychology
and Education.* 6th Edn. New York: McGraw-Hill.

Research methods for applied linguistics

Hatch, E. and A. Lazaraton. 1991. *The Research Manual: Design and Statistics for Applied Linguistics.* New York: Newbury House Publishers.

Johnson, D. 1992. *Approaches to Research in Second Language Learning.*
London: Longman.

Nunan, D. 1992. *Research Methods in Language Learning.* Cambridge:
Cambridge University Press.

Approaches to collecting feedback

Cohen, A. D. 1994. *Assessing Language Ability in the Classroom.* Boston:
Heinle and Heinle.

Færch, C. and G. Kasper. 1987. *Introspection in Second Language Research*. Clevedon, UK: Multilingual Matters.

Nevo, N. 1989. 'Test-taking strategies on a multiple-choice test of reading comprehension.' *Language Testing* 6/2: 199–215 (cited in Cohen 1992).

Sternfeld, S. 1989. *Test Packet for the University of Utah's Immersion/ Multiliteracy Program*. Photocopied materials.

Sternfeld, S. 1992. 'An experiment in foreign education: The University of Utah's Immersion/Multiliteracy Program'. In R. J. Courchêne, J.-I. Glidden, J. St. John, and C. Thérien (eds.): *Comprehension-based Language Teaching/L'enseignement des langues secondes axé sur la compréhension*. pp. 407–32. Ottawa: University of Ottawa Press.

Notes

1   Although the terms 'information' and 'feedback' may convey slightly different meanings, with 'information' relatively neutral and 'feedback' implying purposefulness and focusing on the receiving of information, we will use these terms more or less synonymously. Note that 'pre-test' does not mean 'practice test' (test administered for the purpose of giving test takers practice in taking the test).

2   The term 'pre-test' can be used to refer to the procedure itself, as well as to the activity, so that 'pre-test' is commonly used as either a noun or a verb. Other terms that are commonly used more or less synonymously with 'pre-test' include 'pilot', 'trial', and 'try-out'.

PART THREE

Illustrative test development projects

Introduction

In this part of the book we provide a set of illustrative test development projects, which include a wide variety of task types, and cover a wide range of language abilities. The purpose of these projects is to illustrate different ways in which the considerations and procedures discussed in the first two parts of the book can be applied in practical test development situations, as well as to provide exercises for students to work on. In describing the projects in this part, we follow the design procedures described in Chapters 5–12, systematically going through the three stages of test development (design, operationalization, and administration).

In Project 1, we provide a complete design statement, blueprint, and test. This project is referred to in a number of places in Parts One and Two and can be used when you want to be sure you will find all of the steps in the design and development procedures fully illustrated. In Projects 2–7 we provide examples of partially developed projects, in which some parts of the procedures are fully developed and other parts are either partially developed or not developed at all. Students can work through these and complete them cumulatively as they work through the middle part of the book. Projects 2–3 may be particularly useful, in that they illustrate the kinds of changes in test design that might be needed to reflect minor differences in a single testing situation. Projects 8–10 illustrate how our approach to test development can be applied to the development of classroom achievement tests. First, they illustrate the use of classroom teaching and learning tasks as a basis for developing test tasks. That is, rather than attempting to identify TLU tasks in situations outside the classroom, in these projects the test developers have based test tasks on a language instructional TLU domain, as discussed in Chapter 6 (pages 104–6). Second, they demonstrate the use of syllabus content, in the form of teaching and learning objectives or targets, as a basis for defining the constructs to be measured. Third, they illustrate ways in which our framework of task characteristics can be adapted to suit the needs of a particular situation. The last two projects, developed by students, may use slightly differing terminology and illustrate different ways of defining the construct and specifying TLU tasks.

We suggest that you consider these projects as examples of the process of test design rather than as tasks that you 'should' use for your own testing needs. In addition, we urge you to consider the possibility of using these design techniques for designing different types of tasks for other language testing situations, as well. Our goal is to help you develop flexibility and confidence in your own ability to develop varieties of tests for your own purposes.

Project 1
Fully developed example of high-stakes selection and placement test for students entering a university writing program

Introduction

In this project we describe the development of a test for students entering a university-level sheltered academic writing program for non-native speakers of English in an English-medium university. (The 'sheltered' program includes courses to which only the non-native speakers are admitted. 'Non-sheltered' versions of courses with many of the same general objectives are also offered for native speakers of English.) The test results are to be used to decide whether the students do or do not meet minimum standards necessary to be admitted into the sheltered program, and if they do, whether or not they should be exempted from study in the program and allowed to enter the non-sheltered program for native speakers of English.

To elicit a writing sample, we developed a prompt that provides a context for the writing task and specifies a number of criteria that the writing sample should meet. It also specifies a writing process for the test takers to follow. It is on the basis of the students following these processes and satisfying these criteria that the decisions described above are made. The components of the prompt are patterned after a model of writing currently used in both sheltered and non-sheltered university writing programs.

I Design statement

1 Test purposes

A *Inferences*
About test takers' language ability in a wide range of academic domains in which writing is necessary

B *Decisions*
1 **Stakes:** relatively high; test results used to make decisions about the amount of required course work for test takers.

2 Individuals affected: test takers, teachers in the writing program.

3 Specific decisions to be made
   a *Selection*
     1   admission into sheltered writing program.
     2   exemption from study in the sheltered writing program and admission to the non-sheltered program for native speakers of English.
   b *Diagnosis*
      for students placed in sheltered writing program, tests will be made available to teachers as writing samples for diagnosing writing problems of specific students.

2   Description of TLU domain/s and task types

A   *Identification of tasks*

1 TLU domain: real-life and language instructional

2 Identification and selection of TLU tasks for consideration as test tasks
   a The TLU tasks to be analyzed were identified on the basis of a needs analysis carried out with instructors in the ESL writing program and content courses. The results of such an analysis led us to exclude relatively less crucial tasks, such as 'filling in a course evaluation' or 'writing a note to an instructor explaining why one might have to miss a class' from the set of tasks to be analyzed. (See additional discussion under 'Describing TLU Task Types' in Chapter 6, Section 2, pages 101–10.)
   b On the basis of the following analysis of the characteristics of TLU Tasks 1–4, we would conclude that Tasks 1 and 2 (see Table P1.1) belong to the same task type, 'Term paper', due to the high degree of overlap among the characteristics of the two tasks. We would probably also conclude that Tasks 3 and 4 belong to different task types due to the degree of dissimilarity among the features of the two tasks (see Table P1.2). To show this, we have highlighted the distinctive characteristics of Tasks 3 and 4 in bold type.

B   *Description of TLU task types*

See Tables P1.1 and P1.2.

	TLU TASK 1	TLU TASK 2
	Term paper analyzing a piece of literature	Term paper analyzing a biological process
SETTING		
Physical characteristics	Location: home, library, computer writing lab, classroom. Noise level: varied, including quiet, well-lit conditions (such as in a library) or crowded, noisy conditions such as at a table in the student union. Temperature and humidity: typically comfortable on campus, varied off campus. Seating conditions: varied: individual desks, tables, computer consoles. Lighting: typically good on campus, varied off campus. Materials and equipment and degree of familiarity pencil/pen, paper, word processor, monolingual and bilingual dictionaries, thesauruses, spelling checkers, grammar checkers. Students likely to be familiar with most of these with the exception of word processors.	Same as for Task 1
Participants	Teachers, classmates, friends who might help students with writing, all of whom are likely to be familiar to test takers and have a positive attitude toward them.	Same as for Task 1
Time of task	Varied, including daytime, evenings, and weekends.	Same as for Task 1
INPUT		
Format		
Channel	Audio and visual, but typically visual, could include oral meetings with the instructor, as the term paper topic is refined.	Same as for Task 1
Form	Language	Language and non-language (tables, pictures, equations, etc.)
Language	Generally target	Same as for Task 1
Length	Prompt: variable. Might be short, or very lengthy, including a list of possible topics, or of points that needed to be included. Task: Input used in writing the paper: long.	Same as for Task 1
Type	Prompt and task	Same as for Task 1
Speededness	Unspeeded	Same as for Task 1
Vehicle	Live	Same as for Task 1

	TLU TASK 1	TLU TASK 2
Language characteristics		
Organizational characteristics		
Grammatical	Vocabulary: wide range of general and technical vocabulary. Morphology and syntax: wide range of organized structures. Graphology: generally typewritten.	Same as for Task 1
Textual	Variable: wide range of cohesive devices and organizational patterns.	Same as for Task 1
Pragmatic characteristics		
Functional	Variable: ideational, manipulative, and imaginative.	Variable, but primarily manipulative and ideational.
Sociolinguistic	Dialect/variety: variable standard and regional. Register: formal and informal. Naturalness: natural. Cultural references and figurative language: variable.	Dialect/variety: mostly standard. Register: mostly formal. Naturalness: natural and unnatural (examples of test taker responses). Cultural references and figurative language: variable, but probably relatively restricted.
Topical characteristics	Variable: literary topics.	Restricted: analysis of a biological process.
EXPECTED RESPONSE		
Format		
Channel	Visual	Same as for Task 1
Form	Language	Same as for Task 1
Language	Target	Same as for Task 1
Length	Relatively long: 10–30 typewritten pages	Same as for Task 1
Type	Extended production	Same as for Task 1
Speededness	Generally unspeeded	Same as for Task 1
Language characteristics		
Organizational characteristics		
Grammatical	Vocabulary: general and technical. Morphology and syntax: standard English. Graphology: typewritten.	Same as for Task 1
Textual	Cohesion: cohesive. Rhetorical: extended discussion and analysis, probably without topic headings for a formal outline. Thesis might be stated at end of paper.	Cohesion: cohesive. Rhetorical: deductive presentation with thesis and divisions stated at beginning. Topic headings generally included.
Pragmatic characteristics		
Functional	Ideational, heuristic, possibly imaginative.	Ideational, heuristic
Sociolinguistic	Dialect/variety: standard. Register: formal. Naturalness: natural. Cultural references and figurative language: variable.	Same as for Task 1
Topical characteristics	Variable: literary topics	Restricted: analysis of a biological process
RELATIONSHIP BETWEEN INPUT AND RESPONSE		
Reactivity	Non-reciprocal	Same as for Task 1
Scope of relationship	Extremely broad	Same as for Task 1
Directness of relationship	Indirect	Same as for Task 1

Table P1.1:   Characteristics of TLU Tasks 1 and 2 for Writing Project 1

	TLU TASK 3	TLU TASK 4
	Essay Exam	Proposal
SETTING		
Physical characteristics	Location: classroom. Noise level: quiet. Temperature and humidity: comfortable. Seating conditions: individual desk with arm rest for writing. Lighting: well lit. Materials and equipment and degree of familiarity: bluebooks, pencil, pen. Copy of test question.	Same as for term paper
Participants	Student, teacher, other students. All familiar.	Same as for term paper
Time of task	During class hours.	Same as for term paper
INPUT		
Format		
Channel	Mostly visual	Same as for term paper
Form	Generally language	Same as for term paper
Language	Generally target	Generally target
Length	Prompt: short. Input used in writing the answer: short to medium.	Same as for term paper
Type	Prompt	Prompt
Speededness	Possibly speeded	Generally unspeeded
Vehicle	Live, if there is any spoken input.	Live, if there is any spoken input.
Language characteristics		
Organizational characteristics		
Grammatical	Same as for term paper	Same as for term paper
Textual	**Cohesive prompt, perhaps including background set up for the actual question. Other input used as basis for responding to prompt would vary widely in cohesion and rhetorical organization. More highly focused than with term paper or proposal.**	**Same as for term paper**
Pragmatic characteristics		
Functional	For the prompt: ideational and manipulative. For other input used in responding to exam question: same as for term paper.	Same as for term paper
Sociolinguistic	Same as for term paper	Same as for term paper
Topical characteristics	**More limited than term paper or proposal.**	**Same as for term paper**

	TLU TASK 3	TLU TASK 4
EXPECTED RESPONSE		
Format		
Channel	Visual	Visual
Form	Language	Language
Language	Target	Target
Length	**Relatively short: one paragraph to two pages.**	**Variable: short to long, depending on the nature of the proposal.**
Type	Same as for term paper	Same as for term paper
Speededness	**Somewhat speeded**	**Generally unspeeded**
Language characteristics		
Organizational characteristics		
Grammatical	Same as for term paper	Same as for term paper
Textual	**Perhaps more limited than for term paper, depending on the nature of the prompt.**	**Same as for term paper**
Pragmatic characteristics		
Functional	Ideational, manipulative, or other functions depending on the nature of the prompt.	Ideational and manipulative
Sociolinguistic	Same as for term paper	Same as for term paper
Topical characteristics	Perhaps more limited than for term paper.	Same as for term paper
RELATIONSHIP BETWEEN INPUT AND RESPONSE		
Reactivity	Non-reciprocal	Non-reciprocal
Scope of relationship	Moderately broad	Narrow to broad
Directness of relationship	Indirect	Indirect

Table P1.2:   Characteristics of TLU Tasks 3 and 4 for Project 1 with possible distinctive features in bold type

3   Description of characteristics of test takers

A   *Personal characteristics*

1   **Age:** 18 and above, but mostly between 18 and 23.
2   **Sex:** male and female.
3   **Nationalities:** widely varied.
4   **Immigrant status:** immigrants and international students.
5   **Native languages:** widely varied.
6   **Level and type of general education:** undergraduate transfer students with a minimum of one year's education in a North American junior college, college, or university.

7   **Type and amount of preparation or prior experience with a given test:** many test takers will be familiar with ESL proficiency tests such as the Test of English as a Foreign Language (TOEFL), the University of Cambridge Certificate of Proficiency in English (CPE), and the Michigan Test.

B   *Topical knowledge of test takers*

1   In general, relatively widely varied topical knowledge due to test takers' varying major fields of study.

2   Some highly specific topical knowledge, such as personal experience studying English, personal experience with North American culture, etc.

C   *Levels and profiles of language knowledge of test takers*

1   **General level of language ability:** intermediate to advanced.

2   **Specific writing ability:** more widely varied, low intermediate to advanced, perhaps because test takers are frequently able to use their speaking ability to compensate for very poor writing ability. Some transfer students arrive with very limited writing ability (unorganized prose, frequent errors in structure, frequent errors leading to misinterpretation of meaning, little control of register), despite their having passed English courses at other institutions. These students are at too low a level for the kind of instruction provided in the sheltered writing program for non-native speakers. They are channeled into an intensive English program instead. Others upon arrival can write extremely well (highly organized prose, well supported arguments, excellent complete control of grammar and punctuation, complete control of register, etc.). These students are ultimately exempted from the sheltered writing program altogether.

D   *Possible affective responses to taking the test*

1   Highly proficient test takers: likely to feel positive about taking the test, since it provides them with an opportunity to be exempted from the sheltered writing program, which involves more terms of study than the non-sheltered program.

2   Less proficient test takers: may feel threatened by the test, since they may not meet the minimum standards for admission into the sheltered writing program.

4   Definition of construct(s)

A   *Language ability*

Syllabus-based construct definition. The goals of the sheltered writing program specify that students completing the program should control a number of organizational and pragmatic features of written prose. We thus use a syllabus-based construct definition that includes these areas of language knowledge so that decisions can be made as to whether or not the test takers should qualify for exemption from the program. The description can be quite broad because detailed diagnostic information is not needed. The test is not used to measure control of specific structures or other language elements as might be taught in a course and measured in an achievement test. The specific components of language knowledge that are included in the construct definition are as follows:

1   **Knowledge of syntax**
    a   *Accurate use* of a range of syntactic structures.
    b   *Range and accuracy* of general purpose and specialized vocabulary, including cultural references.
2   **Knowledge of rhetorical organization:** Knowledge of features for organizing information.
3   **Knowledge of cohesion:** Knowledge of features for explicitly marking cohesive textual relationships.
4   **Knowledge of register:** Control of moderately formal register in formulaic expressions and in substantive discourse.

B   *Strategic competence*

Not included in the construct

C   *Topical knowledge*

Not included in the construct because we are interested in making inferences about components of language ability only.

5   Plan for evaluating qualities of usefulness

A   *Reliability*

1   **Setting minimum acceptable levels**
    a   *Relevant considerations*

1 Purpose: relatively high-stakes test, so minimum acceptable level for reliability will be very high.
2 Construct definition: relatively narrow range of components—language knowledge only—included in construct, so realistic to expect high level of reliability.
3 Nature of test task: single test task with only two parts, so realistic to expect high level of reliability.

b *Level*: very high.

c *How specified*: appropriate reliability estimate, adequacy of time allocation, clarity of scoring criteria.

2 **Logical evaluation**: Answer questions 1–5 in 'The logical evaluation of usefulness', Chapter 7 (pages 138–48). (See Table P1.3 at end of project, where answers to these questions are provided.)

3 **Procedures for collecting empirical evidence**

(Refer to procedures described in references in Chapter 12.)

a *Appropriate estimates of reliability*
1 Stage of development when information will be collected: try-out.
2 Procedures for collecting information: administer test twice, at a two-week interval to sample of 30 test takers. Have tests rated twice in random order by four raters. Calculate inter-rater reliability, intra-rater reliability, and test–retest reliability.

b *Adequacy of time allocation*
1 Stage of development when information will be collected: try-out.
2 Procedures for collecting information: interview 30 students

c *Clarity of scoring criteria.*
1 Stage of development when information will be collected: try-out.
2 Procedures for collecting information: interview raters.

B *Construct validity*

1 Setting minimum acceptable levels

Relevant considerations, level, and how specified (Note that for construct validity the relevant considerations and how levels are specified all seem to be integrated, unlike for reliability, where it seems relatively easy to separate them.)

a *Purpose:* relatively high-stakes test, so wide range of evidence needs to be collected in support of the validity of the score interpretations and decisions to be made.

    b *Construct definition:* evidence related to four components of language knowledge needs to be collected.

    c *Domain of generalization:* evidence supporting generalizability of score interpretations to the intended domain of generalization needs to be collected

2 **Logical evaluation:** Answer questions 6–15 in 'The logical evaluation of usefulness', Chapter 7 (pages 138–48). (See Table P1.3 at the end of this project, where answers to these questions are provided.)

3 **Procedures for collecting empirical evidence to evaluate construct validity** (Refer to procedures described in references in Chapters 7 and 12.)

    a *Is the construct definition adequate for the purpose of making exclusion, admission, and exemption decisions?*

       1 Stage of development when information will be collected: operationalization and try-out.

       2 Procedures for collecting information: interview a sample of faculty members teaching courses in which test takers will be doing academic writing and obtain feedback on the adequacy of the construct definition.

    b *Is test task free from bias?*

       1 Stage of development when information will be collected: try-out.

       2 Procedures for collecting information.

          a Interview 30 students in try-out to obtain their opinions on fairness of test task.

          b Develop several other prompts by sampling from a different set of TLU task characteristics and then conduct a concurrent validity study of the relationship among scores on responses to different prompts.

C *Authenticity*

1 **Setting minimum acceptable levels**

    a *Relevant considerations*

       1 Potential for impact on instruction is high, so minimum acceptable level for authenticity needs to be high.

       2 Domain of generalization is broad, so minimum acceptable level for authenticity does not have to be so high.

    b *Level:* moderate. (See Comment 2.)

    c *How specified*

       1 Quantitative indicators of the degree of correspondence between characteristics of TLU tasks and test task.

2   Expected perceptions of test users and test takers.

2   **Logical evaluation:** Answer questions 16–17 in 'The logical evaluation of usefulness', Chapter 7. (See Table P1.3 at the end of this project, where answers to these questions are provided.)

3   **Procedures for collecting empirical evidence to evaluate authenticity**
a   *To what extent do the characteristics of the test task correspond to those of tasks in the target language use situation?*
    1   Stage of development when information will be collected: operationalization and try-out.
    2   Procedures for collecting information: test developer, teachers, and students use checklists to determine degree of correspondence between characteristics of TLU tasks and test tasks. (See Tables P1.1, P1.2, and P1.5.)
b   *To what extent do the test developer, teachers, and students, consider the authenticity of the test task to be 'high'?*
    1   Stage of development when information will be collected: operationalization and try-out.
    2   Procedure for collecting information: use questionnaire with three-point (high, moderate, low) scale to obtain ratings of overall levels of authenticity.

D   *Interactiveness*

1   **Setting minimum acceptable levels**
a   *Relevant considerations*
    1   Involvement of test taker characteristics included in the construct definition should be high.
    2   Involvement of other characteristics of test takers should be as high as possible while not making it difficult to achieve minimum levels of usefulness of the other qualities.
b   *Levels*
    1   Language ability: high.
    2   Topical knowledge: moderate.
    3   Metacognitive strategies: moderate.
    4   Affective response: moderate.
c   *How specified:* expected degree of involvement of test taker characteristics.

2   **Logical evaluation:** Answer questions 18–25 in 'The logical evaluation of usefulness', Chapter 7 (pages 138–48). (See Table P1.3 at the end of this project, where answers to these questions are provided.)

3 **Procedures for collecting evidence of interactiveness:** as with authenticity, information on interactiveness can be gathered during the pretesting cycle of test administration, using the qualitative methods described in Chapter 12. These could address the following questions:
   a *To what extent do test takers and teachers consider the involvement of language knowledge and metacognitive strategies to be high?*
      1 Stage of development when information will be collected: operationalization, try-out, and periodically during operational use.
      2 Procedures for collecting information: have test takers and teachers evaluate the interactiveness of the test by means of a questionnaire in which they rate the degree of involvement of topical knowledge, language knowledge, and metacognitive strategies.
   b *To what extent do test takers and teachers consider the involvement of other characteristics of test takers (topical knowledge, metacognitive strategies, and affective responses) to be at least moderate?*
      1 Stage of development when information will be collected: try-out, and periodically during operational use.
      2 Procedures for collecting information: have test takers fill out a questionnaire on which they rate their affective response to the test tasks.

E *Impact*

1 **Setting minimum acceptable levels**
   a *Relevant considerations*
      1 Kinds of decisions to be made: high-stakes.
      2 Possible effects: misplacement, unnecessary money spent on tuition, for students placed at too low a level insufficient instruction in writing.
   b *Level*: very high.
   c *How specified*: expected specific influences.

2 **Logical evaluation during design and operationalization stages:** Answer questions 26–40 in 'The logical evaluation of usefulness', Chapter 7. (See Table P1.3 at the end of this project, where answers to these questions are provided.)

3 **Procedures for collecting evidence of impact**
   a *For test takers*
      1 Are all test takers informed of the purpose of the test, how it will be scored, and how decisions will be made on the basis of these scores?
         a Stage of development when information will be collected: try-out and test use.

    b Procedures for collecting information.
- i All of the test takers will be given a questionnaire to fill out at the end of the test try-out in which they are asked whether they feel that they were adequately informed of the purpose, scoring, and decisions and whether specific changes are needed. 80 per cent of respondents shall rate this information as 'adequate'.
- ii 10 per cent of test takers will be given the same questionnaire during test use. Same criteria used as in (i) above.

  2 Do 80 per cent of test takers consider the test to be 'relatively free from bias'?
- a Stage of development when information will be collected: try-out and test use.
- b Procedures for collecting information: same as for (b) above

b *For the educational system*
  1 Do teachers agree with 80 per cent of the placement decisions?
- a Stage of development when information will be collected: try-out and test use, two weeks after student has been placed in a teacher's course.
- b Procedures for collecting information: questionnaire that teacher fills in for each student placed in one of her courses.

  2 Do 80 per cent of the teachers agree that the criteria for grading the test are consistent with the objectives of the courses into which the students will be placed?
- a Stage of development when information will be collected: try-out and test use.
- b Procedures for collecting information: questionnaire that each teacher fills in each quarter after teaching in the sheltered ESL writing program.

c *For society*
  1 Do professionals in the community generally agree that the criteria for grading the tests are consistent with goals of society?
- a Stage of development when information will be collected: try-out and test use.
- b Procedures for collecting information: interview a sample of professionals in the community from a specified set of fields (for example, law, business, engineering, the arts).

F *Practicality*

1 Logical evaluation during design and operationalization stages: Answer questions 41–42 in 'The logical evaluation of usefulness', Chapter 7. (See Table P1.3 at the end of this project, where answers to these questions are provided.)

2 **Setting minimum acceptable levels:** relevant considerations.
   a Threshold level of use of resources: see 6.
   b Consequences of exceeding threshold level: not too great for moderate averages.
3 **Procedures for collecting evidence of practicality:** Is use of resources being monitored to insure that sufficient resources will be available to complete the project?
   a *Stage of development when information will be collected:* design, operationalization, try-out, and periodically during operational use.
   b *Procedures for collecting information*
      1 Monetary resources: standard accounting procedures for accounting for use of monetary resources.
      2 Human resources: questionnaire that each member of project development team fills in on a weekly basis to indicate amount of time spent on project.

6   Inventory of available resources and plan for their allocation and management

A   *Assessing demands for resources*

1 What type and relative amounts of resources are required for:
   a the specification stage.
   b the operationalization stage.
   c the try-out and use stage.
2 Are demands on test writers (teachers in sheltered writing program) consistent with the amount of time they have available for test writing?
   a Stage of development when information will be collected: specification
   b Procedures for collecting information: interview teachers in sheltered writing programs.

B   *Identification of resources that will be available for carrying out test development activities at each stage*

1 **Design stage**
   a *Human resources*
      1 Project Director: faculty member at the university teaching a full load of courses and directing the ESL teacher training program.
      2 Test writers: Project Director and five teaching assistants (TAs) currently teaching the sheltered ESL writing courses. Two of these TAs have had a course in language testing. The remaining have not. All are taking a full course load at the university.

    3   Scorers: Same five TAs as described in (2).

    4   Clerical support:

        a One department secretary who will photocopy the test materials during the specification, operationalization, and try-out stages of development.

        b One department administrative assistant who will keep records of test takers' scores.

  b *Material resources*:

    1   Space: office space already provided for the Project Director and TAs.

    2   Equipment: computers that are the personal property of the Project Director and TAs. Copy machine owned by English Department and available to Project Director and test writers.

    3   Time: no released time provided. Test development is considered part of normal work load for Project Director and test writers.

    4   Test materials: adequate paper, pencils and other material supplies.

2 Operationalization stage

  a Human resources: same as for specification stage.

  b Material resources: same as for specification stage.

3 Administration, try-out, and use stage

  a *Human resources:* Same as for specification stage, with addition of two paid test administrators at the university's testing center.

  b *Material resources:* Same as for specification stage. Also chalkboard, chalk, individual desks, large clock visible throughout the room, booklets, pencils with erasers, and a pencil sharpener, and individual chairs with arm rests for writing.

C *Allocation of resources for different test development tasks*

1 Human resources (in number of hours). See Table P1.4.

2 Space

  a Test development: Project Developer's and test writers' offices.

  b Test administration and use: Empty classroom for try-out, testing center.

3 Equipment

  a Computer time: no charge.

  b Photocopier: no charge.

  c Paper: $25.

	Design	Operationalization	Administration	Scoring	Analysis
Project Director	50	25			20
Test writers	10	10			
Editors	5	5			
Raters				30	
Administrators	5	5	3		
Support staff	2	2	2	2	2

Table P1.4:   Human resources in number of hours

D   Costs associated with the project

1   Human resources
   a   *Project Developer:* hourly cost of $50.00.
   b   *Test writers:* 25 hours each, hourly cost of $15.
   c   *Physical resources:* Space already available.
   d   *Fees charged test takers:* $15 per test taker per administration.

E   Test development time line

1   June, 1996: prepare preliminary table of specifications (Project Director).
2   July, 1996: finalize specifications (Project Director and test writers).
3   August, 1996: complete operationalization.
4   September, 1996: complete try-out.

II   Operationalization

In this project the tasks in the TLU domain are highly varied. This is because, upon completing the sheltered writing course, students will go into a variety of academic fields and content courses with different writing requirements. Thus in developing test tasks we cannot start with a single 'most important' TLU task or one that all test takers will be likely to encounter. Nor can we count on all test takers having the same topical knowledge.

Therefore, we decided to develop a more 'neutral' writing task, one that draws upon the test takers' common experience with university procedures rather than experience within a single major field of study. This 'common experience with university procedures' as 'relatively homogeneous topical knowledge' is discussed in Chapter 6. We also decided to build into the prompt the kinds of information and considerations that good writers generally take into consideration when writing. See also the discussion of the role of topical knowledge in the construct definition, Option 1, possible solution 2, in Chapter 6 (pages 112–13).

Blueprint

Test structure

1 **Number of parts/tasks:** the test is organized around a single task with two parts—the comparison/contrast section and the recommendations section (see below). The purpose of the two parts is to require the test takers to demonstrate two methods of rhetorical organization.

2 **Salience of parts:** parts are clearly distinct, as specified in the prompt.

3 **Sequence of parts:** as per sequence normally followed in a proposal of this type.

4 **Relative importance of parts or tasks:** first part of task is more important, since it can stand alone while second part cannot.

5 **Number of tasks per part:** one.

Test task specifications

1 **Purpose:** see design statement.

2 **Definition of construct:** see design statement.

3 **Setting:** see characteristics of individual test tasks.

4 **Time allotment:** two hours.

5 **Instructions**
  a *Language:* the target language (English) because the test takers have a wide variety of native languages. The test takers read the instructions as they are read aloud by the proctor.
  b *Channel:* visual (writing).
  c *Instructions:* (see Appendix 1).

6 **Characteristics of input and expected response.** (See Table P1.5 overleaf)

7 **Scoring method**
  a Criteria for correctness: criterion-referenced language ability scales based upon theory-based definitions of the ability to use language use in writing tasks. Ratable samples of test takers' writing will be scored from 1 to 4 on knowledge of grammar, textual knowledge, knowledge of vocabulary, and knowledge of register. (None of the test takers are at level '0' on any scale, although zero is included in each scale.) (See Appendix 1 for actual scales used.)

b Procedures for scoring the response: all compositions are read and
   rated independently by two trained raters. The raters review the
   scales before each rating session. No rating session lasts longer than
   45 minutes. The raters assign ratings on the four scales and make
   independent decisions on exclusion, admission, and exemption,
   based upon their ratings and the criteria described above. If the first
   two raters disagree on their ratings, additional raters rate the composition until two raters agree. (See Chapter 11 for a discussion of
   procedures for training raters.)

c Explicitness of criteria and procedures: the test takers are informed
   in general terms about the scoring criteria (in the prompt). (See
   Appendix 1.)

TEST TASK CHARACTERISTICS

SETTING

Physical characteristics	Location: university testing center. Noise level: low. Temperature and humidity: comfortable. Seating conditions: individual chairs with arm rests for writing. Lighting: well lit. Materials and equipment and degree of familiarity: large clock visible throughout the room, booklets, pencils with erasers, and a pencil sharpener.
Participants	Paid test administrators in the university's testing center, trained and experienced in test administration, all of whom are unlikely to be familiar to test takers but have a positive attitude toward them.
Time of task	Wednesday afternoon at 3:00 p.m. every other month.
INPUT **Format**	
Channel	Visual
Form	Language
Language	Target
Length	Medium
Type	Complex prompt that provides a context for the writing task and specifies a number of criteria that the writing sample should meet. It also specifies a specific writing process for the test takers to follow.
Speededness	Unspeeded
Vehicle	Live
Language **characteristics**	
Organizational *characteristics*	
Grammatical	Vocabulary: general and specifically related to admissions procedures and characteristics of written prose. Morphology and syntax: standard English. Graphology: typewritten.
Textual	Cohesion: cohesive within each step in the prompt. Organization: list of procedures (for writing an essay).
Pragmatic characteristics	
Functional	Ideational and manipulative (describing, instructing).

Sociolinguistic	Dialect/variety: standard. Register: moderately formal. Naturalness: natural. Cultural references and figurative language: none.
Topical characteristics	Prompt for written proposal: admissions procedures to American universities.
EXPECTED RESPONSE	
FORMAT	
Channel	Visual
Form	Language
Language	Target (English)
Length	Moderate (500 words) in order to provide a writing sample with characteristics that conform to those on which responses will be rated.
Type	Extended production.
Speededness	Depends upon perception of test takers. Not designed to be highly speeded.
Language characteristics	
Organizational characteristics	
Grammatical	Vocabulary: general and technical (specifically related to admissions procedures). Morphology and syntax: standard English. Graphology: typewritten.
Textual	Cohesion: cohesive throughout. Rhetorical: written proposal in essay form.
Pragmatic characteristics	
Functional	Ideational and manipulative (describing, justifying, proposing, arguing, comparing, contrasting).
Sociolinguistic	Dialect/variety: standard. Register: moderately formal. Naturalness: natural throughout. Cultural references: events and procedures associated with admissions problems in two universities. Figurative language: none.
Topical characteristics	Admissions procedures to American universities.
RELATIONSHIP BETWEEN INPUT AND RESPONSE	
Reactivity	Non-reciprocal
Scope of relationship	Somewhat broad (there is quite a lot of input in the prompt).
Directness of relationship	Indirect

Table P1.5:   Characteristics of test task

III   Administration, try-out, and use

1   Administration

A   *Preparing the testing environment*

1   The testing environment will be prepared by the personnel at the university testing center.

2   Go over the instructions with the test administrators at the testing

center. Make sure they understand them and answer any questions they may have.

B   *Communicating the instructions*

Have the test administrators read the instructions aloud while the test takers look at them in their test booklets.

C   *Maintaining a supportive testing environment*

Make sure that the testing center will keep a proctor on hand to answer questions about the instructions or testing procedures.

D   *Collecting the tests*

Have test administrators collect all testing materials with the exception of the test takers' working outline.

2   Try-out

A   *Get information about administrative procedure*

1   Debrief test administrators and test takers about problems with administrative procedures.
2   Hypothetical feedback: many test takers indicate that they prefer to work on a word processor.
3   Hypothetical modification of administrative procedure: develop plan with testing center to provide access to word processors, programs, and clean disks for storing documents. Change test task characteristic 'Characteristic of test task setting: physical setting: materials and equipment' accordingly.

B   *Determine appropriate time allocations*

1   Debrief test takers about time allocation.
2   Hypothetical feedback: test takers indicate that two hours is inadequate. They would prefer two 50-minute writing periods with five-minute breaks, followed by an additional 30 minutes for final revision.
3   Hypothetical modification of time allocations: change test task specification 'time allotment' according to feedback.

C   *Identify problems in task specification*

1   Debrief test takers about task specification

2   Hypothetical feedback: test takers indicate that they do not remember clearly the procedures they followed in getting admitted to the institution from which they transferred, which made it difficult for them to complete the comparison/contrast portion of the essay.

3   Hypothetical modification of task specification: ask test takers to provide a list of alternative processes that they had gone through at the two institutions and develop alternative test task specifications (specifically, changes to topical content of test task input and expected response) based on these processes.

D   *Obtain preliminary information on how test takers react to the test*

1   Debrief test takers about appropriacy and fairness of test as a whole.

3   Use

A   *Scoring*

Testing center sends tests to English Department. Project Director schedules a meeting of teaching assistants to score tests.

B   *Record keeping*

Project Director gives scores to English Department's Administrative Assistant who records them and mails out score reports and recommendations to test takers. A record of scores on each of the scoring scales is kept.

C   *Archiving*

English Department Administrative Assistant keeps tests on file for one year.

Appendix 1: Test for Project 1

Instructions to test taker

Read these instructions as they are read aloud by the proctor.

1   This is a test of your ability to write a proposal.

2   Read the prompt below. Raise your hand if you have any questions about the prompt. A proctor will come to help you.

3   Using the pencil and lined paper provided, write your response on every other line.

4   Your composition will be scored on the clarity with which you make your proposal, the logic of the evidence you provide to support your proposal, your organization, your control of grammar and punctuation, and your ability to tailor your writing to your audience. You will not be graded on your specific opinions.

5   You will have two hours to complete your proposal. Begin now.

Prompt

1   *Situation and role*: As students entering this university, you have been exposed to a variety of requirements. Also, since you have transferred from another university, you have had an opportunity to experience a different set of procedures. The admissions office would like to improve its procedures and welcomes feedback from new students.

2   *Purpose*: Write a formal proposal in which you provide feedback on the admissions procedures used at this university. First compare and contrast the two sets of admissions procedures you have experienced and evaluate them in terms of their efficiency and humanitarian considerations. Then make specific recommendations for changing one or the other to make it more humane without losing efficiency.

3   *Audience*: The director of admissions at the university.

4   *Structure*: Your composition should be written in the form of a formal proposal of about 500 words. The information you present should be well organized with a clearly stated thesis. Your proposal should contain an introduction, several body paragraphs, and a conclusion. Paragraphs should, for the most part, be carefully organized with clear, limiting topic sentences. Ideas should be clearly and explicitly related to one another.

5   *Evidence*: The evidence you use to support your recommendations should include descriptions of specific procedures you have encountered. Evidence can also include reports of other students who have commented on such procedures.

6   *Language*: The language should be moderately formal: avoid both highly formal and highly informal (chatty) language. Use correct grammar.

7   Your composition will be scored on the basis of your control of grammar, your ability to organize your writing, control of vocabulary, and

your ability to write in a moderately formal style suitable for your intended audience.

You will have two hours to complete your proposal. Use the following process.

1 Prepare a rough outline of your proposal. (You do not have to turn in your outline.)

2 Write a rough draft.

3 Read over your rough draft, checking for organization, logic, and clarity.

4 Write a final draft. Write on every other line.

5 Edit your final draft and correct any mistakes in grammar, punctuation, and spelling. Cross out mistakes and write in the corrections above the line. If you believe a word might be misspelled so that you would check it in a dictionary, circle it. (Circled words will not be counted as misspelled.)

Scoring scales

Knowledge of syntax

Note: This example scale is defined in terms of range and accuracy, with five levels.

Theoretical construct definition:	knowledge of syntax
Operational construct definition:	evidence of accurate use of a variety of syntactic structures, as demonstrated in the context of the specific tasks (as specified in the task specifications) that have been presented, and as rated on the following scale:

Levels of ability/ mastery	**Description**
0 None	*No evidence of knowledge* of syntax
	Range: zero
	Accuracy: not relevant
1 Limited	*Limited knowledge* of syntax
	Range: small
	Accuracy: poor, moderate, or good accuracy. If test taker only attempts a very few structures, accuracy may be good.

2   Moderate   *Moderate knowledge* of syntax

Range: medium
Accuracy: moderate to good accuracy within range. If test taker attempts structures outside of the range that is controlled, accuracy may be poor.

3   Extensive   *Extensive knowledge* of syntax

Range: large, few limitations
Accuracy: good accuracy, few errors

4   Complete   *Evidence of complete knowledge* of syntax

Range: evidence of unlimited range
Accuracy: evidence of complete control

Knowledge of vocabulary

Note: This scale is defined in terms of range and accuracy with five levels.

Theoretical construct definition: knowledge of general purpose and specialized vocabulary items, including cultural references

Operational construct definition: evidence of accurate use of a variety of general purpose and specialized vocabulary items, including cultural references, as demonstrated in the context of the specific tasks (as specified in the task specifications) that have been presented, and as rated on the following scale:

Levels of ability/ mastery	**Description**

0   Zero   *No evidence of knowledge* of vocabulary

Range: zero
Accuracy: not relevant

1   Limited   *Limited knowledge* of vocabulary

Range: small
Accuracy: vocabulary items frequently used imprecisely

2   Moderate   *Moderate knowledge* of vocabulary

Range: moderate size
Accuracy: vocabulary items frequently used imprecisely

3   Extensive
Extensive knowledge of vocabulary
Range: large
Accuracy: vocabulary items seldom used imprecisely

4   Complete
Evidence of complete knowledge of vocabulary
Range: evidence of complete range of vocabulary
Accuracy: evidence of complete accuracy of usage

Knowledge of rhetorical organization

Theoretical construct definition:	knowledge of features for organizing information
Operational construct definition:	evidence of accurate use of a variety of features for organizing information, as demonstrated in the context of the specific tasks (as specified in the task specifications) that have been presented, and as rated on the following scale:

Levels of ability/ mastery	Description
0 Zero	*No evidence of knowledge* of rhetorical organization Range: zero Accuracy: not relevant
1 Limited	*Limited knowledge* of rhetorical organization Range: little evidence of deliberate rhetorical organization Accuracy: organization generally unclear or irrelevant to topic
2 Moderate	*Moderate knowledge* of rhetorical organization Range: moderate range of explicit rhetorical organizational devices Accuracy: organization generally clear but could often be more explicitly marked
3 Extensive	*Extensive knowledge* of rhetorical organization Range: wide range of explicit rhetorical organization devices on essay and paragraph levels

Accuracy: highly accurate with only occasional errors in rhetorical organization

4   Complete

Evidence of complete knowledge of rhetorical organization

Range: evidence of complete range of explicit rhetorical organization devices
Accuracy: evidence of complete accuracy of use

Knowledge of cohesion

Note: This scale is defined in terms of range and accuracy with five levels.

Theoretical construct definition:

knowledge of features for explicitly marking cohesive textual relationships.

Operational construct definition:

evidence of accurate use of a variety of features for explicitly marking cohesive textual relationships, as demonstrated in the context of the specific tasks (as specified in the task specifications) that have been presented, and as rated on the following scale:

Levels of ability/ mastery

Description

0   Zero

No evidence of knowledge of textual cohesion

Range: zero
Accuracy: not relevant

1   Limited

Limited knowledge of textual cohesion

Range: few markers of cohesion
Accuracy: relationships between sentences frequently confusing

2   Moderate

Moderate knowledge of textual cohesion

Range: moderate range of explicit devices
Accuracy: relationships between sentences generally clear but could often be more explicitly marked

3   Extensive

Extensive knowledge of textual cohesion

Range: wide range of explicit cohesive devices including complex subordination
Accuracy: highly accurate with only occassional errors in cohesion

4	Complete	*Evidence of complete knowledge* of cohesion

Range: evidence of complete range of cohesive devices
Accuracy: evidence of complete accuracy of use

Knowledge of moderately formal register

Note: This scale is defined in terms of range and accuracy with five levels.

Theoretical construct definition:	knowledge of markers of moderately formal register in formulaic expressions and in substantive discourse
Operational construct definition:	evidence of the appropriate use of a range of markers of moderately formal register in formulaic expressions and in substantive discourse, as demonstrated in the context of the specific tasks that have been presented, and as rated on the following scale:

Levels of ability/ mastery	**Description**
0 Zero	*No evidence of knowledge* of moderately formal register

Range: zero
Accuracy: not relevant

1 Limited	*Limited knowledge* of moderately formal register

Range: formulaic *and/or* substantive language use
Accuracy: poor within either or both formulaic and substantive language use

2 Moderate	*Moderate knowledge* of moderately formal register

Range: formulaic *and* substantive language use
Accuracy: moderate within formulaic *and* substantive language use

3 Extensive	*Extensive knowledge* of moderately formal register

Range: formulaic *and* substantive language use
Accuracy: highly accurate within both formulaic

and substantive language use, with only occasional errors

4   Complete

Evidence of complete knowledge of moderately formal register

Range: evidence of both formulaic *and* substantive language use
Accuracy: evidence of complete accuracy in formulaic and substantive use.

QUESTIONS FOR LOGICAL EVALUATION OF USEFULNESS	Extent to which quality is satisfied	Explanation of how quality is satisfied
RELIABILITY		
1 *To what extent do characteristics of the test setting vary in an unmotivated way from one administration of the test to another?*	Quality completely satisfied	There is no variation in setting. All administrations of test are carried out in the same setting.
2 *To what extent do characteristics of the test rubric vary in an unmotivated way from one part of the test to another, or on different forms of the test?*	Quality completely satisfied	Variations in rubric in Part 1 (compare and contrast) and Part 2 (make specific recommendations) are motivated by the organizational characteristics of proposals.
3 *To what extent do characteristics of the test input vary in an unmotivated way from one part of the test to another, from one task to another, and on different forms of the test?*	Quality completely satisfied	Characteristics of input (in the two parts of the prompt) are completely consistent with purposes of these parts. The only significant variations that exist are in the specific technical vocabulary used to specify the purpose of each part of the response, which cannot be avoided.
4 *To what extent do characteristics of the expected response vary in an unmotivated way from one part of the test to another, or on different forms of the test?*	Quality completely satisfied	Characteristics of the expected responses in the two parts of the test are completely consistent with the purposes of these parts.
5 *To what extent do characteristics of the relationship between input and response vary in an unmotivated way from one part of the test to another, or on different forms of the test?*	Quality completely satisfied	Characteristics of the relationship between input and response do not vary between the two parts of the test.
CONSTRUCT VALIDITY		
6 *Is the language ability construct for this test clearly and unambiguously defined?*	Quality completely satisfied	Construct definition includes three individually described parts which are later used as the basis for developing scoring scales.

7 *Is the language ability construct for the test relevant to the purpose of the test?*	Quality completely satisfied	Construct is defined in consultation with instructors. Construct is consistent with both the instructional goals of the sheltered writing courses and with expectations of instructors in other courses in the non-language instructional domain.
8 *To what extent does the test task reflect the construct definition?*	Quality completely satisfied	The test task is designed to elicit a sample of language use that is long and complex enough (500 words) to allow the test taker to demonstrate language ability in the areas specified in the construct definition.
9 *To what extent do the scoring procedures reflect the construct definition?*	Quality completely satisfied	The four scoring scales (morphology and syntax, vocabulary, textual knowledge, and register) are directly tied to the four parts of the construct definition.
10 *Will the scores obtained from the test help us to make the desired interpretations about test takers' language ability?*	Quality completely satisfied	The required interpretations of language ability (see needs analysis) can be made directly from the test scores.
11 *What characteristics of the test setting are likely to cause different test takers to perform differently?*	None	All test takers should be comfortable in the physical setting and familiar with the writing materials (pencil and paper). If the use of word processing equipment were an option, test takers able to use this equipment might be at an advantage with respect to the ease with which they could revise their writing.
12 *What characteristics of the test rubric are likely to cause different test takers to perform differently?*	None	The instructions are at a level which students at the lower ability levels should be able to understand. Proctors are available to help test takers understand the instructions. Structure, time allotment, and scoring method do not favor different test takers in any obvious way.
13 *What characteristics of the test input are likely to cause different test takers to perform differently?*	None	There are no obvious characteristics in which the input would cause different test takers to perform differently. All test takers are able to process visual input of the type used in the test.
14 *What characteristics of the expected response are likely to cause different test takers to perform differently?*	None	The only characteristics of the expected response that are likely to cause different test takers to perform differently are those directly tied to the construct to be measured.
15 *What characteristics of the relationship between input and response are likely to cause different test takers to perform differently?*	Possibly the scope and directness of the relationship	If different test takers have different amounts of experience with admission procedures, or if their ability to recall their experiences differ, this might bias performance on the test in favor of test takers with more experience.

AUTHENTICITY

16 *To what extent does the description of tasks in the TLU domain include information about the setting, input, expected response, and relationship between input and response?*	Complete	Description of tasks in the TLU domain is presented in Tables P1.1 and P1.2 and includes information about the setting, input, expected response, and relationship between input and response.

| 17 | To what extent do the characteristics of the test task correspond to those of TLU tasks? | Relatively good correspondence | Analysis of correspondence between characteristics of test task and TLU tasks can be performed by comparing distinctive features of TLU tasks in Table P1.2 with features of Test task in Table P1.4. One mismatch might be found in the characteristics of the physical setting (use of pencil and paper in test vs. word processors in TLU tasks). Another possible mismatch might be found in the topical characteristics of the prompt. 'Admission procedures' might not be a typical topic in TLU tasks. |

INTERACTIVENESS

18	To what extent does the task presuppose the appropriate area or level of topical knowledge, and to what extent can we expect the test takers to have this area or level of topical knowledge?	Considerable extent	Test task presupposes an appropriate area of topical knowledge. However, level and extent of topical knowledge may not be appropriate.
19	To what extent are the personal characteristics of the test takers included in the design statement?	Included in considerable detail	Information on a wide variety of personal characerics needed to design appropriate test tasks is included.
20	To what extent are the characteristics of the test tasks suitable for test takers with the specified personal characteristics?	Generally suitable	No obvious inconsistencies between characteristics of test tasks and personal characteristics of test takers.
21	Does the processing required in the test task involve a very narrow range or a wide range of areas of language knowledge?	Wide range	Test task involves all areas of language knowledge, both organizational (grammatical and textual) and pragmatic (functional and sociolinguistic).
22	What language functions, other than the simple demonstration of language ability, are involved in processing the input and formulating a response?	Ideational, manipulative, and heuristic	Test takers express their ideational knowledge of admission procedures, perform the manipulative function of making recommendations for changes, and use language heuristically to work out solutions to problems in the process of writing the composition.
23	To what extent are the test tasks interdependent?	Highly interdependent	Information provided in the compare-and-contrast part of the task is used as background to the recommendations part of the task.
24	How much opportunity for strategy involvement is provided?	Variable, but generally high	Test takers are required to assess their topical knowledge and a wide range of language knowledge. They are also required to plan how they will include this information in their responses. Goal setting is limited because test takers do not have a choice of topics.
25	Is this test task likely to evoke an affective response that would make it relatively easy or difficult for the test takers to perform at their best?	Likely very easy	The task is designed to let the test taker provide information on a familiar topic and express an opinion under supportive physical conditions. The requirements are clearly specified.

IMPACT

26	*To what extent might the experience of taking the test or the feedback received affect characteristics of test takers that pertain to language use (e.g. topical knowledge, perception of the target language use situation, areas of language knowledge, and use of strategies)?*	Considerable	Since the test task is higly authentic, with respect to tasks in both the real-life and language instructional TLU domains, and since the test taker will be provided with a breakdown of performance in the different areas of the construct definition, the feedback should accurately inform the test takers' perceptions of the TLU situation, areas of language knowledge, and use of strategies.
27	*What provisions are there for involving test takers directly, or for collecting and utilizing feedback from test takers, in the design and development of the test?*	Considerable	Test takers are interviewed during the try-out and allowed to provide feedback, which is used to refine the test.
28	*How relevant, complete, and meaningful is the feedback that is provided to test takers? (Are the scores that are reported meaningful? Is qualitative feedback provided?)*	Considerably	Test takers are provided with a breakdown of their quantitative scores by scale. The description of the levels in the scales provides qualitative feedback as well.
29	*Are decision procedures and criteria applied uniformly to all groups of test takers?*	Yes	All test takers follow the same procedures and are scored using the same criteria.
30	*How relevant and appropriate are the test scores to the decisions to be made?*	Highly appropriate	The scores are designed to be directly relevant and appropriate to the decisions to be made. Levels on scoring scales are defined with respect to these decisions.
31	*Are test takers fully informed about the procedures and criteria that will be used in making decisions?*	Reasonably so	Test takers are informed about the areas of language ability upon which their tests will be scored, but not the levels within each area. They are also informed about aspects of language use (their specific topical knowledge and opinions) that will not be scored. They are not informed about the procedures used in scoring the test. The above is consistent with the intent of the test developer to provide enough information to enable the test takers to do their best work but not excessive information for which the test takers have no direct use.
32	*Are these procedures and criteria actually followed in making the decisions?*	Yes	No options for making decisions are provided that deviate from the specified procedures and criteria.
33	*How consistent are the areas of language ability to be measured with those that are included in teaching materials?*	Highly	The areas of language ability evaluated in instructional tasks and test tasks are the same.
34	*How consistent are the characteristics of the test and test tasks with the characteristics of teaching and learning activities?*	Highly consistent	The characteristics of the test task are based upon one of the instructional models used in the sheltered composition courses for L2 speakers.

35 *How consistent is the purpose of the test with the values and goals of teachers and of the instructional program?*	Highly consistent	The test is developed by a team of teachers in the instructional program, working with the director of the program. There is no discrepancy between the values and goals of the teachers and the purpose of the test.
36 *Are the interpretations we make of the test scores consistent with the values and goals of society and the education system?*	Yes	The educational system (the university within which the test will be used) explicitly values competence in writing. In fact, the writing requirement is the only one required of all undergraduates in the university. In addition, society at large values the ability to write, and the areas of language knowledge measured and interpretations made of test scores are consistent with these values.
37 *To what extent do the values and goals of the test developer coincide or conflict with those of society and the education system?*	Essentially complete agreement	The test developer is in spiritual and emotional harmony with the values and goals of society and the education system.
38 *What are the potential consequences, both positive and negative, for society and the education system, of using the test in this particular way?*	——	Potential positive consequences for society and the educational system for using the test in this particular way include letting the test taking experience inform the test takers, from the outset of the goals of the educational system and at least a portion of society as a whole. Negative consequences for society and the education system are hard to predict at this point.
39 *What is the most desirable positive consequence, or the best thing that could happen, as a result of using the test in this particular way, and how likely is this to happen?*	——	The test takers feel comfortable knowing that they are evaluated on exactly what they are expected either to have mastered or to be in the process of mastering in order to complete their writing requirement. This is likely to happen through the process of informing the test takers not only of the purpose of the test but also of the purpose of the courses in the sheltered writing program.
40 *What is the least desirable negative consequence, or the worst thing that could happen, as a result of using the test in this particular way, and how likely is this to happen?*	——	If the personal characteristics of the test takers change over time and the test continues to be used without revision, it may eventually no longer be appropriate for the test takers. Moreover, the continued use of the test will tend to keep the sheltered writing courses from changing in response to the needs of the test takers, the educational system, and society.

PRACTICALITY

41 *What type and relative amounts of resources are required for: (a) the design stage, (b) the operationalization stage, and (c) the administration stage?*	——	A complete list of resources by type and amount is provided in the design statement. This is adequate for the purpose of developing the test. Additional information on required and available resources will be gathered when necessary.
42 *What resources will be available for carrying out (a), (b), and (c) above?*	——	See design statement.

Table P1.3:   A checklist for the logical evaluation of usefulness

Project 2
Partially developed example of a selection/placement test for telephone company employees

Introduction

For this project and Project 3 we move to a completely different testing situation. A telephone company is hiring employees to respond in writing to customers' complaints about phone company service. Both native and non-native speakers of English are applying for the job and a screening test of writing ability in English is needed. Thus, in this project we design a test to measure ability to write in a highly limited TLU domain. The method that we use involves supplying the test takers with very specific topical information dealing with complaints about problems with phone service. The test takers need to include this information in both a formal letter and an informal memo.

Portions of design statement

Purpose of test

The purpose of the test is to make inferences about language ability which will be used as part of the information the phone company takes into consideration in making decisions to hire or not to hire, and if hired to require additional specialized English instruction or not. The test will also be used as an exit exam to help determine whether to move trainees completing the ESP course into job positions.

Description of TLU domain and task types

For this project, we provide only an abbreviated description of the TLU domain task types.

The characteristics of the TLU domain and tasks for a public relations job in the phone company are highly restricted.

With respect to the physical setting, employees of the phone company work in a quiet, well lit working space. Equipment and materials used in this sort of job-related writing includes a desk, chair, word processor with spelling checker, English and bilingual dictionaries, and telephone. Participants include familiar supervisors and co-workers, and unfamiliar customers. Time is normal working hours.

Tasks include responding to complaints on the phone or in writing, writing memos to co-workers, writing business letters, and problem solving via correspondence.

Characteristics of test takers

Personal characteristics

Applicants are at least 21 years of age, and include both males and females, and both native and non-native speakers of English. Non-native English speaking applicants are immigrants, representing a wide range of nationalities and native languages. Test takers' language abilities range from intermediate to advanced. A written questionnaire is used to screen out beginners. Applicants have reasonably comparable ability levels across the four skills.

Topical knowledge

The test takers have highly specific knowledge of standard kinds of service and financial problems, typical solutions, knowledge of departments responsible for carrying out solutions, etc. Applicants are familiar with typical complaints and how to route information to deal with them.

Definition of construct

Language knowledge

The construct to be measured includes the following components of language knowledge:

Knowledge of syntax: Knowledge of a wide range of syntactic structures.

Knowledge of vocabulary: Knowledge of wide range of accurately used general purpose and technical vocabulary items.

Knowledge of rhetorical organization: Knowledge of a range of features for organizing information.

Knowledge of cohesion: Knowledge of a range of range of features for explicitly marking cohesive textual relationships.

Knowledge of register: Knowledge of a range of markers of formal and informal registers in formulaic expressions and substantive discourse.

Topical knowledge

Knowledge of procedures for responding (in writing) to customer complaints to the phone company.

Inventory of available resources and plan for their allocation and management

Considerable resources are required to prepare prompts of this type. We have to think through ways of providing enough information to guide the response without providing too much of the language required to express it. No resources are involved in preparing responses, since responses are constructed. Few resources are involved in administering the test (group administration is possible). Considerable resources are required to develop scoring criteria and to train the raters to interpret the grading criteria and provide consistent ratings.

Operationalization

Test structure

We need to obtain a highly authentic writing sample that can be rated on a broad range of language characteristics. We also want a prompt that will elicit a focused response to highly specific information. To accomplish this we use two contextualized sentence construction tasks. In both tasks we provide the test takers with coherent background information which suggests the content of sentences to be constructed. The constructed sentences then form coherent writing samples. Thus, in these elicitation tasks test takers are provided with specific information to communicate in a writing sample, but the way they do so is uncontrolled.

Scoring method

Responses are scored using scales that describe particular combinations of language knowledge (and levels of topical knowledge) that the phone company finds useful in making decisions about hiring and training.

Procedures for scoring are the same as for Project 1. The test takers are informed explicitly of the general areas of language use on which their responses will be scored.

The first four scales (knowledge of syntax, knowledge of vocabulary, knowledge of rhetorical organization, and knowledge of cohesion) are the same as those used in Project 1. The fifth scale, knowledge of register, needs to be constructed somewhat differently for this project because knowledge of two registers (formal and informal) is involved. The sixth scale, levels of topical knowledge, is specific to this project. The last two scales are given below.

Knowledge of register

Note: This scale is defined in terms of range and accuracy with four levels.
Construct definition: Knowledge of a range of markers of formal and informal register in formulaic expressions and substantive discourse.

Levels of ability/ mastery	Description
0 Zero	*No evidence of knowledge* of register Range: zero Accuracy: not relevant
1 Limited	*Limited knowledge* of register Range: limited distinctions between formal and informal register Accuracy: frequent errors
2 Moderate	*Moderate knowledge* of register Range: moderate distinction between formal and informal registers Accuracy: good, few errors
3 Complete	*Evidence of complete knowledge* of register Range: complete distinction between formal and informal registers Accuracy: no errors

Topical knowledge

Note: This scale is defined in terms of range and accuracy with four levels.
Construct definition: Knowledge of procedures for dealing with telephone company customer complaints.

Levels of ability/ mastery	Description
0 Zero	*No evidence of knowledge* of procedures for dealing with phone company complaints Range: zero, test taker demonstrates no knowledge of procedures for dealing with phone company complaints Accuracy: not relevant

1	Limited	*Limited control of knowledge schemata*
		Range: small to moderate
		Accuracy: frequent use of incorrect strategies
2	Moderate	*Moderate control of knowledge schemata*
		Range: wide to complete
		Accuracy: very good, seldom uses incorrect strategies
3	Complete	*Evidence of complete knowledge* of procedures for dealing with telephone company complaints
		Range: complete
		Accuracy: complete, never uses incorrect strategies

Appendix 2: Test

In the following test, editorial comments are given in parentheses.

Instructions

(The instructions are given in writing in the target language. Specification of procedures and tasks is explicit.)

1 This is a test of your ability to write a short letter and a memo.
2 After you read the directives, write your replies on the word processor provided.
3 Try to make your correspondence as meaningful and accurate as possible. You will be graded on the reasonableness of what you say and on how well you say it.
4 You have 30 minutes to write both the letter and the memo.
5 Your responses will be scored on grammatical accuracy, your control of vocabulary, the organization of your letter to the customer, your ability to write both formally (in the business letter) and informally (in the memo), and your ability to deal with the complaint in a way that follows phone company policy.

Prompt

A co-worker has taken a phone message for you from a dissatisfied customer and has left you his notes. Here is the message:

IMPORTANT MESSAGE

FOR (Test taker's name here)

DATE Sept. 13, 1995 TIME 9:55 AM/PM

Mr. Ray Norris

OF Duck Creek Village

PHONE (111) 555–1234

MESSAGE
– phone rings for whole minute
– no one on other end
– pick it up, doesn't stop
– does this 3–4 times a day, at night too
– called phone company, complained, no help

SIGNED: J. P.

Now do the following, using the information in the message above:

1 Write a formal letter of reply to this customer dealing with his complaints.

2 Write an informal memo to a friend who works in the appropriate department in the phone company explaining the problem and asking your friend to deal with it.

Project 3
Partially developed example of a syllabus-based diagnostic achievement test for students in an ESP program

Introduction

For our third project, the situation is largely the same as in Project 2, except that now we are testing only non-native speakers who have already been accepted into the phone company's training program. We will develop a diagnostic achievement test to determine whether the test takers have mastered specific material in the phone company's ESP program—material dealing with control of grammar in writing. The test task resembles the one used in Project 2, except that we will now control more tightly the exact structures that we want the test takers to use. This will enable us to measure the control and accuracy with which the test takers are able to use a specific set of structures.

The test takers are given specific sets of words to be combined into sentences which together form a business letter similar to the one elicited in Project 2. Omitted from the prompt are a number of grammatical forms such as prepositions, verb endings, and markers of singular and plural, which the test takers must supply. The business letter which the test takers produce is then scored objectively by means of a scoring key.

Portions of design statement

Purpose of test

The purpose of this test is to make decisions about whether or not those job applicants described in Project 2 who have been admitted to the ESP course in the phone company have mastered specific course content. The test will also be used to provide diagnostic feedback to those applicants who are judged not to have mastered the specific course content, as well as information that course designers and teachers can use to tailor the course more closely to the needs of this group of students.

Description of TLU domain and task types

Characteristics of the TLU domain and task types are the same as those for Project 2. The population of test takers is limited to those students who have been accepted into the ESP training program for the phone company.

Description of characteristics of test takers

The personal characteristics and topical knowledge of the test takers remain unchanged. The general level and profile of language ability are more restricted and are equivalent to those for Level 2 test takers in Project 2. Their range of abilities is narrower than for Project 2 due to the screening procedures for admission into the training program.

Definition of construct

For this achievement test, the following syllabus-based construct definition is used: 'knowledge of specified grammatical forms and punctuation marks in writing a formal business letter.' The following specific components are included in the construct definition.

Grammatical forms:

1 Prepositions
2 Participial modifiers
3 Personal and relative pronouns
4 Verb forms
5 Infinitives
6 Adverbs
7 Quantifiers
8 Auxiliary verb forms
9 Coordinating and subordinating conjunctions

Punctuation marks:

1 Comma
2 Semicolon
3 Period
4 Question mark

Inventory of available resources and plan for their allocation and management

Test tasks of this type require considerable resources to prepare. Words and phrases must be selected which restrict the form of the response without providing all of the information needed to phrase the response correctly. Few resources are required for administration, since group administration is possible. Few resources are required to develop scoring keys. Moderate scoring time is required, since test must be individually scored following a procedure that requires considerable attention to detail.

Operationalization

The task type selected for this project is the most restrictive of the three projects illustrated so far. Test takers are provided with frames consisting of sets of words which must be combined into single sentences in the order in which they are listed. These frames exert a very high degree of control over the specific form of the limited production responses.

Consideration of qualities of usefulness for tasks of this type

Reliability

We build scorer reliability into the test by having responses scored objectively with a scoring key. If test takers produce grammatically correct responses that are acceptable and are not included in the scoring key, the key might need to be revised after trialing. We build internal consistency across items by keeping as many as possible of the characteristics of the input and response the same for all of the individual items. For example, the input format is always visual, in language, short, etc.

Construct validity

We build construct validity into the test by defining the construct in a way that is consistent with the purpose of the test and designing test tasks that will allow us to make inferences about language ability consistent with the construct definition.

Authenticity

Authenticity is limited due to lack of match between characteristics of task input in the TLU and testing domains. The input in the TLU domain would be grammatically organized and more cohesive than that in the test itself. Moreover, more input is supplied for the test than would normally be supplied in the TLU domain. Specifically, new information, such as solutions that the phone company personnel would supply in response to letters of complaint, is supplied in the test input.

Interactiveness

Interactiveness is somewhat limited because the test takers' topical knowledge does not play as significant a role in carrying out the test task as was the case in Project 2, since the test takers do not add new information from their on-the-job experience. The processing also requires the test takers to use a narrower range of language knowledge than was the case for Project 2 because more of the response is supplied. The focus here is primarily on grammatical knowledge.

The test tasks are not highly interdependent. Thus involvement of planning is probably limited because of the lack of need to organize information. All parts of the test are thematically unified and cohesive, but there is less need for the test taker to take this into consideration in responding to the prompt than was the case for Project 2. Adequate opportunity (time) for strategy involvement is provided.

Impact

Feedback on impact could be obtained by asking test takers and their teachers for comments on the design specifications, operationalization, and decisions to be made.

The test should make it relatively easy for the test takers to perform at their best. There are no obvious affective barriers to such performance. There is some likelihood that the test takers will find personal significance in the explicit functional goal of the test task. Opportunity for constructed goal setting is limited by the fact that the general task is supplied, and there is little opportunity for flexibility. We might hope for identification with supplied goals.

Scoring method

The test is scored objectively by means of the following key:

Dear Mr. Adams,

Thank you for your letter of May 10 concerning problems you have been having with your telephone service.

You indicate that several times a day your phone rings for two whole minutes, and when you pick it up no one is on the line.

You mention that you have called the phone company to complain several times, with no results.

We sincerely regret any inconvenience this has caused you.

Phone company personnel have checked our switching system and outside lines and can find no problems at our end; therefore, the problem must be in the wiring in your home.

We will be happy to send an investigator to your home to check your wiring and make any necessary repairs.

Please contact our repair department as soon as possible to let us know what time will be convenient for you.

Sincerely yours,

Douglas Smith
Director of Customer Relations
Southern Colorado Bell
Boulder, CO 30402

Scoring procedures

All responses are scored by the teachers, according to the following procedure:

Start with 100 points. Deduct one point for each of the following:

Omitted word
Incorrect form of word (including misspelled word)
Omitted or incorrect punctuation mark
Instructions not followed (test taker writes two sentences instead of one, etc.)

Appendix 3: Test

In the following test, editorial comments are given in parentheses.

Instructions

(The instructions are given in writing in the target language. Specification of procedures and tasks is explicit.)

1 You will be asked to write a short letter.
2 You will be provided with sets of words and phrases from which to construct sentences to make a complete letter.
3 Create *a single sentence* from each set of words.
4 The following is an example the kinds of changes that need to be made. The changes are underlined in the example.

Example:
Thank you / your letter / request information telephone company / extended service contract inter-office systems

Answer:
Thank you <u>for your</u> letter request<u>ing</u> information <u>about the</u> telephone company's extended service contract <u>on</u> inter-office systems<u>.</u>

5   As you can see, you can add endings, small words, and punctuation.
6   Be sure to include all of the information supplied. Write your responses in grammatically correct English. Punctuate your sentences correctly. Remember that you must create only one sentence per set of words.
7   You will have 15 minutes to complete this test.

TEST TASK

You have received a letter of complaint about the phone company's service. You are replying to that letter:

May 14, 1999

Mr. Charles Adams
114 West 23rd
Grand Junction
Colorado

Dear Mr. Adams,

Thank you / your letter / May 10 / concern / problems / have / your telephone service.

_____

_____

_____

You indicate / several time day / you phone / ring / two whole minutes / you pick it up / no one / on line.

_____

_____

_____

You mention / you call / phone company / complain / several times / no results.

_____

_____

_____

We / sincere regret / inconvenience / this cause you.

_____

_____

_____

Phone company personnel / check / switching system / outside lines / find / no problem / our end / problem / must be / wiring / your home.

_____

_____

_____

We / happy / send / investigator / you home / check / wiring / make / necessary repair.

_____

_____

_____

Please / contact / repair department / soon / possible / let know / time / convenient / you.

Sincerely yours,

Douglas Smith
Director of Customer Relations
Western Colorado Bell
Grand Junction, CO 30402

Project 4
Portions of a project to develop an exit test for students in an adult education conversation course for immigrants

Introduction

An Adult Education Program in a large US city offers a series of conversation courses for immigrants wanting to improve their ability to participate in small talk (relatively unserious ideational conversation for the purpose of socialization). An exit test is needed to measure students' ability to converse with native speakers about topics included in small talk. The Adult Education Program will use this test to assign grades, as well as provide a certificate indicating the students' profile of language ability. Test takers might use the certificate to help obtain employment, for admission to another program, or simply for personal satisfaction.

Portions of design statement
Purpose of test

This is a fairly low-stakes test for the purpose of providing evidence of the test takers' ability to participate in small talk. Interpretations of scores will be included in an end-of-course certificate and scores will be used as a basis for assigning course grades.

Description of the TLU domain and task types

Students in the Adult Education conversation courses are going to continue to live in the US. The TLU domain for these students is broadly defined and includes a variety of types of tasks to meet occupational, day-to-day pragmatic and social needs. Tasks to meet social needs include participating in small talk on a variety of topics such as the weather, family, living in the city, shopping, sharing experiences of applying for a job, and so forth.

Characteristics of test takers
Personal characteristics

Test takers are refugees and newly arrived immigrants, 18 years of age and up, male and female, with a wide variety of nationalities and native languages, and from a variety of social classes and educational backgrounds. Their experience with different kinds of tests also varies widely. However, all have signed up for an English conversation course in which one of the stated objectives is to prepare students to engage in small talk.

Topical knowledge

Test takers will have expertise in relatively diverse areas of topical knowledge. We cannot predict what, if any, areas of topical knowledge will be shared by all test takers. We can assume, however, that each test taker will have expertise in one or more areas of topical knowledge, based upon his or her life's experience and interests. (A list of such areas of topical knowledge is provided in the 'Test script for the examiner' under 'Topics to talk about in English', page 304.)

General level and profile of language ability

The test takers' ability to use English to participate in small talk varies from beginning to advanced. Furthermore, some test takers will be able to use English in TLU tasks that involve reading, while some may be preliterate. Profiles of areas of language knowledge also vary widely. Some test takers might be high in organizational knowledge and low in pragmatic knowledge. Some might control several registers, while others may not even control one.

Definition of construct to be measured

Theory-based definition of language knowledge (does not include strategic competence): includes the following components:

Knowledge of vocabulary: Knowledge of a wide range of general purpose and specialized vocabulary items, including cultural references and figures of speech.

Knowledge of syntax: Knowledge of a range of syntactic structures.

Textual knowledge: Knowledge of a wide range of features for organizing information and explicitly marking cohesive textual relationships.

Topical knowledge: Topical knowledge is not included in the construct definition. This is because we are not concerned with measuring how much knowledge the test takers have about the topics covered in small talk.

Allocation of resources

This project places relatively heavy demands on test development (developing the script), somewhat lighter demands on training test givers (since the test is scripted), and heavy demands on time for administration and scoring.

Operationalization

This test, adapted from part of the Bachman-Palmer Oral Interview (Bachman and Palmer 1983), is designed to be adaptable to different test takers at different levels of language ability and with expertise in different areas of topical knowledge. It is thus particularly suitable for situations where test takers from diverse backgrounds are found. Also, it is scripted, making it quite easy for inexperienced interviewers to get started.

Considerations of qualities of usefulness

Reliability

Since the test is scripted, there is likely to be little unwanted variation in the testing procedures. The main source of unreliability will most likely be variation in scoring between examiners. This will be addressed by providing training sessions and regular opportunities for the raters to refamiliarize themselves with examples of interviews at different ability levels. Minimum levels of scorer reliability for this test will be set quite high because the test is scripted (controlling variation in administration) and the test developer will provide raters with a substantial amount of training.

Construct validity

Our main concern here will be whether or not the scripted interview allows us to obtain a sample of speech production adequate for the examiners to rate according to the scoring scales. Minimum levels of construct validity will be set quite high. Even though the test is scripted, examiners will have considerable opportunities to elicit a rateable speech sample, thereby increasing the likelihood of drawing valid inferences about the construct from the test takers' performance.

Authenticity

While the individual prompts in the script are reasonably typical of input likely to be found in small talk situations, as a set, they do not follow ordinary conversational organization, and this may lead to the perception of lower authenticity. One way to improve the authenticity of the test task might be to find a way to simulate more accurately normal conversational style. However, doing so might make the test less practical by requiring more time to get a rateable sample of the test takers' performance. Minimum levels of authenticity will be moderate for this test, since the need to obtain a rateable sample within a reasonably short period of time will make it difficult to provide for more authentic language use on the part of the examiner.

Interactiveness

Minimum levels of interactiveness will be set quite high because the characteristics of the test tasks allow for a high level of involvement of language knowledge, topical knowledge, and strategy use.

Language knowledge: A fairly wide range of language knowledge is involved because of the variation and complexity of the tasks.

Topical knowledge: Significant involvement of topical knowledge is involved because the test takers are allowed to talk about their own areas of expertise.

Strategies: Need and opportunity for strategy use is high initially, when the test takers choose their area of expertise. It is low to the extent that the examiner controls the general structure of the conversation. It is relatively high within responses to many prompts in which test takers can decide what they want to say.

Affect: Affective responses to the test should be relatively positive, since the test takers are given a choice of topics and an opportunity to perform at their best. Some test takers may feel uncomfortable with the increasing complexity of the prompts and their inability to respond to the more difficult ones.

Impact

The test is designed to have a positive impact on test takers and instructors since its language content follows closely the stated objectives of the course. Minimum levels of impact could be set quite high, because of the importance of the test both to the test takers and to the stakeholders.

Practicality

Tests of this type are fairly demanding of development resources, since a separate script must be prepared for each area of expertise. Because the test is scripted, relatively few resources are required to train examiners to give the test, though training examiners to score the test may require more resources. Actual administration and scoring time will be considerable, since this test must be administered separately to each test taker.

Test structure

The test consists of six parts, which are described briefly below. These parts are also listed in the script for the examiner, which indicates the specific types of prompts used and the order in which they are presented.

1 *Warm-up*

After greeting the test taker and explaining the purpose of the test, the examiner determines the test taker's area of expertise—a topic about which the test taker feels comfortable communicating. The test taker is offered a list of topics to choose from, topics for which the examiners have prepared scripts to follow. (See test script for example questions.)

2 *Initial questions*

These are yes/no and *wh*-questions asked to make the topic more specific (if necessary) and as a warm-up for the succeeding section. (See test script for example questions.)

3 *Extended response questions*

These are asked to elicit fairly long answers within the test taker's area of expertise. (See test script for example questions.)

4 *Specialized vocabulary questions*

These questions are asked to determine the depth and breadth of the test taker's vocabulary. (See test script for example questions.) General formats for the questions are as follows:

A   Elaboration questions

These are asked to get a definition by giving a vocabulary item, generally one used by the test taker in the extended response questions above.

Exactly what is (a/an) _____ ?

Tell me more about _____ .

Can you describe (a/an/the/) _____ ?

What does it mean to _____ ?

B   Questions for particular items

These are asked to elicit one or more vocabulary items by giving a definition or description.

What's the word for something that/someone who _____ ?

What do you call it when you _____ ?

C   Comparison and analysis

These questions are asked to check recognition and/or production of exact vocabulary. Some may also elicit speech that is rateable on the cohesion scale.

What's the difference between _____ and _____ ?

Do you know anything about _____ ? (Is it/Are they much like _____ ? How?/Why not?

5 *Textual organization ability test*

This is designed to elicit an organized, extended response that can be used as the basis for assigning ratings or textual organization ability. (See test script for example questions.)

6 *Hypothetical situations and supported opinion*

Questions of these types are asked to elicit speech related to the test taker's area of expertise, but in areas which she/he is unlikely to have talked about previously in English to any great extent. This requires the test taker to speak while thinking about a previously unconsidered problem and thus probes the limits of his/her competence. (See test script for example questions.)

Test script for the examiner

(Illustrative scripts are provided for two different areas of topical knowledge: 'children' and 'teachers and school.')

Instructions

The test takers are told in class that there will be an oral interview test conducted by two of their teachers. They are told about the purpose of the test and about its general format: an opportunity for them to talk about a topic with which they are familiar.

Specific test tasks

1 *Warm-up (for all test takers)*

Good morning/afternoon/evening Mr./Miss/Mrs. X, Please sit down. How are you today/this evening?
[Test taker responds.] [Respond to test taker as appropriate.]

Do you know what the purpose of this test is?
[Test taker responds. If test taker does not know the purpose of the test, explain as follows.]
The purpose of this test is to give you a chance to talk about something that interests you so you can show us what you have learned in your conversation course.

Mr./Miss/Mrs. X, Where do you usually speak the most English now?
[Prompts: At home? Away from home (when you travel)? At work? In church? At school?]

Who do you usually speak English with?
What can you talk about best in English?
[Prompts: show or read list of 'Topics to talk about in English' to test taker.]

Topics to talk about in English

Children	Church
Field of study	Food
Friends and enemies	Hobby
Job	Movies
Parents	Politics
Reading	Shopping
Sports	Spouse
Teachers and school	Television
Travel	Vehicles
Weather	

2 *Initial questions*

(Script used with test takers whose area of expertise is 'children'.)

How many children do you have?
Are they boys or girls?
Are they all here in _____ with you?
Were they born here? Where were they born?
What are their names, and how old are they?

Where do they go to school?
What kinds of games do they like to play?

3 *Extended response questions for test takers whose area of expertise is 'children'*

What are the rules for the game they like to play most?
Do you remember a time when you and your children did something that was a lot of fun? Tell me about it.
Have any of your children ever been very sick or hurt? Tell me about it.
Do any of your children have a job? Tell me about it.

4 *Specialized vocabulary questions for test takers whose area of expertise is 'children'*

What toys do your children play with? What is a _____ like?
Do you make any of your children's clothes? Tell me how you make a _____ .
Do your children have any clothes that they particularly like? What does your child's _____ look like?

5 *Textual organization ability test for test takers whose area of expertise is 'children'*

What are the advantages and disadvantages of being a child in a large family?
What are the similarities and differences between the personalities of two of your children?
What are the similarities and differences between the way children must behave in front of adults in your country and in the United States?
What are the advantages and disadvantages of a child's being raised very strictly?

6 *Hypothetical situation and supported opinion for test takers whose area of expertise is 'children'*

If you could be a child again and relive one week of your life, how old would you want to be? What would you want to do? Why?
If you could have your own children remember only three things about

how to live their lives, what three things would you want them to remember? Why?

[End of script for area of expertise: 'children']

1 *Initial questions for test takers whose area of expertise is 'teachers and school'*

What different schools have you attended?
Were most of your teachers men or women?
Do you like school?

2 *Extended response questions for test takers whose area of expertise is 'teachers and school'*

Was there any teacher you particularly disliked? Tell me about him/her. What did he/she do that you disliked the most? Did you learn a lot in his/her class anyway? Why?
Was there any particular teacher that you really liked? What was he/she like?
How were you selected for admission into school here? In your country? Why did you choose this particular school to attend?

3 *Specialized vocabulary questions for test takers whose area of expertise is 'teachers and school'*

Can you describe a classroom in your school? What else was in the room? Exactly how were grades assigned in one of your classes? [Vocabulary questions: biased, incoherent, irrelevant, procedures, techniques, qualified, unqualified.]

4 *Textual organization ability test for test takers whose area of expertise is 'teachers and school'*

What are the similarities and differences between the way students are admitted into colleges in your country and in the US?
What are the similarities and differences between the way and the time students select a major in your country and in the US?
What are the similarities and differences between the quality of education you receive in a school in your country and in the US?
What are the similarities and differences between two classes you have taken here?
What are the reasons for and against studying in the US?

5 *Hypothetical questions and supported opinion for test takers whose area of expertise is 'teachers and school'*

If you were the foreign student advisor in your school here, how would you prepare students from your country for their experiences here? Why? If you were in charge of the university system in your country, what changes would you make in the way students are chosen for admission? Why?

If you were a teacher, how would you treat your students? [Vocabulary questions: discipline, assignments, grading.] Why? Do you think your attitude has changed because of your educational experience here? How? Why?

Scoring criteria

Criterion-referenced rating scales describing different ability levels within the various areas of language knowledge, such as those used in Project 1, except that control of register is not rated in this test.

Scoring procedures

There are two examiners: the primary examiner, who conducts the test, and the secondary examiner, who simply observes it. These two examiners score the interview separately, both during and immediately following the test. If the examiners disagree by more than one level on each scale, they discuss the interview and their notes in order to arrive at a rating that they can agree upon.

Report form

Scores are reported as a profile of abilities in the different areas included in the construct definition.

Project 5

Portions of a project to develop a high-stakes ESP screening test for making hiring and training decisions

Portions of design statement

Purpose of test

A hotel in Asia is hiring people to take reservations over the phone in English. The hotel needs some means of screening the job applicants in terms of their ability to use English for this purpose. All of the applicants are required to have had experience with the same kind of job, but using their native language.

Three levels of hiring/training decisions will be made: to hire without training, to hire with training, or not to hire. This is a relatively high-stakes test, since results will affect hiring decisions.

Description of the TLU domain and task

These are defined very narrowly (see column 2 of Table P5.1). The test taker's sole task is to take phone reservations (in English) in a fairly large hotel that can afford to hire someone to take reservations and do nothing else.

Characteristics of test takers

Personal characteristics: Test takers are male and female, aged 20 and up, with at least a high school education. All job applicants have had a course in hotel management and at least one year's experience working in a hotel, though not necessarily in a hotel in which the L2 was used.

Topical knowledge of test takers: Relatively highly focused specific knowledge. Test takers are familiar with procedures for registering guests at a hotel.

General level and profile of language ability: Moderate to extensive (intermediate to advanced).

	Characteristics of TLU task: 'taking reservations over the phone'	Characteristics of test task: 'taking reservations over the phone'
SETTING		
Physical characteristics	Location: telecommunications room. Physical conditions: quiet, well lit. Materials and equipment and degree of familiarity: telephone, isolated switchboard, computer terminal providing information occupancy, rate structure, credit card verification device, transportation options, etc., all of which are familiar to language user.	Location: small, private room in hotel. Physical conditions: quiet, well lit, non-distracting. Materials and equipment and degree of familiarity: a functioning telephone headset, a registration form, and a pencil, all familiar to test taker.
Participants	Customers making hotel registrations.	Hotel staff trained to administer the phone role-play test.
Time of task	Day or night	Daytime or evenings
INPUT		
Format		
Channel	Aural	Aural
Form	Language	Language
Language	Target	Target
Length	Relatively short: sentences or short aural paragraphs.	Relatively short
Type	Item	Item
Speededness	Moderate (also depending upon test taker). Input cannot be slowed down too much without a loss in efficiency and risk of upsetting customers.	Moderate (also depending upon test taker. See discussion above.)
Vehicle	Live	Live-
Language characteristics		
Organizational characteristics		
Grammatical	Vocabulary: narrow range of general and specialized vocabulary, frequent and infrequent (some proper names, etc.). Morphology and syntax: narrow range of organized structures.	Vocabulary: general and specialized for hotel reservations, frequent and infrequent, no cultural references. Morphology and syntax: organized.

Textual	Cohesion: cohesive, with a narrow range of cohesive devices. Rhetorical characteristics: narrow range appropriate to a short phone conversation on topic of making hotel reservations.	Cohesion: cohesive, with a narrow range of cohesive devices. Rhetorical characteristics: narrow range appropriate to a short phone conversation on topic of making hotel reservations.
Pragmatic characteristics		
Functional	Ideational and manipulative	Ideational and manipulative
Sociolinguistic	Dialect/variety: standard and local. Register: formal and informal. Naturalness: natural. Cultural references and figurative language: minimal.	Dialect: standard Register: formal and informal. Naturalness: natural. Cultural references: none.
Topical characteristics	Hotel reservations	Hotel reservations
EXPECTED RESPONSE		
Format		
Channel	Aural	Aural
Form	Language	Language
Language	Target	Target
Length	Short, except when test taker recapitulates the details of the reservation.	Relatively short
Type	Limited constructed	Limited constructed
Speededness	Moderate	Moderate (also depending upon test taker. See discussion above.)
Language characteristics		
Organizational characteristics		
Grammatical	Vocabulary: general and specialized for hotel reservations, frequent and infrequent, no cultural references. Morphology and syntax: organized	Vocabulary: general and specialized for hotel reservations, frequent and infrequent, no cultural references. Morphology and syntax: organized
Textual	Cohesion: cohesive. Rhetorical: conversation with features such as markers for getting attention, interrupting, nominating topic, and so forth.	Cohesion: cohesive. Rhetorical: conversation with features such as markers for getting attention, interrupting, nominating topic, etc.

Language characteristics—continued

Pragmatic characteristics

Functional	Ideational and manipulative including accepting, denying, explaining, requesting clarification, interrupting, repeating, etc.	Functional: ideational and manipulative: asking for repetition, repeating, confirming, explaining, describing.
Sociolinguistic	Dialect/variety: standard. Register: primarily formal. Naturalness: natural. Cultural references: minimal.	Dialect: standard. Register: formal. Naturalness: natural. Cultural references: none.
Topical characteristics	Hotel reservations	Hotel reservations
RELATIONSHIP BETWEEN INPUT AND RESPONSE		
Reactivity	Reciprocal	Reciprocal
Scope of relationship	Narrow, since in conversations of this type the hotel employee is typically responding to fairly specific requests.	Narrow
Directness of relationship	Direct and indirect. Responses may provide information not in the input, such as rate structure, etc.	Direct and indirect

Table P5.1:   Characteristics of TLU and test tasks

Definition of construct to be measured

The construct includes both language knowledge and topical knowledge in a single construct, 'ability to interpret specific topical information related to making hotel reservations' (Option 2 in Chapter 6, page 123). Although the task involves reciprocal language use and thus requires both listening and speaking, for our purposes we will only attempt to measure the test taker's ability to interpret information through listening to the input.

Portions of plan for evaluating the qualities of usefulness

Reliability

Minimum levels of reliability will be set rather high since this is a high-stakes test and the scripted nature of the input allows for a great deal of control. To collect evidence for evaluating reliability, we will conduct two studies. In one study, several examiners will give the same test to a group of test takers and calculate the consistency of scores across the different test administrations. In the second study, several raters will score the same tests and calculate the consistency of scores across the different raters.

Construct validity

Minimum levels of construct validity will be set quite high again, due to the high-stakes nature of this test. To collect evidence for construct validity we will keep a record of the job performance of test takers whose test performance was deemed adequate and who were subsequently hired. We will then analyze the on-the-job language of these individuals, to describe the numbers and types of language errors made in registering customers

Authenticity

Minimum levels of authenticity will be set quite high, since the TLU task upon which the test task is based is quite restricted. To collect information for evaluating authenticity, we will ask test users to describe their perceptions of the authenticity of the test tasks.

Interactiveness

Areas of language ability that are involved in the spoken responses include the textual knowledge and strategic competence associated with conversational management, such as interrupting, getting repetitions, getting spellings of names, etc. Because of the rather limited involvement of topical knowledge and the metacognitive strategies, due to the nature of the task, minimum levels of interactiveness will be set rather moderate. To collect information for evaluating interactiveness, we will ask test takers for their opinions on the extent to which their language knowledge, topical knowledge, and metacognitive strategies were involved in taking the test.

Impact

Minimum levels of impact will be set quite high due to the high-stakes nature of the test. To evaluate impact, we will ask employers and test takers to comment on the fairness of the test, and on its appropriateness for making decisions.

Inventory of available resources and plan for their allocation

Resources can be allocated fairly equally between test development and use. A fairly resource-intensive administration procedure is acceptable due to the small number of applicants for jobs and the importance of the decisions made on the basis of test performance.

Portions of operationalization

In this project the test task is modeled very closely after characteristics of the TLU task and is designed to be as authentic as possible. The task consists of a short role-play. The person giving the test plays the role of a customer making a room reservation over the phone. Two scripts are provided, one in which the customer makes a reservation for herself in a very informal register, and the other in which the customer makes a reservation for his employer in a very formal register. The test taker's task is to listen to the 'customer's' request and fill in the information provided on a registration form.

The test taker is allowed to interrupt the 'customer' and request repetitions, clarifications, spelling, etc., as would normally be the case in a reciprocal phone conversation. However, the time allowed for each conversation is limited in order to make reasonable demands on the test taker's efficiency in processing aural input.

The primary emphasis is on listening. The task requires only limited spoken responses in the input, as would be the case in the TLU situation.

Written production responses include writing down the information provided by the customer making the reservation. The test is scored according to the accuracy of the information the test taker writes down on the registration forms, that is, the degree to which it corresponds to the information provided by the test giver.

Blueprint

Test structure

1 *Number of parts*: The test is organized around a single task, to obtain the necessary information for filling in a hotel registration form from a customer registering over the phone. This task is broken down into a number of related sub-tasks, each involving filling in a different piece of information.

2 *Salience of parts*: obvious to test taker due to the registration form which test taker must fill out.

3   *Sequence of parts*: follows natural order of sub-tasks involved in taking
    a reservation.
4   *Relative importance of parts*: equally important.

Test task specifications

1   *Purpose*: to make hiring decisions about applicants for jobs with the
    hotel.
2   *Definition of construct*: ability to interpret specific topical information
    related to making hotel reservations.
3   *Environment*: (See characteristics of test task environment in Table
    P5.1.)
4   *Time allocation*: A limited amount of time (determined after try-out) is
    allotted per each reservation in the role-play. The reasoning behind this
    is that if the test taker is too slow, he or she will likely upset the cus-
    tomer and be inefficient on the job.
5   *Instructions*:
    a   Language: target.
    b   Channel: aural and visual.
    c   Specification of procedures and tasks: explicit.
6   *Characteristics of individual test tasks*: (See Table P5.1.)
7   *Scoring method*: objective
    a   Criteria for correctness: accuracy of information the test taker
        writes on the registration form. The examiner's script is used as
        the scoring key. Start with 100 points. Subtract points as follows:
        error in proper name: 5 points; wrong or missing piece of informa-
        tion (month of arrival, day of arrival, month of departure, day of
        departure, room type, method of payment): 5 points. Note: count
        credit card number as four words.
    b   Procedures: The test administrator reads the registration card and
        scores the responses according to a scoring key developed on the
        basis of the test giver's script.
    c   Explicitness of criteria and procedures: explicit.

Scoring

Accuracy of information the test taker writes on the registration form

The examiner's script is used as the scoring key. Start with 100 points.
Subtract points as follows: error in proper name: 5 points; wrong or missing piece of information (month of arrival, day of arrival, month of depar-

ture, day of departure, room type, method of payment): 5 points. Note: count credit card number as four words.

The test administrator reads the registration card and scores the responses according to a scoring key developed on the basis of the test giver's script.

Appendix 5: Test

Instructions

For this test, you are going to pretend you're working as the reservations clerk at a hotel, a hotel a lot like ours. *I'm* going to pretend to be two different customers. *You* will need to fill out one of the forms here (give candidate two registration forms) with all the information each 'customer' gives you. Do you understand?

I expect you to stop me whenever you need to: have me spell things, repeat things—anything you need to make sure that you get all of the information right. However, you'll only have a short time with each customer. I'll set my timer for two minutes. Then we'll stop and that will be the end of that part of the test. However, you can fill in as much as you need to on the form after the timer rings. Do you understand?

[Instructions to test administrator: Read the following aloud to the candidate. Stop, repeat, spell, etc. as requested by the candidate. Please note that you will need to use the titles, names, and references that correspond to your sex.]

Part 1

OK. Now I'm going to pretend to be the first customer.
[Turn away from candidate. Pretend to talk on phone. Remember. Stop, repeat, spell, or do whatever the candidate asks you to in character as the customer.]

Hi. I'd like to get a room for this weekend. We'll be coming in Friday next week and checking out early Monday morning.
[Note for grading: Any plausible dates should be accepted.]

My name is Robert/Roberta E. Jennsen. My wife/husband and my ten-year-old son will be with me. We'll want a room with two queen-size beds.

I smoke—trying to quit but I haven't been able to yet I'm afraid. And my wife/husband would like a room away from the street, if you've got one. Something quiet, you know.

Oh, hey! I've got some frequent flier points I think I can use at your place. I think they're worth a 25% discount.

Other than that, let me give you my credit card number. It's 7239–double 4–75–1313–double 2–80. It's good 'til January next year.

[This is the end of the first set of customer information.]

Part 2

OK. Now I'm going to pretend to be the second customer.
[Reset the timer for two minutes before continuing.]
Good morning. I'd like to make a reservation for Mr./Ms. Stephen/Stephanie W. Kosciuszko (pronounce /koh-shee-OOS-ko/). He's/She's planning to arrive at your hotel this evening and will stay until the following Wednesday. He/She is the Vice-president of Rexxen Manufacturing and will be traveling alone.

Mr./Ms. Kosciuszko is very tall and absolutely requires a king-size bed. He/She also absolutely requires a non-smoking room, preferably on a non-smoking floor.

Please charge the room to our corporate account. I believe you have that on record.

Expected responses

Written responses are to be recorded on a registration form. [Use an authentic form if possible.]

Name _____			
	last name	first name	initial
Company _____			
Date of arrival _____			
Date of departure _____			
Room type _____			
Special requirements _____			
Method of payment _____			
Credit card _____ _____			
	number	date of expiration	

Project 6
Portions of a project to develop a placement test for an ESL reading course

Introduction

We asked the director of an adult education program about her primary needs for a language test. She indicated that she had a pressing need for a reading test that would provide her with information about her students' ability to read job-related material. She said that she could use this information in two ways:

1 to place her students at appropriate levels in reading courses, and
2 to supply job service case workers with information about students' reading ability, as well as with specific demographic and employment related information.

The following test is designed to accomplish these two purposes.

Portions of design statement

Purpose of test

This is a fairly high-stakes test of reading ability in which inferences about the test takers' ability to perform the test task will be used by job service personnel to make selection (hiring) decisions. Inferences will also be used by adult education program personnel to make placement decisions (to place test takers in ESL reading courses at the appropriate level). At the same time, the test will provide demographic and work-related information about the test takers' experience and objectives.

Description of the TLU domain and task types

The TLU domain is broadly defined as 'workers reading on the job'. The test takers are or will be employed in a wide variety of jobs, ranging from entry level manual labor positions to white collar and professional employment. TLU tasks in these various jobs include reading job applications, instruction manuals, signs and notices, and bulletins.

Characteristics of test takers

Personal characteristics

Test takers are refugees and newly arrived immigrants entering an adult education program in a large US city, 18 years of age and up, male and female, wide variety of native nationalities and native languages, variety of social classes and educational backgrounds. Highly varying experience with different kinds of tests.

Topical knowledge of test takers

Test takers will have relatively diverse topical knowledge due to their varying job-related experiences. However, all test takers will have highly specific knowledge of some prior employment experience, either in the US or their country of origin. They will know about their own personal demographic characteristics, and their own employment experience and needs. Although the test is not designed as a measure of this knowledge, knowledge of this type obtained by job service case workers is used as part of their advising procedures.

General level and profile of language ability

General ability level varies from beginning to advanced. Generally, these test takers can speak a little better than they can read or write. However, some test takers can read much better than they can write.

Definition of construct to be measured

Language knowledge

In this project, the characteristics of the input are described quite precisely and are used to develop a definition of the construct to be measured: knowledge of graphology, knowledge of work-experience-related vocabulary, the grammar of questions, the grammar of phrases, the grammar of subordination, and the organization of paragraphs.

Consideration of qualities of usefulness

Reliability

Reliability-related concerns with this method include consistency of scoring. Although a single scorer is used, the person doing the scoring might change over time, and different scorers might have different ideas of what constitutes a reasonable response to some of the prompts. A plan for empirically evaluating reliability might include having several scorers score a number of tests and comparing the scoring for consistency. Perhaps examples of 'reasonable' responses could be provided to the scorers.

Construct validity

A plan for empirical investigation of construct validity might include developing several other prompts by sampling from a different set of TLU task characteristics and then conducting a study of the relationships among scores on responses to different prompts.

Authenticity

Filling out an employment questionnaire is a task that the majority of these test takers will have done, or will need to do. However, it is unlikely that the average questionnaire would include input with a systematically graduated range of complexity comparable to the input in this test. In addition, the test task is only one of many kinds of reading tasks that the test takers are likely to encounter on the job.

Interactiveness

Language knowledge: A fairly wide range of language knowledge is involved, with the possible exception of knowledge of organization of long texts and sociolinguistic variation.
Topical knowledge: The role of test takers' personal topical knowledge in carrying out test tasks is highly involved, because the test takers respond to input from personal experience.
Strategies: We would expect there to be involvement of strategies in accessing different bits and pieces of topical knowledge, or in deciding which of several answers to put down (for example, in questions 23–25 in Chapter 7).

Impact

We want the test to affect test takers and job service case workers positively. The opportunity for positive impact might be increased by carefully explaining the rationale behind the test and the steps that have been taken to promote relevance, appropriateness, and fairness. Feedback on impact could be obtained by asking the test takers, the staff of the language program, job service personnel, and employers for feedback on the design specifications, method, and decisions to be made.

Practicality

The information from which the input is created is the authentic information needs of the job service case worker. Some time and effort is needed to develop the actual input for interpretation and try it out. No resources are required to prepare constructed responses. The test can be administered to a group of test takers by an untrained proctor. Scoring procedures are straightforward. Scorers can be trained by providing them with samples of tests and an opportunity to discuss the distinction between responsive and non-responsive answers to the questions.

Inventory of available resources and plan for their allocation

More resources are available for test development than for test use. Therefore, the test should require few resources to administer and score.

Operationalization

The test consists of a written questionnaire for the students to read and respond to. The main difference between the questions is the complexity of the language in which they are worded. The early, easy questions consist of one-word items using high frequency vocabulary such as 'name', 'age', etc. The later, more difficult questions are much longer, involve complex syntax, and contain less frequent vocabulary. All of the questions in the questionnaire deal with demographic information or work-related experience.

The input is created in two steps. First, we give a list of the kinds of information that job services case workers need to obtain in their counseling. We then convert this list into questions of increasing linguistic complexity. We try to develop questions for which the reasonableness of the answer can be easily determined.

All of the questions can be responded to in a word, phrase, or short simple sentence, so few demands are made on the students' ability to produce written language. The topical information in the responses comes from the test takers' prior work experience and current expectations.

The answers to the questions are scored on the basis of their reasonableness, the idea being that if the test takers can supply a reasonable answer to a question, they must have understood it.

Scoring criteria

Reasonableness of response only. Credit is awarded if answer makes sense. No credit is given if answer does not make sense.

Scoring procedures

Scorers familiarize themselves with a list of example correct and incorrect responses prior to scoring the test. Each test is scored once.

Report form

Question number	Credit	Non-credit
1	_____	_____
2	_____	_____
3	_____	_____
4	_____	_____
5	_____	_____
6	_____	_____
7	_____	_____
8	_____	_____
9	_____	_____
10	_____	_____
	Etc.	
TOTAL	_____	_____

Actual copies of the test are provided along with the score report form, since the information provided by test takers may be of value to test users.

Appendix 6: Test for Project 6

Instructions

The instructions will be translated into the test takers' native languages, since we cannot assume that test takers will be able to read them.

1 In order for us to place you in a reading course, and in order for Job Services to help you find a job, we need some information about your job experience and needs.
2 The test consists of a short form for you to read and fill out. You can answer each question in just a few words. Answer all of the questions that you can. If you cannot understand the question, just leave it blank.

Don't worry if you cannot answer a question. We will talk with you later and get any additional information we might need.

3   Write your answers to the questions below in the space provided.

Employment information form

General Information

1   Name? _____

2   Age? _____

3   Address? _____

4   Nationality? _____

5   Place of birth? _____

6   Date of birth? _____

7   Date of arrival in the US? _____

8   Are you married? _____

9   How long have you lived in (name of city)? _____

10   How long did you live in the country in which you were born?

_____

11   Do you have any children? _____

Job information

12   Have you held a job in the US? _____

13   Have you held a job in your native country? _____

14   List the names of the first and second jobs you have held.

_____

15   Which of the above-mentioned jobs did you hold for the longest time? _____

16   How many years of schooling did you have prior to working on your first job? _____

17   What was your salary on the last job you held? _____

18   Of all of the jobs you have held, for which one did you feel the greatest personal satisfaction? _____

19 If you were applying for another job in the US, what is the minimum salary for which you would be willing to work? _____

20 What kinds of hours would you be willing to work if offered a job here in (name of city)?_____

21 For what kind of job do you feel the most qualified? _____

22 What kinds of benefits did you receive in the last job you held?

_____

23 If you were unemployed, what are the consequences that you would fear the most? _____

24 What aspect of your working environment in the last job that you held did you find most appealing? _____

_____

25 If you were offered a job in the US, what kind of insurance would you most want your employer to provide? _____

_____

26 Some employers do very little to take care of their employees outside of factors which directly affect their ability to perform their job. Others tend to involve themselves more directly in their employees' personal lives and take various steps to help promote their employees' sense of well being. Which kind of employer would you prefer to work for? _____

_____

27 What do you think should be the two most important factors for an employer to consider when deciding whether or not to promote an employee within an organization? _____

_____

28 What proportion of one's total employment time do you believe an employer should allow an employee to be absent from work with no justification needed? _____

_____

29   Of the various factors involved, such as language ability, job experi-
      ence, flexibility, adaptability, and willingness to involve oneself in job
      training, which do you believe places the least demands upon one's

      language ability? _____

      _____

Project 7

Employment/placement/achievement test for immigrants in a government-funded vocational training ESL course

Introduction

The following is an extended example illustrating the process by which we might develop portions of a design statement and blueprint of an ESP test. Here is the situation. Suppose we were brought in as consultants to help develop a test for immigrants in a government-funded vocational training ESL course. The course is designed to enable them to communicate accurately and appropriately when speaking with customers, supervisors, and co-workers about repairs to the customers' automobiles. Also, suppose results from the test would be used by potential employers as well as by the vocational training school. In this project, we need to use a number of TLU tasks as the basis for developing test tasks because no single TLU task will allow us to design a test with adequate overall usefulness.

Design

Comments on the process

Developing the description of the tasks in the TLU domain

We would consult with subject-matter specialists (such as people who are master mechanics or managers of parts departments, as well as non-specialists, who are likely to have been customers in an auto repair shop), and come up with a list of the types of tasks the mechanic would be likely to perform in carrying out the job.

Developing the construct definition

We would develop the construct definition in consultation with both personnel from the vocational training school and potential employers. We might suggest a number of areas of language knowledge that we could measure and ask them what was important. We could also discuss with them the amount of resources needed to develop test tasks that would allow us to measure various areas of language and topical knowledge.

Considering qualities of usefulness

In determining the appropriate balance among the qualities of usefulness, we need to recognize that although the decisions to be made on the basis of the test are relatively low-stakes, we are accountable to the funding agency, and hence will need to demonstrate the reliability and construct validity of our test.

At the same time, since the entire course will be focused on job-related tasks that involve speaking, we want the test to correspond as closely as possible to the test takers' potential work environment, and so want to include speaking tasks that are as authentic and interactive as possible. In addition, we need to be concerned with the impact of the test, the consequences for both employer and applicant of making the wrong employment decision. Since it is designed for multiple administrations in a federally funded program, or possibly by a number of similar programs, considerable resources might be devoted to developing this test.

Portions of the design statement

1 *Purposes of test*

To place immigrants in a government funded vocational training ESL conversation course designed to enable individuals to communicate accurately and appropriately in speaking with customers and co-workers about repairs to the customers' automobiles; to help potential employers make employment decisions.

2 *Description of tasks in the TLU domain*

The following is a list of TLU task types. The characteristics of these tasks would need to be described in a complete design statement.

   a Explaining to customers what kinds of diagnostic tests need to be performed on their automobiles.

   b Explaining to customers the nature of mechanical problems encountered.

   c Explaining to customers what needs to be done to repair the problems.

   d Explaining to customers the basis for repair charges.

e Consulting with or seeking the advice of co-workers and super-visors on the kinds of diagnostic tests that need to be performed, on the nature of mechanical problems encountered, etc.

f Ordering parts.

g Negotiating compromises when the customer is dissatisfied with repair.

h Asking the employer for time off.

3 *Construct to be measured*

Ability to communicate with correct syntax and correct technical and non-technical vocabulary in speaking in appropriate registers with customers and co-workers about repairs to the customers' automobiles. The construct definition also includes correct topical knowledge of mechanical procedures for repairing automobiles.

The construct to be measured includes:

1 knowledge of syntax,
2 knowledge of technical and non-technical vocabulary,
3 knowledge of registers appropriate for communicating with customers and co-workers, and
4 topical knowledge of procedures for performing automobile repairs.

Portions of operationalization

Comments on the process

To create our test tasks, we would begin by making a list of the characteristics of the TLU tasks to determine what, if any, characteristics these tasks have in common, so as to describe the tasks in the TLU domain. We would then be in a position to select or modify actual TLU tasks, or to create test tasks that have characteristics similar to those of the TLU tasks, for example, a simulated role-play in which several examiners interact with test takers. The first examiner might pretend to be a customer who has brought his car in for repair. The customer/examiner would describe a problem in general terms and the test taker would be expected to use her topical knowledge of automobile mechanics to ask appropriate questions to obtain more detailed information. The second examiner might pretend to be a supervisor who asked the test taker to explain the progress of the repairs: what had been done and what work still remained. The third examiner might be a clerk at an auto parts store taking an order for parts needed in the repair.

In considering TLU tasks for possible use in developing test tasks, we would again use the aspects of usefulness as criteria.

We might first ask which of these TLU tasks would allow us to develop test tasks that would provide us with *reliable* information. If we asked the test taker to make up an explanation of what she did in repairing a mechanical problem, and why, without supplying any particulars, variation in what the test taker decided to say from one test administration to the next might lead to unreliability.

We would also require *valid* information about the construct to be measured. For example, do any of the tasks involve responses that would not provide information about knowledge of syntax? Tasks that require only one-word responses to yes/no questions might not provide us much useful information about this. For example, although the list of TLU tasks includes asking the employer for time off, we might decide to omit this task because it could be accomplished by using a set formula that would not allow us to make judgments about knowledge of syntax.

An additional requirement for construct validity is that the client, the owner of an automobile repair company, needs to be able to make inferences about the test taker's control of various kinds of vocabulary items related to automobile repair. One of the TLU tasks involves describing to the customer what repairs have been made to the automobile and what parts have been replaced. This task by itself might provide useful information about the test taker's control of the specific vocabulary for this language use task, but it might not in and of itself be adequate to allow us to make inferences about the test taker's ability to use the more precise technical names of parts in conversations with supervisors or when ordering parts from the distributors.

All of the tasks in the list of TLU tasks could be expected to be relatively *authentic* because they are based on an analysis of the characteristics of the TLU tasks gathered from content area specialists—people familiar with the kinds of tasks automobile mechanics engage in.

Some of the tasks in the list of TLU tasks might be less *interactive* than others. For example, asking for a day off might be accomplished with a formula that would not require a high level of involvement of topical knowledge, language knowledge, or high levels of use of strategic competence, so we might decide not to include this task in our test.

We would ask which tasks would have a positive *impact* on the test taker (the immigrant automobile mechanic) and other users of test results (the teachers in the ESP program and potential employers). We might ask the teachers in the ESP course which tasks would provide them with the most useful information on ability to use correct syntax and appropriate vocabulary, and which tasks might provide useful models for the development of teaching/learning tasks. We might also ask the test takers to what extent they feel the test tasks are relevant to their future language use needs.

Some of the tasks described above might involve the use of an actual car, and multiple examiners, both of which might be less practical in this testing situation.

Portions of the blueprint

1 *Test structure*

A Number of parts/tasks: This test is organized around three tasks: a role-play with a customer, a role-play with a supervisor, and a role-play with an auto parts clerk. The purpose of the three parts is to require the test takers to demonstrate control of syntax, vocabulary, register, and topical knowledge in tasks that involve communicating with customers and co-workers on the topic of automobile repair.

B Salience of parts: parts are clearly distinct.

C Sequence of parts: as per sequence normally followed in repairing an automobile:
1 taking the customer's description of the problem and arriving at a possible repair to solve it;
2 discussing the proposed repair and parts to be ordered with the supervisor, and
3 ordering the parts in the parts department.
Note that control of topical knowledge could be measured in Part 1.

D Relative importance of parts or tasks: all parts equally important.

E Number of tasks per part: one.

2 *Test task specifications*

A Purpose: as stated in the project, this test will be used for a single purpose: to place immigrants in a government funded vocational training ESL conversation course designed to enable them to communicate accurately and appropriately in speaking with customers, supervisors, and co-workers about repairs to the customers' automobiles. Thus, the purpose for each test task will be the same.

B Definitions of construct
1 *Task 1*: Construct definition would include ability to describe the nature of specific problem 1 using correct technical and non-technical vocabulary in a register appropriate to interaction with a customer.

2 *Task 2*: Construct definition would include ability to describe the nature of specific problem 2 using correct technical vocabulary in a register appropriate to interaction with a supervisor, as well as the ability to provide a description of the status of the repair to the defective part.

3 *Task 3*: Construct definition would include ability to name specific parts to be ordered using correct technical vocabulary in a register appropriate to interaction with personnel in the parts department.

C Setting: There are a number of possible settings for the test tasks, for example, in an actual auto repair shop with actual automobiles, parts, etc. as props, or in a classroom using pictures as props. Another option would be to conduct the test in a language laboratory using audio-visual equipment to provide some of the necessary input and record the responses. The description of the test tasks in Table 7.1 is based upon a version of the test designed to be administered in an actual auto shop.

D Time allotment

1   *Task 1*: 5 minutes
2   *Task 2*: 5 minutes
3   *Task 3*: 5 minutes

E Instructions

1 *Language*: the target language (English) because the test takers have a wide variety of native languages. The test takers read the instructions as they are read aloud by the proctor.
2 *Channel*: aural and visual.

F Scoring method

1 Criteria for correctness: criterion-referenced, language ability scales. Ratable samples of test takers will be scored from 1–4 on separate criterion-referenced scales for range and accuracy of use of syntax, technical and non-technical vocabulary, register, and topical knowledge.
2 *Procedures for scoring the response*: all role-play tasks are video-taped and rated on all four scales by two raters. The raters review the scales before each rating session. No rating session lasts longer than 45 minutes. The raters assign componential ratings on the four scales.
3 *Explicitness of criteria and procedures*: the test takers are informed in general terms about the scoring criteria (in the prompt).

G Characteristics of individual tasks: see Table P7.1.

	TEST TASK 1: Role-play with customer	TEST TASK 2: Role-play with supervisor	TEST TASK 3: Role-play with auto parts clerk
SETTING			
Physical characteristics	Location: auto shop, area where customers bring vehicles in for service. Noise level: quiet at time of testing. Temperature and humidity: somewhat cool with smell of chemicals and exhaust fumes. Seating conditions: varied: no seating. Lighting: generally well-lit but mechanics' flash lights provided for under-the-hood work. Materials and equipment and degree of familiarity: mechanic's tool set with which test takers are likely to be familiar.	Location: supervisor's counter in auto shop. Noise level: quiet at time of testing. Temperature and humidity: somewhat cool with smell of chemicals and exhaust fumes. Seating conditions: varied: no seating. Lighting: well lit. Materials and equipment and degree of familiarity: 'supervisor's' file of work orders and pen. Test taker likely to be familiar with materials.	Location: by telephone on wall of auto shop. Noise level: quiet at time of testing. Temperature and humidity: somewhat cool with smell of chemicals and exhaust fumes. Seating conditions: varied: no seating. Lighting: well lit. Materials and equipment and degree of familiarity: telephone connected to phone used by examiner; a list of numbers of auto-parts suppliers. Test taker will likely be familiar with materials and equipment
Participants	Test taker and examiner playing role of customer. Examiner will be unfamiliar to the test taker but likely to have a positive attitude toward him/her.	Test taker and second examiner playing role of supervisor. Examiner will be unfamiliar to the test taker but likely to have a positive attitude toward him/her.	Test taker and third examiner playing role of auto parts clerk on another phone. Examiner will be unfamiliar to the test taker but likely to have a positive attitude toward him/her.
Time of task	Evening, after closing time	Evening, after closing time	Evening, after closing time
INPUT			
Format			
Channel	Aural (customer's description of problem) and visual (customer's car with defective starter).	Aural (supervisor's question) and visual (test taker will be given a partially repaired starter motor which he will examine. On the basis of this examination he will construct his reply to the supervisor).	Aural (auto parts clerk's responses) and visual (list of phone numbers of auto parts suppliers).
Form	Language and non-language	Language and non-language	Language
Language	Target	Target	Target
Length	Short to medium (several sentences).	Short to medium (several sentences).	Short to medium (several sentences).
Type	Prompt: customer describes problem.	Prompt: 'What's status of repair?'	Prompt: 'Can I help you?' Input for interpretation (whether or not parts are available and their prices).

	TEST TASK 1: Role-play with customer	TEST TASK 2: Role-play with supervisor	TEST TASK 3: Role-play with auto parts clerk
Degree of speededness	Generally unspeeded	Generally unspeeded	Generally unspeeded
Vehicle	Live	Live	Live
Language characteristics			
Organizational characteristics			
Grammatical	Vocabulary: narrow range of general and technical vocabulary. Syntax: moderate range of organized structures.	Vocabulary: narrow range of general and technical vocabulary. Syntax: narrow range of organized structures.	Vocabulary: narrow range of general technical vocabulary. Syntax: narrow to moderate range of organized structures.
Textual	Cohesion: textually cohesive. Organization: sentences and oral paragraphs with visual points of reference.	Cohesion: textually cohesive. Organization: individual sentences to request information and ask for additional details of scope of repairs.	Cohesion: textually cohesive. Organization: individual sentences to request information and ask for additional details of scope of repairs.
Pragmatic characteristics			
Functional	Ideational and manipulative, with perhaps some heuristic functions as 'customer' thinks through the problem while he talks.	Manipulative: requesting information.	Ideational: supplying information.
Sociolinguistic	Dialect/variety: regional. Register: formal. Naturalness: natural. Cultural references and figurative language: none.	Same as for Task 1	Same as for Task 1
Topical characteristics	Electrical problems with intermittent starter motor.	Same as for Task 1	Same as for Task 1
EXPECTED RESPONSE			
Format			
Channel	Aural and visual	Aural	Aural
Form	Language	Language	Language
Language	Target	Target	Target

	Task 1	Task 2	Task 3
Length	Relatively short: sentences and short paragraphs.	Relatively short: sentences.	Relatively short: sentences.
Type	Extended production	Limited production	Limited production
Speededness	Generally unspeeded	Generally unspeeded	Generally unspeeded
Language characteristics			
Organizational characteristics			
Grammatical	Vocabulary: technical, associated with problems with starter motor. Syntax: standard English.	Same as for Task 1	Same as for Task 1
Textual	Cohesion: cohesive. Rhetorical: limited and extended description and explanation, and prediction.	Cohesion: cohesive. Rhetorical: one-sentence requests for information.	Cohesion: cohesive. Rhetorical: questions and answers.
Pragmatic characteristics			
Functional	Ideational, manipulative, and some heuristic (using conversation to figure out what problem might be).	Manipulative: requests for information.	Manipulative: requests for information.
Sociolinguistic	Dialect/variety: standard. Register: formal. Naturalness: natural. Cultural references and figurative language: none.	Same as for Task 1	Same as for Task 1
Topical characteristics	Electrical problems with car associated with intermittent and noisy operation of starter motor.	Same as for Task 1, but can be more technical because of supervisor's background knowledge.	Same as for Task 1
RELATIONSHIP BETWEEN INPUT AND RESPONSE			
Reactivity	Reciprocal	Reciprocal	Reciprocal
Scope of relationship	Narrow	Narrow	Narrow
Directness of relationship	Mostly direct	Indirect	Indirect

Table P7.1: Test task specifications for Project 7

Projects 8–10
Classroom achievement tests

Introduction

The next three projects illustrate how our approach to test development can be applied to the development of classroom achievement tests. First, they illustrate the use of classroom teaching and learning tasks as a basis for developing test tasks. That is, rather than attempting to identify TLU tasks in situations outside the classroom, in these projects the test developers have based test tasks on a language instructional TLU domain, as discussed in Chapter 6 (pages 103–6). Second, they demonstrate the use of syllabus content, in the form of teaching and learning objectives or targets, as a basis for defining the constructs to be measured. Third, they illustrate ways in which our framework of task characteristics can be adapted to suit the needs of a particular situation. Finally, they illustrate the applicability of our approach for developing tests to languages other than English.

Project 8
Classroom achievement test for an introductory German course

Introduction

In this project we illustrate the development of one task in a syllabus-based test for students in a first year university level course in German in an American university. The textbook on which this test is based (Donahue and Watzinger 1990) is, in the words of the authors, 'a new, functionally communicative, proficiency oriented program for beginning college German' (page iii). The general goals of the course are to enable the student 'to learn to speak German that is reasonably fluent, spontaneous, grammatically and culturally accurate, and easily understood by a native speaker of German' (page iii). Functional goals include initiating and sustaining simple conversations that center on topics and experiences with which the students are already familiar, such as family and friends, life as a student, free-time activities, and daily routines. Students should also be able to handle situations typically encountered by tourists. Some of the specific functional goals include ability to ask and answer questions, make requests, give commands, provide explanations, and express attitudes. In addition to the functional goals, the course focuses on building a large vocabulary and becoming aware of customs and values of native speakers of German as well as the linguistic features of the language that reflect those values. Finally, the course emphasizes grammatical accuracy, which involves learning the forms of words and the order in which to use them to construct sentences and larger units of discourse.

In this project we focus on the development of one test task which might be included in a syllabus-based achievement test covering some of the material in Chapter 5 of the German textbook. (This task would be used in combination with other tasks to form a complete test.) One of the more distinctive aspects of this project is the discussion of two TLU domains—language-instructional and real-life—and how the consideration of these influences the test task characteristics. Another distinctive aspect is that the test is based on a specific commercially available text, which may add to the realism of the project. Finally, this is a test of language ability in German, which helps support our position that this book is relevant to the development of tests for all languages, not just English as a second or foreign language.

Stage 1: Specification

Purpose of test

The purpose of this test is to measure students' control of specific lexical and grammatical forms used to perform a particular function. In this relatively low-stakes test, results are to be used to make a number of decisions. Decisions about test takers include progress and grading: the degree to which students meet minimum standards of mastery of the content of a single instructional unit. Decisions about instruction include determining what portions of a unit have been effectively taught, and what portions might require review. No decisions about teachers, supervisors, or the program are involved.

Description of task in the TLU domain

The characteristics of the test task ('ordering a meal') are based on the characteristics of the TLU task of ordering a meal in German, which is found in both the real-life TLU domain and the language instructional TLU domain. (The chapter in the German textbook for which this test is being developed includes specific instructions on how to order a meal in German.) The language-instructional task (ordering a meal) is consistent with the general functional goals of the text, which the authors state, include handling situations typically encountered by a tourist in Germany.

Column 1 of Table P8.1 provides an analysis of the characteristics of the TLU task, 'ordering a meal'.

Description of test takers' characteristics

Personal characteristics

Personal characteristics of test takers are fairly restricted. Most test takers are undergraduate students in an American university. Students in the introductory German class are at least 18 years of age, mostly between 18 and 23, and both males and females. Most are US citizens and native speakers of English. Those whose native language is not English usually control English very well. Students can be expected to be familiar with test tasks of the type we propose since previous unit tests would be likely to include similar test tasks.

Topical knowledge

All test takers have highly specific topical knowledge of procedures for ordering a meal in restaurants found in the US. While these procedures are

	Characteristics of relevant TLU task	Modifications to test task
	Ordering a meal in a restaurant	Ordering several items in a meal in a restaurant
SETTING		
Physical characteristics	Location: restaurant in Germany. Noise level: varied, but probably not quiet. Lighting conditions could vary from well lit to subdued (candle lit). Temperature and humidity: typically comfortable. Seating conditions: typically at a table for two or four, though possibly at a larger table or at a counter. Materials and equipment: place setting, menu, and possibly a sign or chalkboard on which the daily special is written.	Location: language laboratory where students normally practice course material responses (practicality). In addition to a sample menu, the test takers are also provided with a test booklet containing written instructions.
Participants	Tourist and possibly a companion, server.	Test taker only
Time of task	Varied, but typically during mealtimes.	Regularly scheduled class period.
INPUT **Format**		
Channel	Audio (from the server) and visual (menu and chalkboard with daily specials).	Audio and visual (to help insure that test takers understand the procedures they are to follow).
Form	Language (menu) and non-language (items on a buffet).	Language only (practicality)
Language	Target (German)	German on the menu and during the instructions. English is also used in the instructions to insure that test takers understand the instructions.
Length	Generally short but might include a fairly long list of daily specials.	Short
Type	Input for interpretation.	Input for interpretation.
Speededness	Unspeeded	Unspeeded

Vehicle	Live (oral input)	Reproduced: to increase practicality and reliability (consistency in administration).

Language characteristics

Organizational characteristics

Grammatical	Vocabulary: narrow range of specialized vocabulary associated with ordering a meal. Syntax: narrow range of organized structures. Graphology: might be typewritten or handwritten.	Same as for TLU task
Textual	Narrow range of cohesive devices and organizational patterns.	Same as for TLU task

Pragmatic characteristics

Functional	Ideational (describing options) and manipulative (for eliciting an order for a meal). Politeness formulae.	Same as for TLU task
Sociolinguistic	Dialect/variety: variable, depending upon the region of Germany being visited.	Dialect/variety: standard
	Register: moderately formal and informal. Naturalness: natural. Cultural references and figurative language: names and descriptions of dishes typically found in German restaurants but not in US restaurants.	Same as for TLU task
Topical characteristics	Limited: ordering a meal	Same as for TLU task

EXPECTED RESPONSE

Format

Channel	Audio	Same as for TLU task
Form	Language	Same as for TLU task
Language	Target (German)	Same as for TLU task

Length	Short (words, phrases, short sentences).	Same as for TLU task
Type	Limited production	Same as for TLU task
Speededness	Generally unspeeded	Same as for TLU task
Language characteristics		
Organizational characteristics		
Grammatical	Vocabulary: mostly technical vocabulary associated with items on a menu or ways the items might be prepared. Syntax: standard German.	Same as for TLU task
Textual	Cohesion: cohesive. Rhetorical: list containing different parts of meal being ordered.	Same as for TLU task
Pragmatic characteristics		
Functional	Ideational, manipulative	Same as for TLU task
Sociolinguistic	Dialect/variety: standard. Register: moderately formal. Naturalness: natural. Cultural references and figurative language: none.	Same as for TLU task
Topical characteristics	Limited: ordering meals in a restaurant.	Same as for TLU task
RELATIONSHIP BETWEEN INPUT AND RESPONSE		
Reactivity	Reciprocal	Non-reciprocal (practicality)
Scope of relationship	Narrow	Same as for TLU task
Directness of relationship	Direct and indirect. While responses often include information provided in the menu or by the server, there might be situations in which a tourist ordering a meal would need to be familiar with German culture in order to know specific details of what kinds of food are normally offered and how they are normally ordered.	Same as for TLU task

Table P8.1: Characteristics of TLU task and modifications to related test task similar to procedures for ordering meals in German restaurants, specific differences might be found in the kinds of food generally available in German and US restaurants. For example, for breakfast Germans often eat a hard roll with butter and jam (along with coffee, tea, etc.), whereas hard rolls are not generally found on breakfast menus in restaurants in Ephraim and Panguitch, Utah, where most of the students live.

General level and profile of language ability

All test takers are at a beginning level of language ability in German, and their speaking ability is very limited.

Possible affective responses to taking test

We would hope that the students would feel positive about taking the test since it is based upon material they have been taught and is likely to be perceived as based upon a task which they might, some day, be performing in German.

Definition of construct to be measured

For this achievement test, a syllabus-based construct definition is used. This includes the following components of language knowledge: knowledge of singular and plural present tense forms in first and third person of the linking verb *mögen*.

Considerations of some qualities of usefulness

Authenticity

The authenticity of the test task is probably only moderate with respect to the real-life TLU task. Although the function of the test task (ordering a meal) and some of the input (a menu) are consistent with characteristics of a real-life TLU task, additional written instructions, including instructions indicating whom the speaker is to order for, specific ways to start the order, and instructions to use a specific linking verb are not very authentic. They are, however, consistent with the way the instructional tasks are cued in the text, and are thus relatively authentic with respect to the language-instructional TLU, so that the test task should not come as a surprise to the test takers.

Impact

We would hope that test takers would have a positive affective response to the test task because it is consistent both with the instructional tasks and with TLU tasks they would likely need to perform if they traveled in Germany. In addition, we would expect the impact on the instructors to be positive because they are likely to feel that their students are being tested fairly on material that has been emphasized in the instruction.

Inventory of available resources and plan for their allocation

Unit tests of this type are prepared by either the course supervisor, a committee composed of course instructors, or both. Tests are administered to all sections of the course on a single day and then scored by members of the testing committee or other course instructors. Time to develop and score the tests is considered to be part of the instructors' normal teaching requirements.

Stage 2: Operationalization

Some portions of test task specifications

Setting

The test as a whole, including the example task, is administered in the language laboratory using audio-visual equipment. Test takers are provided with a test booklet and tape for recording their responses. The tape with the instructions and input is prepared by the instructors. The test is administered during the ordinary class period.

Rubric

The time allotted for the example task needs to be adequate for test takers to read and listen to the instructions, think about their response, and record their responses to the task. This will be determined by pretesting the task on three students, one from each of three ability levels: high, medium, and low.

This specific task is scored objectively by a single instructor according to a scoring key. Instructions are provided in the students' L1 (English) both orally and in writing.

Input

Input is both oral and visual, in the L2 (German). It consists of a printed restaurant menu in German and short spoken requests for information related to ordering a meal in a restaurant. Additional input is also provided which instructs the test taker to use a specific word when ordering the meal. The form of this additional input is consistent with input in the instructional materials.

Expected response

The response is recorded on the student's test tape. It consists of a series of short sentences in which the test taker orders parts of a meal (in German) for him or herself and several other non-German-speaking companions. The purpose of this is to measure the ability of the test taker to use a variety of forms of the linking verb *mögen* in ordering a meal.

Relationship between input and response

Non-reciprocal, narrow in scope and relatively direct. The responses are framed directly from information provided in the menu according to explicit instructions.

Example test task

See Appendix 8 for the actual test.

Stage 3: Administration

The entire unit test will be tried out on three students at different ability levels prior to actual use and adjustments to test tasks will be made if necessary.

The test will be improved by debriefing teachers and a sample of students following each use and making appropriate modifications. The revised test will be reused during subsequent quarters.

Appendix 8: Test for Project 8

Instructions

(In English, both recorded and written)

You, your friend to whom you have been speaking in English, and several other non-German-speaking friends sit down to eat at the Café Kranzier. You are the only person in your party who speaks German. The waiter addresses you, and you place the orders for everyone in your party. Listen to the questions from the waiter and place your order for yourself and the others according to the information provided. Record the following parts of your order on the tape.

Items

(The English translations, given in parentheses, are not recorded on the tape and are provided only for readers of this book.)

Item 1

Recorded input: 'So, guten Tag. Was möchten Sie trinken?'

'Good day. What would you like to drink?'

Instructions: Order something to drink for yourself from the menu. Use a form of the verb 'mögen'.

Item 2

Recorded input: 'In Ordnung. Und Ihre Bekannte? Was darf's für sie sein?

'All right. And your friend? What will she have?'

Instructions: Order something different to drink from the menu for your friend. Use a form of the verb 'mögen'.

Item 3

Recorded input: 'Und was möchten Sie gern essen?'
'And what would you like to eat?'

Instructions: Select any main dish from the menu and order it for *both* you and your friend. Start your order with 'Wir . . .'. Use a form of the verb 'mögen'.

Item 4

Recorded input: 'Und was möchten die anderen trinken?'
'And what would the others like to drink?'

Instructions: Select any drink from the menu and order it for the other two people at your table. Start your order with 'Sie . . . '. Use a form of the verb 'mögen'.

Item 5

Recorded input: 'Und was möchten die anderen gern essen?'
'And what would the others like to eat?'

| Instructions: | Select any main course from the menu and order it for the other two people at your table. Start your order with 'Sie . . . '. Use a form of the verb 'mögen'. |

Item 6

(At end of meal)

Recorded input:	'Hätten Sie auch gern einen Nachtisch?'
	'And would anyone like dessert?'
Instructions:	Tell the waiter 'No thank you' in German.

Conclusion

Recorded input:	'Vielen Dank. Ich bringe Ihnen sofort Ihre Getränke.'
	'Thank you very much. I'll bring your drinks right away.'
Instructions:	Thank the waiter.

Scoring

Responses are scored objectively and indicate whether the test taker uses the correct forms of the linking verb 'mögen'. Scoring criteria are essentially the same for all items in the task: 2 points if the student uses the correct suffix in the appropriate person and number, including pronouncing the umlaut correctly if needed, 1 point for the correct inflectional suffix in the appropriate person and number and incorrect use of umlaut, if needed, and 0 points for incorrect form of linking verb and incorrect use of umlaut. Item 6 is included to increase the authenticity of the task but is not scored.

One instructor scores this task for all students. The instructor listens to each item once and awards variable credit for each item according to the scoring key provided above.

Project 9

Classroom achievement test for the reading component of the Korean–English Two-Way Bilingual Immersion Program[1]

Introduction

The Korean/English Two-Way Immersion Program (KETWIP) was started in 1993 in three elementary schools near Los Angeles' Korea Town (Rolstad et al. 1993, 1994). There is one class in the program in each school, and students in this class are kept together and will move from kindergarten through graduation from high school. In the initial stage of the program about 75 per cent of all instruction is in Korean, with the rest in English. As the students progress to the higher grades, instruction in Korean will never be less than 50 per cent of the total class time. Unlike traditional 'transitional' bilingual education, this program is a 'two-way' bilingual immersion program, with equal focus on Korean and English. KETWIP's aim is to help Korean-Americans retain and improve their native Korean language, while providing an opportunity for native English speakers to acquire Korean as a second language.

The test is designed for first graders in the KETWIP program and focuses on assessing students' ability to use language to comprehend academic textbooks written in Korean for first graders.

Stage 1: Design

Purpose of test

The purposes of the reading tests for the first grades in this program are described specifically as follows:

1 To assess the effect of the Korean-English Two-Way Bilingual Immersion Program instruction with regard to students' development in the ability to comprehend academic textbooks written in Korean for first graders (i.e. products).
2 To provide meaningful feedback to enhance instructional practice and students' learning with respect to reading academic textbooks written in Korean for first graders (i.e. processes).

Description of TLU domain and list of TLU tasks

The TLU domain is a set of settings and tasks that the students in this program are likely to encounter and that require target language use. Since the KETWIP program is at its *initial* stage of curriculum, namely the first grade, it is appropriate at this level to focus the instructional goals on the ability to comprehend the textbooks that the students use daily in class. Extending the domain to a long-term goal such as the ability to comprehend literature other than the textbooks would be more appropriate to the upper level students. Thus, at this initial stage the domain is limited more or less to the instructional situation and tasks.

Setting

The setting is Korea Town in Los Angeles, where two languages and two cultures (mainly Korean and English) coexist. In Korea Town, the setting where all students are commonly exposed to academic Korean textbooks is a *classroom* with classroom-related material, equipment, and time. The setting also includes the home where they will do homework assignments using their Korean textbooks. Materials include textbooks, notebooks, pencils, pens, etc. The Korean textbooks were written in Korean by the Institute of Korean Educational Development. These textbooks are based on the national syllabus policy and are used by first graders nationwide in Korea. The KETWIP adopted these textbooks as the primary reading material.

Instruction is given in Korean during the three morning class periods, followed by English instruction in the afternoon. During the Korean instruction, the teacher uses these textbooks regularly throughout the morning session. Other adapted materials are utilized for decoding practice. Time also includes afternoon and evening when students do homework related to reading.

Input

Format

The language arts, including reading, listening, speaking, and writing, are not subjects taught in isolation, but integrated process skills that help promote all students into higher levels of critical thought. Input presentation also occurs in the integrated processes with other language skills in natural discourse. Although discrete items are presented by the teacher (for example, phonemes, morphemes, and vocabulary learning in class), the items occur in a stream of naturally connected language use.

Channel of input is visual, mode is receptive, form is language (Korean), and length of input is usually short.

Language of input

Language of input is Korean. The vocabulary and syntax are simple and adapted to the beginner level. The input is organized grammatically and is occasionally presented in the form of code-mixing by the teacher and peers (i.e. Korean and English).

Pragmatic characteristics of input vary widely. Depending on subject content, topics include language arts, science, ethics, math, and social studies. With the exception of math and science, the topics include general areas such as etiquette, school life, family, children's games, food, friends, birthdays, hobbies, etc.

Genres frequently appearing in the textbooks consist of prose, diaries, and letters. Expositions, poems, signs, and notices appear less frequently.

Vocabulary includes general and subject content-related vocabulary. Vocabulary and picture content in Korean textbooks is simple and restricted according to the child's age. The degree of cultural references depends on the topic, with more cultural references likely to be found in the texts related to Korean holidays, food, clothes, and customs.

Classroom activities concerning discrete items involve the decoding of individual phonemes and morphemes, identification of written words, and recognizing and matching written words with their meanings.

Extended classroom tasks and homework include reading aloud and answering teachers' comprehension check-up questions regarding the text. 'Simplified' book reviews under subheadings such as a title, a theme, and topics are taught and assigned regularly to develop reading ability.

Two distinctive registers are found in the texts: language between students and their elders is written in the honorific register, whereas language between peers occurs in the non-honorific register.

Expected response

Format of response

The form of responses includes the Korean language or code-switching, mixing with English, as found in writing short answers to comprehension questions in the students' first language. The form of responses also contains non-language such as nodding, matching, and circling commonly found in the subject learning activities. The channel of response is visual (for example, writing, physical responses) and oral (for example, verbal expressions of a book's content). Type includes limited (such as short answers) and extended production (such as book reviews). Length is usually short, and speed is variable.

Language of response

Organizational and pragmatic characteristics of responses are simple and not as diverse as those found in input characteristics, which is typical for young learners.

Relationship between input and response

The relationship between input and response is non-reciprocal. However, there are 'interactions' between the language user and the input. The language user is 'involved' in the text, negotiating the meaning of the graphic system. This involvement uses interactive processes which include the text, the language user's language ability, topical knowledge, affective schemata, and metacognitive strategies.

Characteristics of test takers

Personal characteristics

Students' ages range from five to seven. Most of them have been born in the US. About 50 per cent of the students in the program are Korean-Americans and about 50 per cent are Tagalog, Spanish, or English speakers.

The test takers do not have highly specific topical knowledge in a particular subject because they are too young to have developed expertise in one subject area. However, due to the diversity of their ethnic backgrounds, the test takers have different topical knowledge to varying degrees (for example, knowledge associated with their own sub-cultures). Topical knowledge commonly shared by all test takers includes language, course content, games, and hobbies which are relevant to their age.

General level and profile of language ability

Test takers' general level of language ability varies substantially. The reading ability of Korean-Americans is at the beginning to intermediate level. However, this ability level varies substantially depending on their home environment and their parents' philosophy regarding their child's Korean language education. As for non-Koreans, they are at the beginning level in reading skills. Most of them are at a discrete vocabulary item and simple sentence level.

Definition of constructs to be measured

The construct, broadly defined, is 'the ability to use language to read and understand academic textbooks written in Korean for the first graders'. This definition is based on the syllabus used in the Korean course, and includes the following sub-skills:

1 ability to recognize written vocabulary and comprehend its meaning
2 ability to grasp the main idea of written words and sentences
3 ability to recognize specific details

Plans for evaluating the qualities of usefulness

Feedback to teachers, learners, parents, the program, and society will include qualitative information. Qualitative information will be in verbal descriptions, based on logical analysis, to help interpret test tasks and performance on these tasks.

Inventory of available resources and plan for their allocation

Materials needed for instructions and test administration include textbooks, papers, and other writing instruments. A Korean teacher is also a test administrator. The teacher will be the main interpreter and feedback provider regarding student performances on the tests.

Stage 2: Operationalization

Blueprint

Setting

The test takers' home is the place where they take exams. The home should be quiet, comfortable, and familiar to them.

Test organization

The following two tests will be given as take-home tests:

1 Monthly reading comprehension test: 8–10 questions.
2 Final exam of simple book review based on two chapters (or titles) from students' textbooks.

Time allocation

1   Reading comprehension test: two days.
2   Simple book review: to be submitted two weeks before the end of the semester to allow time for regular feedback.

Characteristics of test tasks

Input

Two sample tasks are given in Appendix 9.

The reading text will have a variety of topics sampled from the students' Korean textbooks. Topics include Korean, science, social studies, and ethics. Text length will be one chapter (or one title) of two to three pages. Textual organization is simple but grammatically correct. The genres of the passages comprise letters, diaries, and prose (poems will be excluded). The content of reading passages will not be overly exciting or disturbing. It will not be culture bound, so as to prevent bias against a particular ethnic group. If cultural references are embedded in the passages, it should be ensured that all students have learned and understood the cultural references.

Questions for comprehension check-up will be presented in the order in which the information was presented in the text. Questions which students are likely to be able to answer without understanding the text should be avoided. Questions dealing with lower-level processing skills, more related to reading comprehension skills *per se*, will be prioritized (i.e. literal under-standing and propositional meaning rather than inferences, interpretations, predictions, and extensions).

Expected response

Students will write their answers in either English or Korean, or with code-mixing. Form of response will be in Korean, English, or both. Channel of response is visual. Types are short answers, as in answering the reading comprehension questions, and extended writing as in the book reviews.

Relationship between input and response

As described in the specifications of the TLU domain, the relationship between input and response is manifested as an interactive process between the input and the test taker's mind while he or she is performing the tasks. Reactivity: non-reciprocal, Scope: narrow (reading comprehension questions), broad (book review), Directness: direct (reading comprehension questions), relatively broad (book review).

Usefulness of the test

Reliability

Since the tests are take-home, the students are likely to consult their parents. Some assistance is acceptable and sometimes necessary. We emphasize that the testing should be a service to learning. The ultimate purpose of these tests is to provide feedback to enhance student *learning* of Korean reading. We hope the students and parents understand the importance of integrity and trustworthiness involved with these take-home tests. Therefore, we will not be concerned with unreliability problems due to help seeking.

Construct validity

The following can be collected as evidence of construct validity:

1 A clear theoretical definition of the construct to be measured, namely clarity of description of measured behavior. This evidence is demonstrated in the construct definition portion of the design statement.
2 Relationship between theoretical construct definition and operational definition. This concerns content coverage, namely sampling a set of representative items and tasks which are congruent with the content domain definitions. This evidence is demonstrated in the characteristics of the TLU domain, construct definition, and characteristics of test tasks portions of the design statement.
3 Relevance of construct to the purpose and use of the test, namely content relevance to justify the test use for the intended purpose: this quality has been and will be obtained by consulting and reflecting relevant theories, content experts' opinions, instructional objectives, educational values and policies.
4 Unbiased test scores. Culture and language cannot be divorced in nature. Considering the heterogeneity of students' backgrounds, however, the tasks will not include culture-specific items, so that the tests will not give unfair advantage or disadvantage to students from different cultural groups.
5 Domain of generalization. The program is at an early stage, and learners are at the beginning level. It is not appropriate at this stage to expect them to read academic Korean textbooks other than the textbooks that they use in class. Our expectation, therefore, is the reading ability of the Korean textbooks that they study in classes. In other words, as for first graders, we will focus the domain of generalization on the instructional TLU domain described in the previous section.

Authenticity

Authenticity involves

1   a rich description of the TLU domain, and
2   the degree of correspondence of tasks in the TLU domain to test tasks.

These two are illustrated in the descriptions of the TLU domain and test tasks (above).

Interactiveness

This is demonstrated in the sections of the input–response relationship and the characteristics of test takers and of test tasks.

Impact

The stakeholders are students, teachers, parents, the program, and the society. When we design the tests, first of all we confirm that the book review and the comprehension check-up tasks used in class are 'appropriate' tools for reading instruction in this program. The next step is to adopt these tasks as test tasks, which will indicate the correspondence of test tasks to the TLU tasks. This correspondence provides evidence of content relevance and content coverage, which are essential elements of achievement tests. The impact of this match up is, accordingly, motivating the learners to approach their daily learning activities more positively and, thus, to bring beneficial washback effects to the instruction and the stakeholders. Again, this congruency and the accompanying positive impact are indicated throughout the series of the descriptions in this paper.

We can extend the discussion of impact to the far-reaching consequences of the test use in society. However, we would prefer to turn the topic of impact to the following point. The validity of test use is first based on the evidential basis of validity, which is based on content relevance, content coverage, and/or authenticity. Also, the validity of test use is based on reliability. The tests which do not have these qualities will not be able to insure the appropriateness of interpretations and of test use for the intended purposes.

Practicality

It will take a considerable amount of time for one teacher to read all of the comprehension test answers and the book reviews. However, an additional teacher to read the students' answers is not easily feasible. Two Korean teachers per class is not desirable, either. Therefore, although it will take time on the part of the teacher, scoring by the teachers is worthwhile to give relevant feedback and thus have a positive impact on stakeholders.

The cost of not achieving a positive influence will be greater. Understanding from partners, learners, and the school administrators concerning the teachers' work is needed to encourage and motivate them.

Note

1 This material is an adaptation of a test development project carried out by Jungok Bae for the TESL/AL 222 course taught by Lyle Bachman at UCLA in the Spring of 1994 and used with the permission of the author. Minor editorial changes have been made to keep the use of technical terms consistent with those in Parts One and Two of this book.

Appendix 9

Sample Tasks

Book review

Write a 1–2 page book review as you practiced in class for each of the following:

1 'Title here'
2 One chapter (or title) of your own choice.

In your review, include the following:

1 Source of the chapter (title)
2 Brief reason why you chose it
3 Author, if any
4 Topic
5 Several sentences regarding the content

You may write in English or Korean. Your evaluation will based on content relevance only.

Reading comprehension question

Read pages 0 to 0 of the textbook, '_____'. Then read the questions written on the exam sheet. Write your short answers on the exam sheet. You may write your answers in either Korean or English.

Project 10

Portions of a syllabus-based EFL progress test for primary school children[1]

Introduction

The Department of Education in an Asian country is implementing a new English language teaching syllabus for schools, in which the assessment of students' progress will be classroom-based, with teachers preparing the tests and test tasks. This syllabus is sequenced for the primary and secondary schools with several 'key stages' at which summative assessment will take place to provide a summary of learners' achievement and to help teachers check whether the learning targets have been covered. The test developed in this project is for Key Stage 1 (KS1), which includes primary grades 1–3. To facilitate the preparation of tests by teachers, the Department has developed sets of specifications based on the content of the new syllabus, from which individual teachers or groups of teachers in schools can develop tests and test tasks for their own classes. The actual specifications for an assessment task that were developed by the Department of Education are reproduced in 'Stage 2: Operationalization'.

Stage 1: Specification

Purpose of test

The overall purposes of these tests are to help teachers to:
– understand how their students are progressing
– find out students' strengths and weaknesses
– work out ways of helping the students
– use information from the assessment as a basis for future lesson planning.[2]

Portions of description of the TLU domain and tasks

The classroom setting and the teaching/learning tasks that are used constitute the TLU domain and tasks for this test. These learning tasks are intended to correspond to situations outside the classroom in which students might possibly use English, or can imagine themselves using English. The teaching tasks in the syllabus are organized into modules, such as 'Me, my family, and friends', and 'Places and activities'. Within each module there will be a number of units which are thematically or conceptually related. The module 'Places and activities', for example, includes units such as 'in the school', 'in the shop', and 'going to the zoo'.

Characteristics of test takers

Personal characteristics: Test takers are boys and girls in primary grades 1 through 3, ages five through eight. They come from a wide range of socio-economic backgrounds. Although the majority are native Cantonese speakers, a variety of ethnic and linguistic communities is represented.

Topical knowledge: These children, having just begun their academic careers, will have relatively little 'academic' knowledge, but will be well-versed in the areas of the family and friends, the local environment, living arrangements, and transportation.

General level and profile of language ability: Some students come from homes in which English is spoken by one or both parents, and thus will have moderate English ability. The majority, however, will have very little working knowledge of English, except for a few words and phrases that they may have acquired informally from radio, television, or street signs.

Definition of construct to be measured

The constructs to be measured are specified in terms of target learning objectives that are provided in the syllabus. These are grouped into three categories:

Dimension targets

Interpersonal dimension: To develop an ever-improving capability to use English
- to establish and maintain relationships
- to exchange ideas and information
- to get things done.

Knowledge dimension: To develop an ever-improving capability to use English
- to provide or find out, interpret, and use information
- to explore, express, and apply ideas
- to solve problems.

Experience dimension: To develop an ever-improving capability to use English.
– to respond and give expression to real and imaginative experience.[3]

Language skills: (listening, speaking, reading, and writing).

Language items and communicative functions

Language items include the major categories of grammar in English (for example, adjectives, adverbs, nouns, prepositions, verbs). Communicative functions for Key Stage 1 (KS1) include items such as greetings and bidding farewell, introducing oneself, describing oneself, expressing thanks, stating opinions, making simple requests, and recognizing common signs in English.

Plan for evaluating qualities of usefulness

Not included in this example. Instead, we provide a brief, preliminary discussion of the potential reliability and construct validity of this test.

Reliability

One source of measurement error in this test will be inconsistencies across tasks, and given the nature of the tasks, which are often integrative, involving a number of learning objectives and more than one language use activity, this will be difficult to eliminate entirely. However, with carefully prepared task specifications and training workshops to assist teachers in the task writing process, it should be possible for teachers to write highly comparable tasks. An additional mechanism in place to check for inconsistencies in tasks will be the various moderation teams who will regularly review tasks that teachers have prepared. Since the tests will be scored by individual teachers, scorer inconsistency is a second potential source of measurement error. However, with carefully constructed scoring keys and guidelines, this should not be a major concern, and can be checked regularly by comparing the scores given by different teachers to the same test tasks, and by asking individual teachers to go over their marks regularly to insure consistency. Given the relative low-stakes nature of this test, a high level of reliability is not absolutely essential, and the procedures suggested here for investigating reliability should be sufficient.

Construct validity

To address the question of construct validity, probably the most relevant evidence in this situation will be that of content relevance and coverage. Linking the specifications directly to the learning objectives of the syllabus should provide for a high degree of content relevance. In order to check this, the specifications developed by the different moderation teams could be exchanged and evaluated in terms of how closely they correspond to the relevant learning objectives. The question of content coverage is more complicated, but could involve a system whereby the tests prepared by individual teachers were regularly sampled and evaluated in terms of how well they covered the learning objectives that the teachers actually covered in class. This could be done within schools, with teachers exchanging their tests, and externally, by the Inspectorate for English.

Inventory of available resources and plan for their allocation

The Department of Education has organized a committee to oversee the development of test specifications, and has formed several test writing and moderation teams consisting of officials from the Curriculum Development Institute, Department of Education, selected headmasters/mistresses, and teachers who are heads of departments from schools. These teams will be responsible for writing and moderating specifications and exemplar test tasks for all the learning objectives in the syllabus. Individual classroom teachers or groups of teachers in schools will then write test tasks for their own classes. Classroom teachers will also score the tests and report the results to students, parents, and school administrators.

Stage 2: Operationalization

Blueprint

Here are the actual specifications for one example task that the Department of Education has prepared for teachers to use in developing test tasks of their own.

Assessment task specifications

1   *Title:*

Going to the zoo (Part 2)

2   *Purpose:*

To assess student progress in using simple information

3   *Language focus:*

Dimension targets

Knowledge dimension: To use simple information
– to provide or find out, interpret, and use information
– to explore, express, and apply ideas
– to solve problems.

Language skills:

Reading and writing

Language items and communicative functions:

Use nouns to identify animals

4   *Language use context:*

A language use situation in which students extract simple information from texts with the help of visual clues.
Participants: Daddy, Mummy, children, and other visitors
Location: at the zoo

5   *Duration of tasks:*

Reading input and writing responses: 5 minutes

6   *Input format:*

Form: Written language (verbal) and pictures of different animals (non-verbal)
Language: English
Length: Rubrics: About 20 words
Text prompt: Written, about 55 words
Type: Written and pictorial input for interpretation and items to elicit limited constructed response

7   *Input language characteristics:*

Vocabulary: Topical vocabulary related to the unit 'In the Park and Playground'
Syntax: Simple sentences and questions
Function: To identify common animals in the zoo

8   *Output format characteristics:*

Form: Written language
Language: English
Length: One word
Type: Limited production

9   *Output language characteristics:*

Vocabulary: Specific vocabulary related to the unit 'In the park and playground'
Syntax: One-word answers
Functions: To identify common animals in the zoo

10   *Scoring procedure:*

Method: Individual items to be scored according to the criteria below. Whole part to be assigned against Bands of Performance
Criteria: e.g. all correct   = ✓ Generally able to
              2–3 correct   = ✗ Partially able to
              fewer than 2 correct = ✗ Not yet able to

As noted above, this blueprint illustrates how terminology and frameworks can be adapted to suit the needs of the particular testing situation. In this blueprint, the phrase 'language focus' is used rather than 'definition of constructs', and the areas included here correspond to the three areas of target learning objectives that are included in the syllabus. Next, the term 'language use context' is used rather than 'TLU domain', and this is described in terms of language function (extracting simple information from texts with the help of visual cues), participants (Daddy, Mummy, children, and other visitors) and location (at the zoo).

Teacher's notes

A   *Level*: Key Stage 1, Primary 1

B   *Time limit*: 35 minutes

C   *Aims*: This assessment task assesses students' ability to:
   1   interpret simple information (Knowledge Dimension)
   2   use simple information (Knowledge Dimension)

D   *Materials required*
   1   Test paper
   2   Tape
   3   Tapescript

E   *Procedure*
　　1   The teacher gives the students the overview of the task. Tell them there are four parts.

　　　　Part 1: students fill in the speech bubbles in a given context
　　　　Part 2: students complete a dialog
　　　　Part 3: students do a listening task
　　　　Part 4: students read a short text and answer the questions

　　2   In Part 1, the teacher introduces the Lee family, who are going to the zoo. Students study the pictures carefully and fill in the time in the speech bubbles.
　　3   In Part 2, students study the pictures, identify the names of the animals and then complete the speech bubbles. (This is the only part of the test illustrated in this example project.)
　　4   In Part 3, the teacher tells the students that Daddy is buying some ice-cream for the children and their mother. Students listen to the tape and color the different ice-creams.
　　5   In Part 4, students read a short text. They are required to complete a quiz card for the Lee family.

F   *Scoring procedure*
Students' performances are marked according to the Task Specific Criteria.
✓ (generally able): name all the animals correctly
✗ (partially able): name two to three animals correctly
✗ (not yet able): name fewer than two animals correctly

Specific test tasks for Part 2 of the test

Scoring criteria and scoring procedures are the same as for Part 1.
See pages 366–70 for extracts from the test.

Notes

1   This project is an adaptation of an example assessment task specifications and tasks developed by the Subject Project Group (English) on Evaluation of Target Oriented Curriculum Assessment Mechanism, as reported in *Target Oriented Curriculum Assessment Guidelines for English Language. Key Stage 1 (Primary 1–3). Annex B.* Education Department, Hong Kong. June 1995.
2   Hong Kong Education Department 1995: 13.
3   *Target Oriented Curriculum Programme of Study for English Language. Key Stage 1 (Primary 1–3).* Hong Kong: Curriculum Development Council. Education Department: page 4.

Assessment Task

Class: _____

Name: _____   Date: _____

Part 1

The Lee family is going to the zoo today. Study the pictures and fill in the bubbles.

1.

Good morning, Daddy. What's the time?

It's eight o'clock.

2.

Mummy, what's the time?

It's _____ _____. Come and have your breakfast.

Part 2

The people are talking about the animals.

Write down the names of the animals they are talking about.

Part 3

The children are tired. They are having a rest. Daddy buys ice-creams for them. Daddy is asking them what ice-cream they like. Listen to the tape and colour the ice-creams.

Part 4

They are leaving the zoo now. Before they go, they get a quiz card and finish it together. Write the answers for them.

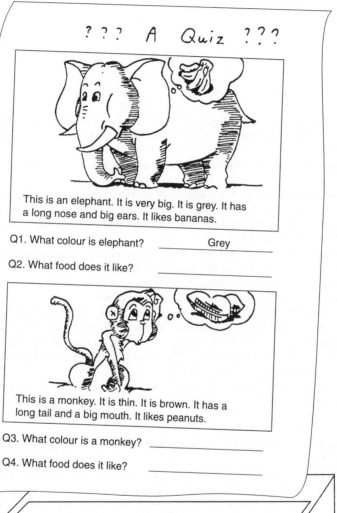

? ? ? A Quiz ? ? ?

This is an elephant. It is very big. It is grey. It has a long nose and big ears. It likes bananas.

Q1. What colour is elephant? _____ Grey

Q2. What food does it like? _____

This is a monkey. It is thin. It is brown. It has a long tail and a big mouth. It likes peanuts.

Q3. What colour is a monkey? _____

Q4. What food does it like? _____

Put your card here.

You will get a [gift] for all correct answers.

References

Alderson, J. C. and A. H. Urquhart. 1985. 'The effect of students' academic discipline on their performance on ESP reading tests.' *Language Testing* 2, 2: 192–204.

Alderson, J. C. and D. Wall. 1993. 'Does washback exist?' *Applied Linguistics* 14: 115–29.

American Psychological Association (APA). 1985. *Standards for Educational and Psychological Testing*. Washington, DC: American Psychological Association.

Bachman, L. F. 1990. *Fundamental Considerations in Language Testing*. Oxford: Oxford University Press.

Bachman, L. F. and A. S. Palmer. 1982. 'The construct validation of some components of communicative proficiency.' *TESOL Quarterly* 16, 4: 449–65.

Bachman, L. F. and A. S. Palmer. 1983. *Oral interview test of communicative proficiency in English*. Los Angeles, CA: Photo-offset.

Baker, E. L., H. F. O'Neil Jr., and R. L. Linn. 1993. 'Policy and validity prospects for performance-based assessment.' *American Psychologist* 48: 1210–18.

Berwick, R. 1989. 'Needs assessment in language programming: from theory to practice' in R. K. Johnson (ed.): *The Second Language Curriculum*. Cambridge: Cambridge University Press: 48–62.

Bialystok, E. 1990. *Communication Strategies*. Cambridge, MA: Basil Blackwell.

Brindley, G. 1989. 'The role of needs analysis in adult ESL programme design' in R. K. Johnson (ed.): *The Second Language Curriculum*. Cambridge: Cambridge University Press: 63–78.

Brown, G. and G. Yule. 1983. *Discourse Analysis*. Cambridge: Cambridge University Press.

Brown, H. D. 1994. *Principles of Language Learning and Teaching*. Third edition. Englewood Cliffs, NJ: Prentice-Hall Regents.

Brown, J. D. 1980. 'Newly placed students versus continuing students: Comparing proficiency' in J. C. Fisher, M. A. Clarke, and J. Schachter (eds.): *On TESOL '80. Building Bridges: Research and Practice in Teaching English as a Second Language*. Washington, DC: TESOL: 111–19.

Canale, M. 1983. 'On some dimensions of language proficiency' in J. W. Oller (ed.): *Issues in Language Testing Research*. Rowley, MA: Newbury House: 333–42.

Canale, M. 1988. 'The measurement of communicative competence' in R. B. Kaplan *et al.* (eds.): *Annual Review of Applied Linguistics*, Vol. 8. New York: Cambridge University Press.

Canale, M. and M. Swain. 1980. 'Theoretical bases of communicative approaches to second language teaching and testing.' *Applied Linguistics* 1: 1–47.

Carroll, B. J. and P. Hall. 1985. *Making Your Own Language Tests: A Practical Guide to Writing Language Performance Tests.* Oxford: Pergamon Press.

Carroll, J. B. 1961. 'Fundamental considerations in testing English proficiency of foreign students' in: *Testing the English Proficiency of Foreign Students.* Washington, DC: Center for Applied Linguistics: 30–40.

Carroll, J. B. 1968. 'The psychology of language testing' in A. Davies (ed.): *Language Testing Symposium: A Psycholinguistic Approach.* London: Oxford University Press: 46–69.

Carroll, J. B. 1993. *Human Cognitive Abilities: A Survey of Factor Analytic Studies.* Cambridge: Cambridge University Press.

Christison, M. A. 1995. 'Multiple intelligences and second language learners.' *Journal of the Imagination in Language Learning*, Vol. 3. Jersey City, NJ: Jersey City State College.

Clark, J. L. D. (ed.): 1978. *Direct Testing of Speaking Proficiency: Theory and Application.* Princeton, NJ: Educational Testing Service.

Cohen, A. D. 1994. *Assessing Language Ability in the Classroom.* Second edition. New York: Heinle and Heinle.

Cronbach, L. J. 1989. *Essentials of Psychological Testing.* Fourth edition. New York: Harper and Row, Publishers.

Crookes, G. and S. M. Gass. (eds.): 1993a. *Tasks and Language Learning: Integrating Theory and Practice.* Clevedon, Avon: Multilingual Matters.

Crookes, G. and S. M. Gass. 1993b. 'Introduction' in Crookes and Gass 1993a: 1–8.

Davidson, A. 1986. *Readability, and Questions of Textbook Difficulty.* Champaign, Ill.: University of Illinois at Urbana-Champaign. Cambridge, MA: Bolt, Beranek and Newman Inc.

Donahue, F. E. and J. Watzinger. 1990. *Deutsch Zusammen: A Communicative Course in German.* Englewood Cliffs, NJ: Prentice-Hall.

Duff, P. 1993. 'Tasks and interlanguage performance: An SLA research perspective' in Crookes and Gass 1993a: 57–95.

Færch, C. and G. Kasper. 1987. *Introspection in Second Language Research.* Clevedon, UK: Multilingual Matters.

Glass, G. V. and K. D. Hopkins. 1984. *Statistical Methods in Education and Psychology.* Second edition. New York: Prentice-Hall, Inc.

Gronlund, N. and R. L. Linn. 1990. *Measurement and Evaluation in Teaching.* 6th Edn. New York: Macmillan.

Guilford, J. P. and B. Fruchter. 1978. *Fundamental Statistics in Psychology and Education.* Sixth edition. New York: McGraw-Hill Book Company.

Hatch, E. and A. Lazaraton. 1991. *The Research Manual: Design and Statistics for Applied Linguistics.* New York: Newbury House Publishers.

Heaton, G. B. 1988. *Writing English Language Tests.* Second edition. London: Longman.

Hong Kong Education Department. 1995. *Target Oriented Curriculum Assessment Guidelines for English Language. Key Stage 1 (Primary 1–3).* Hong Kong: Education Department.

Hong Kong Education Department. 1995. *Target Oriented Curriculum Programme of Study for English Language. Key Stage 1 (Primary 1–3).* Hong Kong: Curriculum Development Council. Education Department.

Hughes, A. 1989. *Testing for Language Teachers.* Cambridge: Cambridge University Press.

Hymes, D. 1972. 'Models of interaction of language and social life' in J. J. Gumperz and D. Hymes (eds.): *Directions in Sociolinguistics: The Ethnography of Communication.* New York: Holt, Rinehart and Winston: 35–71.

Johnson, D. 1992. *Approaches to Research in Second Language Learning.* London: Longman.

Lado, R. 1961. *Language Testing.* New York: McGraw-Hill.

Linn, R. L. 1994. 'Performance assessment: Policy promises and technical measurement standards.' *Educational Researcher* 23, 9: 4–14.

Linn, R. L., E. L. Baker, and **S. B. Dunbar.** 1991. 'Complex, performance-based assessment: Expectations and validation criteria.' *Educational Researcher* 20, 8: 15–21.

Lowe, P. Jr. 1982. *ILR Handbook on Oral Interview Testing.* DLI/LOS Joint Oral Interview Transfer Project. Washington, DC.

Lowe, P. Jr. 1988. 'The unassimilated history' in P. Lowe and C. W. Stansfield (eds.): *Second Language Proficiency Assessment: Current Issues.* Englewood Cliffs, NJ: Prentice-Hall: 11–51.

McNamara, T. 1996. *Second Language Performance Measuring.* London and New York: Longman.

Messick, S. 1989. 'Validity' in R. L. Linn (ed.): *Educational Measurement.* Third edition. New York: American Council on Education and Macmillan: 13–103.

Messick, S. 1994. 'Alternative modes of assessment: Uniform standards of validity.' Paper presented at a Conference on evaluating alternatives to traditional testing for selection, Bowling Green State University, October 25–26.

Morrow, K. 1979. 'Communicative language testing: revolution or evolution?' in C. J. Brumfit and K. Johnson (eds.): *The Communicative Approach to Language Teaching.* Oxford: Oxford University Press: 143–57.

Morrow, K. 1986. 'The evaluation of tests of communicative performance' in M. Portal (ed.): *Innovations in Language Testing.* Windsor: NFER-Nelson: 1–13.

Moss, P. A. 1992. 'Shifting conceptions of validity in educational measurement: Implications for performance assessment.' *Review of Educational Research* 62: 229–58.

Munby, J. 1978. *Communicative Syllabus Design.* Cambridge: Cambridge University Press.

Nevo, N. 1989. 'Test-taking strategies on a multiple-choice test of reading comprehension.' *Language Testing* 6, 2: 199–215.

Nunan, D. 1992. *Research Methods in Language Learning.* Cambridge: Cambridge University Press.

O'Malley, M. J. and **A. U. Chamot.** 1990. *Learning Strategies in Second Language Acquisition.* Cambridge: Cambridge University Press.

Oxford, R. L. 1990. *Language Learning Strategies.* New York: Newbury House.

Palmer, A. S. 1972. 'Testing communication.' *International Review of Applied Linguistics and Language Teaching* 10: 35–45.

Palmer, A. S. 1981. 'Measurements of reliability and validity in two picture-description tests of oral communication' in A. S. Palmer, P. J. M. Groot, and G. A. Trosper (eds.): *The Construct Validation of Tests of Communicative Competence*. Washington, DC: TESOL: 127–39.

Pardee, J. 1982. *ILR Handbook on Oral Interview Testing*. Washington, DC: DLI/ LOS Joint Oral Interview Transfer Project .

Pica, T., R. Kanagy, and J. Falodun. 1993. 'Choosing and using communicative tasks for second language instruction' in Crookes and Gass 1993a: 9–34.

Richterich, R. (ed.). 1983. *Case Studies in Identifying Language Needs*. Oxford: Pergamon Press.

Richterich, R. and J. L. Chancerel (eds.). 1980. *Identifying the Needs of Adults Learning a Foreign Language*. Oxford: Pergamon Press.

Rolstad K., R. Campbell, C. Kim, O. Kim, and C. Merrill. 1993, 1994. *Korean/ English Bilingual Two-Way Immersion Program: Title VII Evaluation Report*. Washington, DC: US Department of Education. (Federal grant number T003c20062).

Savignon, S. 1983. *Communicative Competence: Theory and Classroom Practice*. New York: Addison-Wesley.

Searle, J. R. 1969. *Speech Acts: An Essay in the Philosophy of Language*. Cambridge: Cambridge University Press.

Shohamy, E. 1984. 'Does the testing method make a difference?' *Language Testing* 1, 2: 147–70.

Skehan, P. 1989. *Individual Differences in Second-language Learning*. London: Edward Arnold.

Snow, C. and C. Ferguson (eds.): 1977. *Talking to Children: Language Input and Acquisition*. Cambridge: Cambridge University Press.

Sternberg, R. J. 1985. *Beyond IQ: A Triarchic Theory of Human Intelligence*. New York: Cambridge University Press.

Sternberg, R. J. 1988. *The Triarchic Mind: A New Theory of Human Intelligence*. New York: Viking.

Sternfeld, S. 1989. *Test Packet for the University of Utah's Immersion/Multiliteracy Program*. Photocopied materials.

Sternfeld, S. 1992. 'An experiment in foreign language education: The University of Utah's immersion/multiliteracy program' in R. J. Courchêne, J.-I. Glidden, J. St. John, and C. Thérien (eds.): *Comprehension-based Language Teaching/ L'enseignement des langues secondes axé sur la compréhension*. Ottawa: University of Ottawa Press: 407–32.

Stufflebeam, D. L., C. H. McCormick, R. O. Brinkerhoff, and C. O. Nelson. 1985. *Conducting Educational Needs Assessments*. Boston: Kluwer-Nijhoff Publishing.

Swain, M. 1985. 'Large-scale communicative language testing: A case study' in Y. P Lee, A. C. Y. Fok, R. Lord, and G. Low (eds.): *New Directions in Language Testing*. Oxford: Pergamon Press: 35–46.

Test of English as a Foreign Language. 1995. *TOEFL Test and Score Manual*. Princeton, NJ: Educational Testing Service.

Underhill, N. 1982. 'The great reliability/validity trade-off: Problems in assessing the productive skills' in J. B. Heaton (ed.): *Language Testing*. London: Modern English Publications.

University of Cambridge Local Examinations Syndicate. 1995. *Certificate of Proficiency in English: Handbook*. Cambridge: University of Cambridge Local Examinations Syndicate.

University of Michigan. (ND). *Michigan Test of English Language Proficiency*. Ann Arbor, MI: English Language Institute, University of Michigan.

Upshur, J. A. 1969. 'Measurement of oral communication' in IFS Dokumentation: *Leitungsmessung im Fremdsprachenunterricht (Zweite internationale Expertkonferenz über Testmethoden im Fremdsprachenunterricht)*. Marburg/Lahn: Informationszentrum für Fremdsprachenforschung: 53–80.

van Dijk, T. A. 1977. *Text and Context: Explorations in the Semantics and Pragmatics of Discourse*. London: Longman.

Vaughn, C. 1991. 'Holistic assessment: What goes on in the raters' minds?' in L. Hamp-Lyons (ed.): *Assessing Second Language Writing in Academic Contexts*. Norwood, NJ: Ablex: 111–26.

Wall, D. and **J. C. Alderson.** 1993. 'Examining washback: The Sri Lankan impact study.' *Language Testing* 10: 41–69.

Weir, C. J. 1990. *Communicative Language Testing*. New York: Prentice-Hall.

Wenden, A. 1991. *Learner Strategies for Learner Autonomy*. Englewood Cliffs, NJ: Prentice-Hall.

Widdowson, H. G. 1978. *Teaching Language as Communication*. Oxford: Oxford University Press.

Widdowson, H. G. 1983. *Learning Purpose and Language Use*. Oxford: Oxford University Press.

Wiggins, G. 1994. 'Assessment: Authenticity, context and validity.' *Phi Delta Kappan* 83: 200–14.

Zakaluk, B. L. and **S. Jay Samuels** (eds.). 1988. *Readability: Its Past, Present, and Future*. Newark, Delaware: International Reading Association.

Index

Bold type indicates a major reference.